Advance praise for
The Souls of White Jokes

"Drawing from a rich array of primary source materials, Pérez offers a lucidly written and arresting sociological treatment of how jokes reproduce and sanction white supremacy. This is not just an exploration and indictment of racist humor and the institutions and organizations that allow it; it is an intellectual smackdown on the oft-used excuse "it was just a joke" when confronting the humor that maintains the racial caste system in the United States."
—Rebecca Krefting, author of *All Joking Aside:*
  American Humor and Its Discontents

"It is a commonplace assumption that humor is always harmless fun and vital for our everyday well-being. In this important new book, Raúl Pérez cogently argues that this is not invariably the case, and that jokes and joking relations can be hostile, divisive, alienating, and dehumanizing – or, in other words, very harmful. Within a strong and well-woven theoretical framework, *The Souls of White Jokes* offers a major contribution to the critical sociology of ethnicity and racism as well as to the study of humor in key institutions and organizations."
—Michael Pickering, author of *Blackface Minstrelsy in Britain*

"This timely and important intervention shows that racism is not about ignorance or hate, but about pleasureful solidarity, which shifts the conversation about what white supremacy is and why it persists."
—Michael P. Jeffries, author of *Behind the Laughs*

The Souls of White Jokes

THE SOULS
OF WHITE JOKES

*How Racist Humor Fuels
White Supremacy*

Raúl Pérez

STANFORD UNIVERSITY PRESS
Stanford, California

STANFORD UNIVERSITY PRESS
Stanford, California

Printed in the United States of America on acid-free, archival-quality paper

Library of Congress Cataloging-in-Publication Data

Names: Pérez, Raúl, author.
Title: The souls of white jokes : how racist humor fuels white supremacy / Raúl Pérez.
Description: Stanford, California : Stanford University Press, 2022. | Includes bibliographical references and index.
Identifiers: LCCN 2021052381 (print) | LCCN 2021052382 (ebook) | ISBN 9781503611481 (cloth) | ISBN 9781503632332 (paperback) | ISBN 9781503632349 (ebook)
Subjects: LCSH: Racism—United States. | Wit and humor—Social aspects—United States. | Wit and humor—Political aspects—United States. | Whites—United States—Attitudes. | Whites—Race identity—United States. | United States—Race relations.
Classification: LCC E184.A1 P3885 2022 (print) | LCC E184.A1 (ebook) | DDC 305.800973—dc23/eng/20211102
LC record available at https://lccn.loc.gov/2021052381
LC ebook record available at https://lccn.loc.gov/2021052382

Cover type: (Title) Vocal Type Marsha, Tré Seals, (Subtitle, author) Device Korolev, Rian Hughes
Typeset by Newgen North America in 10/15 ITC Galliard Pro

"'But what on earth is whiteness that one should so desire it?' Then always, somehow, some way, silently but clearly, I am given to understand that whiteness is the ownership of the earth forever and ever, Amen!"

W. E. B. Du Bois, "The Souls of White Folk"

TABLE OF CONTENTS

Note on Terminology   ix

1   The Racial Power of Humor   1
2   Amused Racial Contempt, or a Theory
    of White Racist Humor   22
3   Hiding in Plain Sight: The Violent Racist
    Humor of the Far Right   50
4   Blue Humor: The Racist Insults and
    Injuries of the Police   85
5   President Chimp: The Politics of
    Amused Racial Contempt   123
    EPILOGUE
    Racist Humor and the Cult(ure) of Whiteness   159

Acknowledgments   173
Notes   179
Index   207

NOTE ON TERMINOLOGY

The following chapters reference explicit racial slurs and include offensive, racist, and violent imagery. Used as insults, even in the form of "jokes," these words and images are harmful and painful as they convey and carry the history, weight, and continuity of racial hatred, violence, and white supremacy. While damaging when used in this way, these words and images will not be censored in the analysis that follows, as I do not wish to downplay or "whitewash" their intent and impact. It is important to feel and grapple with the ugly aspects of their original usage and meaning when critically examining their circulation in society. The one exception will be the use of the "N-word," a word that is perhaps the most racist, painful, and violent in the English language. As a Latino who does not identify as white or Black, this decision took a moment of reflection and consideration in light of recurring public debates and controversies regarding its usage by those of us who are not Black. I do not wish to cause the reader any additional pain or discomfort in ways that may detract from fully engaging with the important and serious analysis that follows, and I do not believe this decision undermines or diminishes the arguments made in this book in any way.

The Souls of White Jokes

THE RACIAL POWER OF HUMOR

"This assumption that of all the hues of God whiteness alone is inherently and obviously better than brownness or tan leads to curious acts. . . . Its first effects are funny: the strut of the Southerner, the arrogance of the Englishman amuck. . . . After the more comic manifestations . . . come subtler, darker deeds . . . that every great thought the world ever knew was a white man's thought; that every great deed the world ever did was a white man's deed; that every great dream the world ever sang was a white man's dream. . . . Here it is that the comedy verges to tragedy."

W. E. B. Du Bois, "The Souls of White Folk"

IN 2017, SERGEANT CLEON BROWN of the Hastings (Michigan) Police Department filed a federal civil rights lawsuit against his department, charging that he was the victim of racist joking, taunting, ridicule, and harassment by fellow officers and city officials. Brown, a "white"[1] police officer working in an all-white police department, never imagined he would be the target of such racism. "I just never thought it would be in Hastings, saying, like, racist comments to me. . . . All the years I've been there we never joked about race," Sergeant Brown stated.[2] A year before filing his grievance against the Hastings PD, Brown, a military veteran and law enforcement officer of twenty years, took a DNA test from Ancestry.com.[3] Brown had long assumed his family was part Native American, although with the name "Cleon" he was often teased as being part Black throughout his life. According to his Ancestry.com results, Brown found that he did not have Native American ancestry but was 18 percent sub-Saharan African. Brown was surprised by the results and shared them with his fellow officers.

His newfound racial identity became a running joke at the station. The racial taunting and mockery came from up and down the chain of command. For instance, Police Chief Jeff Pratt now referred to Brown as "Kunta," in reference to Alex Haley's character Kunta Kinte from the television miniseries *Roots*. Fellow officers began to whisper "Black Lives Matter" and pump their fists when walking past Brown. And during the holiday season, an officer put a Black Santa figure that had "18%" written on its beard in Brown's Christmas stocking at the station. Hastings's mayor, Frank Campbell, was also in on the joke. Brown reported that the mayor told him jokes that referred to African Americans as "Negroids."[4] The racist jokes went on for months. His attorney, Karie Boylan, stated that Brown felt emotionally distressed and "bullied" by his colleagues and that the stress of the ongoing incident impacted his mental health and ability to work. Brown sued the police department for racial harassment and sought at least $500,000 in damages.

The city disputed Brown's allegations, responding that it was Brown himself who initiated the "racial banter." According to city attorney Michael S. Bogren, Brown freely and jokingly shared his results with fellow officers. The city's statement provided by Bogren also reported that Sergeant Brown had allegedly commented that he "now understood why he 'likes chicken so much,'" mentioned that "the 18 percent is all in my pants," and further, that Brown "had a long history of making rude comments about black people." Brown denied these accusations, stating that he "has always tried to take a race-neutral approach to policing" and that he developed a new understanding of the effects of racism from this experience.[5] In 2018, the city awarded Brown $65,000, although Jeff Mansfield, city manager for Hastings, noted that "the city did not believe the lawsuit had merit. . . . But when comparing the settlement to the cost and disruptive effect of defending the case . . . it was in the city's best interest

to resolve the case on the terms in the mediated settlement agreement."
Part of Brown's settlement stipulated that he would have to resign.[6]

How should we understand this peculiar incident? Many will certainly
find this story ironic, comical, and perhaps ridiculous. It is not often we
hear about a white police officer being racially harassed and ridiculed as a
Black man in the workplace. More often, it is officers of color and civilians
of color who are the victims of mocking and insulting racist police discourse.[7] So, there is temptation to see this incident as "just a joke." This is
the way the city of Hastings attempted to frame this particular case, and it
is the way these incidents are characterized more generally by elected officials, law enforcement officers, entertainers, and so on, when their "jokes"
go "too far." Viewing such an incident as "just a joke" suggests that no
real harm has been done, that we should not take ourselves so seriously,
and that we should see the incident for what it really is and for how it was
intended: funny.

In many ways, Brown's case is a satirical allegory for the prevalence of
racism within our criminal justice system. Indeed, this peculiar incident is
perhaps the perfect premise for a 21st-century interracial buddy cop comedy, where the white cop who takes a DNA test learns that he is also the
Black cop. Hilarious, right? Or, perhaps, it could be the premise for a dark
comedy, an episode in the Netflix series *Dark Mirror*, or a new film by
comedian and director Jordan Peele, where the white officer who shares
his DNA test results becomes not only the victim of racist jokes by fellow
white officers, but is later the victim of police brutality when he is beaten
nearly to death at a traffic stop by a white police officer who mistook him
for a "criminal."

This incident is also reminiscent of journalist John Howard Griffin's
book *Black Like Me* (1961), in which Griffin recounts his experience travel-
ing in the Deep South after temporarily darkening his skin and documenting his encounters with racism. Griffin offered his observations to argue
that the only way white people could truly understand what it was like to
be a "Negro" in the United States was "by becoming one." As Sergeant
Brown expressed, while the ongoing racist joking and taunting humiliated
and angered him, he believed it gave him greater insight into the problem

of racism in law enforcement in the country. "This is why we have a great divide in this nation," he told the *New York Times*. "I feel my eyes are being opened now to that."[8]

However, in contrast to Griffin's account, Brown did not temporarily darken the color of his skin, which is often used to ridicule rather than to empathize with Black people, and his Ancestry.com results did not alter his complexion. In this case, Brown's racialization was created not by a DNA test but by the racist jokes, teasing, and ridicule that he endured from his fellow white officers and city officials. In other words, it was the racist joking rituals and practices that took place in this setting that changed Brown's racial experience in an otherwise "white space."[9]

Brown momentarily endured what sociologist Elijah Anderson refers to as the "n***** moment"—those moments of "acute disrespect" that Black people routinely experience in white spaces, where all whites have the power to humiliate, degrade, and mark them as racialized outsiders. As Anderson observes:

> Among themselves, black people often refer to this experience after the fact in a light-hearted manner and with an occasional chuckle as "the n***** moment." It is something of an inside joke. At the time it occurs, however, the awareness of this act of acute insult and discrimination is shocking; the victim is taken by surprise, caught off guard. . . . This moment is always insulting, and even a relatively minor incident can have a significant impact.[10]

These seemingly minor incidents, often described as racial "micro-aggressions," routinely occur under the guise of humor.[11] But such incidents are neither minor, micro, nor benign. Racist joking practices in the United States have long played a significant role in shaping how racialized groups and individuals are viewed and treated as inferior subjects and outsiders, while simultaneously forging and maintaining social order, cohesion, and boundaries among white participants and "in-group" members as superior. In the case of Cleon Brown and the Hastings PD discussed above, we see that the use of racist humor changed the social and racial experience of a white, male law enforcement officer, arguably one of the most powerful social positions an individual can occupy in the United States today.

If racist humor has the power to impact the social and racial experience of a white male police officer in the 21st century, what has it done to the people of color who have long been, and continue to be, the prime targets of such humor? And what does the use of racist humor *do* for those who partake in its forbidden pleasure, past and present? From the history and legacy of blackface minstrelsy—in which Blacks were comically ridiculed and portrayed by whites as stupid and buffoonish—to the current circulation of racist jokes and insults in the media, among colleagues in the workplace, within far-right groups and organizations, and among politicians and leaders in the public arena, I argue that racist humor is a discourse that has long played, and continues to play, a powerful role in generating and maintaining racialized feelings, hierarchies, and worldviews. In other words, racist humor has social power.

How racialized groups and individuals are socially defined and treated, and who gets to define and take action upon them, is what racial theorists Michael Omi and Howard Winant call "racial formation," or the process of socially constructing and making race.[12] In this book, I offer another piece in the puzzle of racial formation, one that has been little explored and that is often disregarded as relatively minor, peripheral, or benign. Over the last two centuries, racist humor—its political and discursive evolution and organized opposition to it—has played a critical role in shaping how many Americans think, feel, and act on race. The way in which racist humor has circulated and been challenged in U.S. society is a clear example of how "race" has been, and continues to be, socially and politically constructed in everyday life.

The Comic Construction of Race and Racism

Over a century ago, in his essay, "The Souls of White Folk" (1920),[13] sociologist W. E. B. Du Bois offered an insightful and provocative theoretical argument about the social and political construction of race, racism, and whiteness at a time when many of his highly regarded white peers understood race as a biological reality.[14] For Du Bois, race was a manu-factured illusion that played a powerful role in shaping European, U.S., and global society through the ranking, subordination, and exploitation of people along a rigid spectrum of skin color, geographic origin, and presumed racial traits and predispositions, with whiteness placed atop this artificial and unjust racial hierarchy. Du Bois keenly understood how these notions of race facilitated racial slavery and the continuation of racial op-pression, even after emancipation, and he argued that race and racism were tied to the development of European and Anglo-American imperialism and capitalist development. He clearly saw how race and racism, through oppression and exploitation, contributed to the enrichment of European and U.S. society at a time when many of his white contemporaries in so-ciology viewed racial inequality as an unfortunate but biologically prede-termined problem.

In some ways, Du Bois also saw race as a comical farce with tragic con-sequences, especially when he observed the division, hierarchy, inequal-ity, and conflict that existed not only between whites and non-whites in general but *within* so-called white society in particular. This instability and conflict among whites, Du Bois noted, culminated in "world war" during the early twentieth century, as white nations fought and brutalized other white nations while they competed to secure greater slices of territory in Asia, Africa, and Latin America, to gain greater access to raw materials and the exploitable cheap labor of colonized bodies of color in the so-called third world.

With this critical perspective, Du Bois understood how race and rac-ism worked as a political and ideological tool for ruling-class whites in power, by creating and maintaining social division and control within white-dominated societies. This racial divide, Du Bois noted, was also used to diffuse and redirect class conflict, anger, and violence between working-class whites and ruling-class whites, by shifting class tension and hostility towards racialized targets. Colored bodies, Black and Indig-enous in particular, were placed at the bottom of this manufactured social, cultural, political, and economic hierarchy in order to elevate a sense of "natural" *superiority* among struggling and suffering poor working-class whites. Du Bois referred to this process as the "public and psychological wages of whiteness,"[15] whereby whiteness gave working-class whites an emotional and psychological "ego-boost" in the absence of economic capital and power, while white political and economic elites rechanneled conflict, anger, and hatred away from themselves and towards racialized people of color.

Today, a century after Du Bois published "The Souls of White Folk," we are witnessing the resurgence and spread of an angry white resentment, the politics of white nationalism, recurring forms of racial violence, and a political populism supported by nativism, racism, and xenophobia, in the midst of historic levels of economic inequality, wealth concentration,[16] and other crises not seen in nearly a century. Du Bois's observations on the intersections of race, class, and whiteness are as relevant as ever.

Yet, this is not the Du Bois that is typically engaged by scholars today, if he is engaged at all.[17] The more familiar, and tamer, Du Bois is the one described by his earlier work, on the *Souls of Black Folk* (1903). This Du Bois is the one who gave us greater insight into the internal conflict, consciousness, and emotions of racially oppressed people through what he called "double-consciousness," or the complicated socio-emotional and interactional experience of being a racialized subject in a white-dominated society. As Du Bois observed:

> It is a peculiar sensation, this double-consciousness, this sense of always looking at one's self through the eyes of others, of measuring one's soul by the tape of a world that looks on in *amused contempt* and pity.[18]

Du Bois focused his attention on the complicated and conflicting emotional, psychological, and interactional experience of Blacks in the United States to highlight a significant way in which race and racism shape how Blacks, and other people of color, experience and navigate racial oppression in a white society, in ways that whites rarely notice or experience. But even in this well-established observation that centered on the Black experience, Du Bois hinted at the affective state of the white imagination, where a white world gazes upon and alienates non-whites through a feeling of "amused contempt," or a pleasurable and enjoyable feeling and practice that regards racialized "others" as inferior, worthless, and beneath consideration.[19]

Philosophers—such as Plato, Aristotle, and Thomas Hobbes—long ago observed that feelings of superiority, and the viewing of others as inferior, can be pleasurable and amusing—and are often expressed by laughing at the perceived misfortune of others, what the Germans call "schadenfreude."[20] Today, humor scholars refer to these observations as the *superiority* theory of humor, though these philosophical observations were little more than venerable insights from esteemed thinkers rather than a fully developed social theory. Yet, when applied to the *humor of white folk* over the last two centuries, a pattern emerges, a pattern that illustrates how whites have continued to derive amusement, pleasure, and solidarity from laughing *at* non-whites—a *white schadenfreude*—which has long worked to enhance and maintain feelings of racial superiority and amused contempt among whites.

This shared emotional state, what I call *amused racial contempt,* is the central affective mechanism that I wish to theorize and examine throughout this book. Looking at the way racist humor operates today through this lens sheds light on crucial dilemmas that continue to plague American society, while highlighting how specific "racialized emotions" maintain these historically inscribed racial hierarchies into the 21st century.[21]

Amused Racial Contempt

Scholars who study the psychology of emotions have outlined a small list of what are considered universal primary emotions: anger, fear, sadness, and happiness.[22] These emotions are considered universal and are believed to be physiologically "hard-wired," as researchers find that people in cultures around the world recognize the display of these "affective states" at various levels of intensity. Secondary emotions (e.g., shame, guilt, jealousy, respect, admiration, hatred, contempt, etc.) are considered to be some combination of these primary emotions. Sociologists, drawing on these models but moving beyond isolating emotional states primarily within individuals, argue that emotions are, ultimately, a social phenomenon. As Eduardo Bericat wrote in 2016, the "majority of our emotions emerge, are experienced and have meaning in the context of our social relations."[23] Sociologists have increasingly studied how emotions shape and *structure* social experience, social interactions, and social order. From this perspective, in a racialized social system,[24] where race continues to structure social outcomes, we would expect racialized emotions to play a central role in maintaining and structuring racial experiences, interactions, hierarchies, and order.[25]

Over the last several decades, the study of *racialized* emotions has received little attention among sociologists of emotion. But in a world where racialized emotions appear to be central to how we understand and filter all aspects and inequalities of our current social, cultural, and political era, there is an urgent need for sociologists to address this issue. As Paula Ioanide has argued, it is important to center "emotion and affect in the contemporary expressions of racial violence and discrimination" in order to develop a better understanding of the ways that racial feelings trump facts in the current political moment.[26] This book, which shows how the affective state of amused racial contempt has shaped how Americans think and act, draws on these and other theoretical insights from scholars who have aimed to focus our attention towards the ways emotions operate as social and racial phenomenon.

Sara Ahmed's critical work on the "affective economy of emotions" is invaluable in this regard. Echoing the sociological assertion that emotions are more than a "private matter," Ahmed also goes beyond the claim that emotions are socially shared. For Ahmed, emotions are transactions that circulate in the social, cultural, and political arena by signaling affective states (e.g., love, hatred, fear, joy, etc.) to *align* and *bind* some bodies against others. As Ahmed observes:

> In such affective economies, emotions *do things*, and they align individuals with communities—or bodily space with social space—through the very intensity of their attachments. Rather than seeing emotions as psychological dispositions, we need to consider how they work, in

concrete and particular ways, to mediate the relationship between the psychic and the social, and between the individual and the collective.[27]

According to Ahmed, particular affective states can also "accumulate" the more they are circulated (e.g., racial or religious hatred). In this way, shared affective states give particular bodies greater or lesser social value, which in turn (re)produce social affect, or the way shared emotions shape social reality. Ahmed's insights into these issues are particularly helpful when thinking about how racist humor has long worked to assign social value in ways that align and bind some bodies against others in a white-dominated society like the United States. Moreover, this insight also guides us in thinking about the ways that amused racial contempt continues to evolve alongside broader social and cultural change.

Ahmed's critical work on "happiness" and "happy objects," for example, provides a useful lens for understanding how amusement and pleasure influence the reproduction of racism. Happy objects are simply those that give us pleasure and good feeling and that "become imbued with positive affect as good objects."[28] Happy objects, such as jokes, exist within larger "affective economies" and circulate in ways that are intended to enhance "good" feelings. In turn, as Ahmed notes, when we feel pleasure from happy objects, the belief is that "we are aligned; we are facing the right way."[29] In this way, happy objects are particularly important in social bonding and affiliation, as "[w]e align ourselves with others by investing in the same objects as the cause of happiness."[30] Racist jokes, as I discuss throughout this book, provide a similar type of opportunity for social affiliation and alignment against individuals and groups that are dehumanized and devalued.

Yet, despite this important and critical insight, humor itself is often regarded as a "happy object," and the old notion that "laughter is the best medicine" is increasingly echoed and affirmed through commonsense advice, popular culture, and even across scholarly disciplines—from biology to neuroscience. Researchers are continually exploring and highlighting the role of humor and laughter in enhancing our socio-affective, emotional, and cognitive functioning. They regularly focus on how humor

helps us talk about difficult personal and social issues and how it contributes to our social and individual health and well-being.[31] In other words,
such findings emphasize the positive, even emancipatory, benefit and importance of humor and laughter in social life.

But in pursuing this rather celebratory approach to understanding humor, what is often ignored or downplayed is how humor and laughter can
also shape and impact our social reality in ways that reinforce boundaries around inclusion and exclusion, reproduce dominant ideologies and
practices, and harm social and individual well-being.[32] As Ahmed contends
in her critique of happiness and happy objects, when we are "out of line
with an affective community—when we do not experience pleasure from
proximity to objects that are already attributed as being good," we experience "alienation."[33] In this book, I track this alienating feature of humor
in the context of several areas of American life today—far-right extremist
communities, police culture, and the political arena—to show how dehumanizing humor, rather than being harmless fun, can play a central role in
reinforcing and mobilizing racist power and ideology under the guise of
laughter and amusement.

In addition to Ahmed, other scholars have made crucial interventions
in our understanding of humor and its broader social impact within organizations. For example, Cecily Cooper has highlighted how humor can
increase or disrupt group and organizational cohesiveness because of the
impact it has on "affect reinforcement."[34] "Humor," Cooper argues, "is
one form of social communication which acts as a reinforcing or punishing
event, since humor manipulates affect."[35] In other words, manipulating affect and emotions to *align* and *bind* some bodies against others gives certain bodies greater or lesser social value.[36] In the context of racist humor,
as this book documents, racial ridicule and insult, or aggressive humor, can
work to split, discipline, dehumanize, and ostracize targeted groups and
individuals within social contexts and organizations, or in society at large.[37]
But while humor rooted in social distancing and exclusion works to foster
discrimination and alienation against targeted individuals and groups, it
can also be used to *simultaneously* nurture affiliation, solidarity, pleasure,
and entertainment among in-group members through the denigration and

"othering" of targeted individuals or out-groups.[38] Therefore, it is important to understand that the humor and "joking relations" that take place and shape within society are also expressions of social power relations.[39]

In this way, racist humor works as a form of affective currency in the "public and psychological wages of whiteness," as Du Bois puts it, aligning those who engage in the social ritual of racial ridicule and amused contempt against those who are racialized, mocked, and alienated as targets, in both conscious and unconscious ways. Sociologist Joe Feagin has added to this perspective by conceptualizing the notion of a "white racial frame"—a socially shared worldview that produces, maintains, and aligns a "positive orientation" of whites and whiteness and a "negative orientation" of non-whites.[40] A white racial frame, Feagin suggests, is often expressed through racist joking, because such joking is a racial pleasure that works as an "emotion-laden" type of "social glue" that is rooted in maintaining notions of racial superiority and inferiority.[41] This book explores several important ways that this kind of white racial frame emerges in the form of racist joking in different contexts and the ways that racist humor, underpinning such a racial frame, is actively shaping and encouraging specific forms of social emotions, ideologies, and behaviors.

It is worth pointing out that it is not only whites who are potentially aligned in this process, as the use of racist humor by non-whites, through self-deprecation or the ridicule of other non-whites, can also work to orient non-whites in ways that reinforce a white racial frame, systemic racism, and other forms of inequality.[42] This was revealed in 2016, for instance, when Tom Angel, the former chief of staff for the Los Angeles County Sheriff's Department, was found to have forwarded dozens of racist, sexist, and homophobic jokes to his staff while he was second in command in the Burbank Police Department in 2012 and 2013. "I took my Biology exam last Friday. . . . I was asked to name two things commonly found in cells. Apparently 'Blacks' and 'Mexicans' were NOT the correct answers," was one of numerous examples included in an independent investigation.[43] Angel, who identifies as Mexican American, was hired to help reform the Burbank PD after various allegations of racism, sexual harassment, and police brutality were raised against the department. Yet, he circulated jokes that mocked and dehumanized the very communities disproportionately impacted by police racial abuse and violence. The shared use of racist humor among white and non-white officers, as I discuss in Chapter 4, can function to align white and non-whites officers as colleagues within an organization complicit in systemic racial abuse, in ways that further alienate the racialized targets of such humor.[44]

This book highlights the role of humor in the social and political construction of race and racism. I examine how the use of amused racial contempt is a centuries-long mechanism that continues to contribute to social alignment and alienation, via the affective production of difference between "us" and "them," and show how this process is connected to the emotional maintenance and reproduction of racism, whiteness, and white supremacy. In turn, this book offers a critical reply to the familiar response that these are "just jokes"—a common and pervasive dismissal of the need for critical analysis of the social meaning and impact of racist and other disparaging forms of humor in society.

The Humor of White Folk

Racist humor, like all humor, changes over time. In Du Bois's time, the humor of white people was perhaps most visible in the arena of popular culture, as blackface minstrelsy was one of the most popular forms of entertainment in the United States at the time.[45] Decades earlier, Frederick Douglass had articulated his own anger and displeasure against what he described as the "filthy scum of white society, who have stolen from us a complexion denied to them by nature, in which to make money, and pander to the corrupt taste of their white fellow-citizens."[46] Douglass took serious issue with the way Blacks were rendered routine objects of racial ridicule in a white-dominated society built on the backs of Black slaves, although it would take another century before his opposition to blackface minstrelsy would be channeled more broadly.[47] For Du Bois, this form of amused racial contempt was so deeply embedded that it not only impacted how Blacks were viewed and how they viewed themselves, but it also structured and framed white feelings and worldviews. Over the last several decades, critical scholarship on blackface has emphasized the role that this ritualized form of racial ridicule played in forging and popularizing notions of racial superiority and inferiority in early U.S. society. Such work has revealed how racist humor played an important social function in maintaining and reproducing notions of anti-Blackness, whiteness, and white supremacy in the United States and beyond.[48]

In one sense, the subordinating power of humor grew more pervasive as the subordinating power of slavery diminished. From the pre–Civil War period to the civil rights era, blackface minstrelsy grew as a prominent and unproblematized source of humor and entertainment in the country, what I have previously referred to as the "national sense of humor."[49] This form of organized comic racial ridicule greatly contributed to the racialization and inferiorization of Blacks in the white imagination and was, in many ways, the first genre of race-based popular culture in U.S. and British society.[50]

This genre of humor was developed during the early 1800s by white entertainers who painted their faces black while routinely imitating, mocking, and caricaturing Black people as stupid, buffoonish, inarticulate, and childlike. Urban, northern, middle-class white performers like Thomas D. Rice and Dan Emmet were some of the first to popularize the genre by ostensibly sharing "'authentic" portrayals of southern plantation life on theater stages in northern cities during the early to mid-19th century.[51] These and other performers developed popular stage characters like Jim Crow, Tambo and Bones, and Sambo—figures that were projected as genuine portrayals of Black people in America. By blackening up their faces, often with the ash from burned corks or greasepaint, while engaging in "Negro dialect, song and dance," white entertainers advertised their performances as true and "authentic" portrayals of Blacks. Other characters, like Zip Coon, the free northern "dandy" prone to malapropisms and other speech problems, were depictions of Black people as unassimilable and unfit for freedom and city life.[52]

Blackface minstrelsy was a comprehensive form of entertainment that included music, song and dance, acrobatics, and other kinds of performance. But the central feature of a blackface performance, the main attraction, was the "racist pleasure" and laughter it provoked from a predominantly white male audience. Historian Eric Lott describes the "triangulated" racist pleasure that an early blackface show generated as one "in which blackface comic and white spectator shared jokes about an absent third party . . . the joker personifying the person being joked about."[53] Historian Karen Sotiropoulos also describes a typical performance:

> An interlocutor sat in the center and bantered with the endmen (Tambo and Bones). The endmen played the roles of comedic buffoons and mocked the interlocutor's pomposity in speech laden with malapropisms; in turn the interlocutor corrected the endmen's ignorance, thus allowing for multiple jokes to be made at the expense of African Americans.[54]

Blackface performers also wore ill-fitting clothing for comedic effect and worked to infantilize Blacks and project them as clownish and childlike to the audience. As Lott describes, "This is the sense in which 'the African,' a 'child in intellect' . . . might become an object of screaming fun and games."[55] In the end, the rhetorical and emotional impact of a blackface performance was there to reassure whites that Blacks were inferior, ill equipped for freedom and civilization, and content with slavery and racial domination.

By the end of the 19th century, blackface minstrelsy soared in popularity. As historian Alexander Saxton notes, blackface minstrelsy became the most popular form of entertainment in the nation during the 19th century, in part because its spread coincided with the rise of mass circulation newspapers and white political populism.[56] Moreover, it was a popular form of entertainment that defended racial slavery and a racial hierarchy. By portraying narratives of happy slaves, it ridiculed calls for emancipation, portrayed Blacks as inarticulate and dysfunctional buffoons, and reinforced the political ideology of white supremacy throughout the 19th and early 20th centuries through the reproduction of what Patricia Hill Collins calls "controlling images." As Collins notes, such images are "designed to make racism, sexism, poverty, and other forms of social injustice appear to be natural, normal, and inevitable parts of everyday life."[57]

A central feature of these comic-controlling images was the "racist plea-sure" they provoked among a predominantly white male audience. The rhetorical and affective impact of blackface reassured white men across various class and ethnic backgrounds that Blacks were an inferior race of people. Amused racial contempt worked to normalize this sentiment while desensitizing white audiences to the brutality of human bondage, chattel slavery, and racial oppression.[58] In this way, blackface "cultivated a proslav-ery imagination" among whites by reproducing and reinforcing common-sense notions of Black inferiority, which served to undermine calls for Black freedom and human dignity.[59] While Black artists would later enter this genre of comedy and become successful blackface performers in their own right, and there is evidence of ironic and subversive humor by Blacks in blackface that was readily consumed by Black audiences, to survive within this racist culture industry and succeed, Black artists and entertainers had to reproduce white renditions of blackness—by participating in Black racial ridicule and "self-caricature" and perpetuating "vile stereotypes" for a pre-dominantly white audience within a white-owned entertainment industry.[60]

But blackface was more than the denigration and dehumanization of Blackness. It was also a powerful form of racism that played a key role in the formation of a sense of "whiteness" before and after the Civil War pe-riod. As historian David Roediger has pointed out, the ridicule of Blacks helped achieve "a common symbolic language—a unity—that could not be realized by racist crowds, by political parties or by labor unions."[61] This "common symbolic language" among various European descendants, citi-zens and immigrants, from different class backgrounds was the shared, amused racial contempt that whites collectively practiced and enjoyed at the expense of Black people.

Throughout the 19th and early 20th centuries in the United States, racial ridicule was a pleasurable social activity that allowed whites from various class, national, and ethnic backgrounds—with distinct interests, cultures, religions, traditions, and languages—to view themselves not only as "white," but as racially superior *through* the ridicule of Blacks. This racial ridicule allowed working-class whites in particular to feel racially superior to Blacks, despite their own lack of social, political, and economic power and status in an early Anglo-American capitalist society, fostering the *feeling* that although they were poor, exploited, and powerless in a fiercely brutal and unequal capitalist society, at least they were "not slaves" and "not black."[62]

The racist pleasure of amused racial contempt shared among various ethnic European immigrants and citizens helped them build racial affiliation, cohesion, and solidarity as "whites"—not only through the reproduction of a shared racial ideology, but through the process of engaging in *ritualized* social laughter directed at an inferiorized and racialized target, contributing towards their own group alignment and formation. Therefore, the social practice of amused racial contempt worked to forge what sociologist Emile Durkheim called "collective effervescence," or the way ritualized collective practices can "strengthen emotions . . . to bring all those who share them into more intimate and more dynamic relationship."[63] The racist pleasure gained from the ridicule of Blacks contributed to the reproduction and maintenance of a sense of "whiteness" by allowing all whites to place Blacks and other non-whites at the bottom of the social, political, economic, and racial hierarchy as the natural order of society. In this way, the reproduction of whiteness and white supremacy during the 19th and early 20th centuries was manufactured, in part, through the collective practice of amused racial contempt. In the United States, white racist humor was the "national sense of humor."[64]

Examining Racist Humor Today

Moving through and beyond the historical uses and functions of amused racial contempt in the arena of popular culture, this book looks at the way racist humor operates within three relevant settings and subcultures: far-right extremist groups, law enforcement, and political organizations. By doing so, this book highlights the problems associated with recent efforts by scholars, politicians, and cultural commentators to elevate the positive importance of humor and laughter in everyday life on the one hand,[65] while trying to make sense of the seeming "re-emergence" of racism and white supremacy on the other. Although confronting this issue may be difficult and unsettling for several reasons, as this book demonstrates, racism in America today continues to be engaged in and practiced in ways that are amusing, pleasurable, and enjoyable—not only in the distant past or in the realm of entertainment (as has been the case for centuries and continues today), but within organizations and institutions that wield significant influence and power in the everyday lives of white people and people of color in U.S. society. Highlighting how racist humor operates in these contexts also points to an issue that is often overlooked when discussing the intersection of racism and emotions: racism is more than hatred. It is also a practice deeply rooted in a pleasurable solidarity grounded in an amused contempt for racialized others.

In some ways, it is comforting to think that racism is primarily motivated by negative feelings and emotions, such as hatred, fear, anger, and so on, or that it primarily exists in the past or at the social margins. We might even imagine that being filled with racial hate, anger, and rage might prevent racists from experiencing joy in their lives. We pity the racist. By illustrating the powerful role of racist ridicule in reproducing and reinforcing shared notions of race and racism within institutions like law enforcement or the political arena, however, this book shows that racist humor is not a peripheral, marginal, or harmless form of discourse, as some scholars have suggested.[66] Rather, racist humor has been, and continues to be, a powerful mechanism for reinforcing boundaries of inclusion, exclusion, and dehumanization. An amused racial contempt plays a critical role in efforts to maintain and reproduce racism and white supremacy in the current social and political moment, often in ways that remain under-theorized and under-investigated.

In this way, this book's critical approach to racist humor is a detour from other contemporary and influential studies of "ethnic humor," which have buried an examination of racist humor by advancing more universal, inclusive, or benign claims about the uses of ethnic humor in society.[67] The influential sociologist and humor scholar Christie Davies, for instance, insists that jokes have "no social consequence" and that they are "just jokes," even though he largely ignores the centuries-long relationship between white supremacy and sense of humor.[68] At the same time, this project is also a departure from those scholars who have focused on the more positive aspects of "racial humor" that highlight the ways in which such humor is used to challenge or subvert dominant hegemonic racial meaning.[69] Such studies are important as they illustrate the fact that jokes are not "just jokes" and that the use and interpretation of humor is often a political struggle over meaning, (mis)representation, and identity. But these studies and observations also fall prey to centering and celebrating the "positive" side of humor, while they tend to ignore or downplay the use of humor as a vehicle for racial and social harm.

Chapter Outline

In the chapters that follow, I argue that we need to take humor and laughter seriously, as it is an affective form of communication and social engagement tied to the past and present reproduction of racism and white supremacy. In Chapter 2, I develop my theoretical framework of racist humor as a mechanism of racialization and dehumanization. What does racist humor *do* in society? Little has been said about the role of humor in racism and racialized emotions, and this project is an effort to help fill this void.[70] I draw from social theories of humor to examine the fundamental role of social amusement in facilitating social affiliation and alienation. I connect these theories to the study of racial formation and racism, which provide greater theoretical clarity for understanding the role that racist humor plays in the affective construction of racial affiliation and dehumanization, historically and today.

In Chapter 3, I explore the use of racist humor by the old far right and the recent alt-right to illustrate how leaders in these movements have relied on humor as a strategy to circulate racist ideologies and imagery. This is not a novel phenomenon by the far right, as recent authors have argued, but a strategy decades in the making. I show how white supremacist leader Tom Metzger, for instance, played a leading role in developing this strategy within the far right during the late 1980s and 1990s, as Metzger intentionally, deliberately, and regularly included racist cartoons in his white supremacist paper, *White Aryan Resistance*. Metzger made strategic use of racist humor, during the post–civil rights period, as a political statement, to spread violent racist notions and as a mechanism for political outreach and recruiting. This strategy laid by Metzger, I argue, has been more recently embraced and mobilized by leaders in the alt-right movement during an ostensibly colorblind era. This is illustrated in efforts by white nationalists to repurpose and weaponize online humor, particularly in the form of memes, such as "Pepe the Frog," which the Anti-Defamation League and the Southern Poverty Law Center identified as a repurposed "hate symbol."[71] In other words, since the civil rights period, the far right has made intentional use of racist humor to make their racist messages more appealing and palatable to a wider audience in order to spread white supremacist ideology.

In Chapters 4 and 5, I examine the consequences of racist humor in action, by looking at the use of racist humor within the criminal justice system and in the political arena. In Chapter 4, I examine the prevalence of racist humor among law enforcement officers and department leaders. Numerous police departments have come under investigation following high profile cases of police racial abuse and violence, and racist jokes have been found circulating among the ranks in many police departments across the country. Here, I explore the use and function of racist humor among officers and connect this humor to a context of mass incarceration, police violence, and racism within law enforcement. I draw upon theories of symbolic and cultural violence to expand my theory of racist humor as a form of violence, and I offer an empirical examination of how racist humor within law enforcement can be used as a mechanism of dehumanization that legitimizes structural and direct violence. I analyze news media, public records requests, legal documents, and federal reports, such as the Department of Justice report of the Ferguson Police Department, in my examination of the current prevalence of racist humor in law enforcement. I compare these findings with earlier newspaper coverage and research on the use of racist humor by police, along with proposed efforts to remedy and discipline such behavior by police departments.

Finally, in Chapter 5, I examine the use of racist ridicule in the political arena, during the 2008 presidential election in particular. I examine numerous memes, cartoons, images, and racist jokes that circulated online, in social media, and in newspapers/news media during this presidential election cycle. I look at how depictions of Barack Obama, particularly as an ape, were grounded in anti-Black racial ridicule. Such images circulated not only among the far right but among millions of internet users, various mainstream and conservative news media, as well as conservative politicians and government officials, in the United States and around the world. Data scientist Seth Stephens-Davidowitz finds that "racist jokes" were the top search hits for racially charged Google searches during the Obama elections, and he argues that "racial animus" cost Obama a significant amount of the white vote during both election cycles.[72] This widespread racist ridicule of Obama, I contend, laid part of the affective groundwork for the accelerated rise of a popular amused racial contempt, which facilitated the expansion of a political populism that relied on ridicule and insult as a political tool during the 2016 presidential election. In turn, I argue that racist ridicule in the political arena is a powerful social and political mechanism that has worked to strengthen an ideology of white nationalism, by reinforcing racial boundaries of inclusion and exclusion via racial comic dehumanization.

Together, these chapters demonstrate that the use of racist humor has significantly popularized and advanced racist notions and ideologies within the institutions studied as well as other institutions and organizations in U.S. society in recent decades. In developing my theoretical and empirical argument about the role of humor as a mechanism in racial dehumanization, I do not claim that this is the sole function of humor, or that such humor contains only one interpretation or meaning. However, in an unequal society, not all forms of interpretation are given equal validity or attention, and critical readings are often disregarded. This has often been the case for racist humor, which has not been taken seriously as an object of analysis in recent decades. It is often denied as a serious form of racism and is continually regarded as "just a joke." Part of what makes racist humor so powerful and insidious is that it appears as something other than it is—harmless and delightful rather than socially destructive. Moreover, critical analysts of humor have been viewed as misguided, or as politically or ideologically motivated, and are often seen as humorless killjoys.[73] But as Sara Ahmed contends, we must be "prepared to kill some forms of joy" and "question what is appealing in the appeal to happiness and good feeling," so that we may find "an alternative model of the social good."[74]

CHAPTER 2

AMUSED RACIAL CONTEMPT, OR A THEORY OF WHITE RACIST HUMOR

"It is interesting to notice the great pleasure white people in all classes take in . . . stereotyped jokes and in indulging in discussions about the Negro and what he does, says and thinks. It is apparently felt as a release. . . . [J]okes give release to troubled people. . . . The main 'function' of the joke is thus to create a collective surreptitious approbation for something which cannot be approved explicitly because of moral inhibitions. To the whites the Negro jokes further serve the function of 'proving' the inferiority of the Negro."

Gunnar Myrdal, *An American Dilemma*

WHAT DOES RACIST HUMOR *do* in society? Over the last century, many have commented and speculated on the social impact, or lack thereof, of racist joking and humor in society—that it is wrong, inappropriate, offensive, innocent, harmless, and so on. Yet, even as esteemed scholars and writers have pointed to the role of racist humor in reinforcing notions of racial inferiority and superiority, few have aimed to develop a fuller theoretical analysis of racist humor or what it does in society. When scholars and writers do consider such humor, it is most often discussed anecdotally or anachronistically. Yet, as the history of blackface minstrelsy underscores, racist humor, particularly in the entertainment industry, played a powerful role in reproducing white racist pleasure, white supremacist ideologies, and an affirmation of white identity during the late 19th and early 20th centuries. While the prevalence of such humor was widely challenged during and after the civil rights era, the reality is that such humor never went away.

Today, concern with racist humor arises periodically, particularly when public officials, celebrities, employees, and/or students engage in the faux pas of blackening-up and snapping pictures to memorialize the taboo racist fun or are found circulating racist jokes and memes on social media. Such incidents are routinely reproached as inappropriate, unacceptable, and offensive. But these and countless other incidents are rarely given deeper theoretical consideration and are seldom connected to a fuller understanding of the intimate relationship between racialized emotions and systemic racism. In other words, despite the continuous pleasure and revulsion that such humor produces, even in an ostensibly colorblind society, racist humor has generally not been taken seriously enough as a significant site for the sociological analysis of the reproduction of racism and white supremacy in a more sustained way.

In order to understand how racist humor operates, and to be able to speak about its methods, goals, and impact, it is necessary to briefly discuss some of the larger conceptual issues associated with humor in general, including how it has been previously understood and analyzed by influential American and European scholars and thinkers. These broader insights on humor are useful, but also limiting, in understanding and addressing the problem of racist humor and its relationship to white supremacy and systemic racism. To better understand what racist humor is and what it does, theories of humor will need to be coupled with, and further conceptualized by, theories of race and racism.

Any scholarly project looking at humor usually highlights three standard psychological theories of humor: superiority, incongruity, and relief. The superiority theory, often attributed to Aristotle or Thomas Hobbes, suggests that laughter stems from a sense of superiority over another, that we laugh *at* the misfortunes of others. The incongruity theory, on the other hand, illustrated by philosophers like Immanuel Kant and Henri Bergson, suggests humor results from witnessing unusual or incongruous ideas, objects, or events and drawing an unexpected symbolic or metaphorical relation between them. Finally, the relief theory, articulated by Sigmund Freud and Herbert Spencer, suggests humor and laughter result from the expression of otherwise unacceptable ideas or behaviors that may be readily censured or suppressed in serious discourse by civil society.[1]

While these theories have greatly influenced humor scholarship in general across the disciplines, and I draw on them throughout, in this book I aim to offer a different theoretical and empirical analysis of humor that centers on its role in creating and structuring racial boundaries, hierarchies, sense of belonging, and other social or affective implications. Moreover, rather than treating humor as primarily a psychological or individual phenomenon, drawing on Sara Ahmed's insights on the "cultural politics of emotions," I will focus on the social role of humor in producing collective feelings of "alignment" and "alienation."[2] Racist humor plays a significant role in reproducing social alignment and alienation, as the social function and pleasure of humor works not only to amuse and bring people closer together, but to reinforce a social hierarchy and division between in-group and out-group, Us and Them.

Humor and Social Alignment

It has long been noted and theorized that humor use is first and foremost about sociality. Social humor and laughter bring people together by fostering greater social affiliation and affection among and between individuals.[3] Social humor is a form of social communication that facilitates group cooperation, social bonding, and group formation by decreasing social distance and creating a collective *affect* of fun, pleasure, and enjoyment.[4] Social theories of humor have determined that humor has an emotional impact on how individuals and groups *feel* about themselves, each other, and "others." This theoretical assessment is increasingly observed by scientists today. For instance, laughter and humor are found to positively impact human physiology and emotions through the "affective reward networks in the brain."[5] Moreover, it is increasingly found that laughter produces, releases, and elevates neuropeptides, endorphins, and opiates in the body.[6] These affective reward networks and mechanisms facilitate human social bonding and affiliation because they make us *feel good* when sharing a laugh in the company of others.[7]

With the emergence of scientific testing of older theories of humor and laughter, social theories of humor have also begun to develop in a more systematic, empirical, and theoretically informed way. The connection between humor and laughter remains extremely complicated, and other scholars have examined this connection far more closely than I do in this book.[8] But one of the key connections that this book does home in on relates to the role of humor and laughter in uniting interlocutors.

There is a growing consensus across various disciplines regarding the role of humor and laughter in operating as a sort of "social glue." Evolutionary theorists suggest laughter and humor work to cultivate social cohesion and group formation. Charles Darwin, for instance, who referred to humor as the "tickling of the mind,"[9] speculated that the evolutionary function of laughter is to enhance individual and group pleasure, cooperation, solidarity, and group formation. More recently, Guillaume Dezecache and Robin Dunbar have theorized that a unique evolutionary function of humor and laughter among humans is in increasing group size through "grooming at a distance."[10] As a form of social communication, they contend, humor allowed for social pleasure and fun to be extended and for larger social groups to be potentially formed and maintained. Philosopher John Morreall echoes these observations by suggesting that humor and laughter can be understood as a "play signal" that enhances social pleasure, facilitates socialization, and contributes to social cooperation and interaction.[11]

Social scientists have made similar observations with regard to this particular social function of humor in contemporary life. However, they suggest that culture mediates the use and impact of humor. That is, the kinds of humor that are shared socially, that participants and societies find acceptably funny or unfunny, and that aid in group formation and boundary maintenance are dependent on the social, historical, and political norms and social contexts within which participants and group members exist.[12] Sociologists Gary Alan Fine and Michaela De Soucey, for instance, suggest that over time, social groups develop their own "joking cultures," or the norms, contents, styles, and traditions that are reflective of the particular "communities of practice" that engage in particular forms of humor. Many social observers have made the same point.[13] Different cultures, scholars suggest, have different rules, norms, and practices concerning what can be joked about, what the jokes mean, and who can do the joking.

These theories and observations on the social power of humor in social affiliation and alignment are theoretically relevant and important when considering the racist joking culture of whites, and non-whites, in the United States. In this case, we can think about the joking culture of whites alongside the history of whiteness in the nation, to examine how the use and function of racist humor is a "social fact" that is connected to the history and development of race, racism, and white supremacy. Moreover, we can also begin to think about an examination of racist humor in much broader terms, for instance, by drawing on the history of racial minstrelsy in ways that are rarely linked to the contemporary practice of racist humor in everyday life across different social contexts and institutions, such as the workplace, online, among peers, and so on.[14]

As many of the scholars' works discussed above underscore, humor holds significant affiliative power—something that is equally true in racist humor. This affiliative power enables humor to function as a mechanism that contributes to social alignment, building solidarity, and maintaining and reproducing a shared worldview. But while a key function of social humor is in drawing some people closer together, an equally significant aspect is the capacity of humor to keep us apart.

Humor and Social Alienation

There is a common misconception that racism is always motivated by hate. Although white supremacy draws heavily on a skewed and hateful worldview, as many scholars have shown, it is also strongly motivated by people's desire to attach themselves to others, to a privileged social group or class. Racism has historically provided a powerful tool for whites, and non-whites seeking the status of whiteness, to maintain and develop the social boundaries of that hierarchy and privilege. Because of humor's affiliative power and ability to serve as a social glue, racist humor is deeply woven into Americans' racialized drive to belong, but also to exclude.

Humor, then, is both pro-social and anti-social, as we can laugh *with* others and *at* others.[15] Ridicule, in particular, is a powerful form of social humor and communication that is used to target, humiliate, discipline, mock, and alienate groups and individuals who are "othered" or "marginalized" in some way, often through an emphasis of preexisting stereotypes and social fissures, such as race, class, gender, sexuality, and other social inequalities.[16] Those sharing a laugh at the expense of a ridiculed out-group can foster greater social alignment and decrease social distance with an in-group, as discussed above, while simultaneously creating and/or increasing social distance against the targets of ridicule and insult. In this way, ridicule is a powerful form of communication that works to position, align, and alienate bodies in society. It plays a significant role in reinforcing social hierarchies, social divisions, and thus a *social order.*

In his book, *Laughter and Ridicule: Towards a Social Critique of Humour,* social theorist Michael Billig suggests that laughter and humor are also forms of affective rhetoric. That is, humor is a form of social communication intended to persuade, align, or win people over to your side. By analyzing the social power and impact of humor and ridicule in this way, a different social function of humor is revealed. The dark side of humor functions as a social and political mechanism that can be used to divide social groups and reinforce existing social divisions, particularly when the ridicule of "others" is connected to deep rooted and naturalized social inequalities, hierarchies, and boundaries.

From this perspective, we can see that focusing on humor as primarily a "happy object" or force for good reveals only half the story, the half that tends to be overemphasized and celebrated in contemporary society. The scholarly field of humor studies, and contemporary discourse more generally around humor and laughter, have also embraced this positivity regarding humor. From reinforcing commonsense notions like "laughter is the best medicine" or the "subversive power of humor," to current research that supports these ideas by pointing to the physiological, psychological, emotional, and social benefits and impacts of laughter and humor in every-day life, humor is often viewed as inherently "good." The growth of "posi-tive psychology" under postindustrial capitalism is partly to blame, Billig suggests, because "positive identities and positive selves" should be what we are all striving for, even during times of stark economic inequality, oc-cupational precarity, and growing societal anxiety.[17]

But the overemphasis on humor's positive nature also appears to be a process a few centuries in the making. Some scholars have argued that this approach to the understanding of humor is also connected to the contra-dictions brought about by the Enlightenment, ideas that have been exac-erbated by the positivism of late-stage capitalism. For example, in many European societies, up until the end of the 17th century or so, "it was socially acceptable to laugh at individuals who were deformed or mentally ill, and the exchange of hostile witty remarks was a popular form of inter-action in fashionable society."[18] During the 18th century and the Victorian era, however, views on this kind of humor in Europe began to change, and Enlightenment and humanistic thinkers began to question the "hostile" and "aggressive" uses of humor and laughter as a means to disparage and marginalize. They began to view such forms of humor and laughter as "unrefined" and "vulgar" and sought to redefine and conceptualize the "sense of humor" in a more "virtuous" or "benevolent" way, to seemingly rescue it from its more negative uses.[19]

Although a liberal and moral sensibility about the ethics of humor began to gain more influence during this era, Enlightenment views on the sense of humor, much like those of freedom and democracy, co-existed alongside the realities of colonialism, empire, and racial slavery. During this same period, racial caricature and ridicule were also increasingly be-coming one of the dominant forms of humor and entertainment on both sides of the Atlantic.[20] For instance, the racial ridicule of Africans, slaves, and Blackness was increasingly prevalent in late 18th and early 19th century English art, carrying over from generation to generation, across art forms, and across geographical space. The resilience of these forms of racial ridi-cule, paired with a lack of critical examination of them, belies a deep-seated hypocrisy in modern western ideals, a problem that is still widely evident in the United States and other western societies today. As the art historian Temi Odumosu potently noted, "[These jokes and caricatures] seem to expose a weak spot in the European psyche, a space of deeply familiar pleasure and power play in the imaginative relationship with the other."[21]

As I describe in detail in the following chapters, ethnic and racial ridicule continue to serve a similar purpose in America today, propping up historically hegemonic racial ideologies, reinforcing an ethnocentric worldview, and upholding notions of ethnic and racial superiority and inferiority. Consequently, it is essential for any study of humor to also look closely at its intersection with systems of power and social control. This book's findings underscore how thoroughly racist humor is woven into the very fabric of America's systems of racial power, and it highlights the need to continue to develop new theoretical innovations for understanding what racist humor is, what it does, and how it impacts U.S. society today.

Acknowledging White Racist Humor

During the early 1940s, as the United States entered the global war against fascism in Europe, the problem of white supremacy and systemic racism continued rampantly at home. Gunnar Myrdal, the Swedish economist and sociologist, was commissioned by the Carnegie Corporation to examine the "Negro Problem" in Anglo-American society. As an outsider, it was believed that Myrdal could offer an "unbiased" perspective on race relations in America, even though Black American scholars like W. E. B. Du Bois had been critically examining and articulating this problem for decades, as we discussed in Chapter 1. In Myrdal's influential book, *An American Dilemma: The Negro Problem and Modern Democracy*,[22] Myrdal focused on the contradiction of the United States calling itself a democratic society even as whites in America had enforced and maintained a system of racial domination through the subordination of Blacks across virtually all aspects of social, cultural, political, and economic life. This systematic oppression and subordination, Myrdal argued, contributed to the "poor performance" of Black Americans and their inability to fully "racially integrate" into U.S. society—a problem that was further reinforced by the way whites viewed and treated Black Americans as an inferior group, thus perpetuating a vicious cycle of white racial domination. But Myrdal also made the point that such subordination was not always explicit or institutional, that it was also accomplished through more quotidian social practices. In his book, Myrdal briefly highlighted what he described as a "white sense of humor" in the United States—a practice that he felt revealed much about a white racial imagination and social habits—and how this kind of humor related to broader status and identity formation among whites and their general outlook and domination over Black Americans and other racialized groups.

Indeed, during the time that Myrdal was working on this study in the decades preceding the civil rights movement, white racist humor was a widespread and typical indulgence across the United States in both private and public spheres, including popular films, books, and television.[23] In other words, this form of racist humor was more than an attitude or merely a form of racial prejudice. It was an expression of an amused racial contempt that can be seen as operating through what sociologist Joe Feagin would later call a "white racial frame."[24] This racial frame—which centers whiteness and white culture as "normal" and at the top of the American social hierarchy—developed in tandem with the broader historical, social, political, and economic development of U.S. society. A white racial frame sustains structural and systemic racism via a shared worldview that produces and maintains a "positive orientation" of whites and whiteness as "superior, virtuous, and morally good," and is upheld by developing and maintaining a "negative orientation" of non-whites as "inferior" and "bad."[25] From this perspective, a white racial frame is useful for understanding how white social affiliation and alignment operates and is connected to systemic racism.

This shared racial frame has been crucial for legitimizing and rationalizing systemic racism across social institutions, as it allows whites (and non-whites) to advocate for white advantages and privileges as normative, rather than a result of unjust historic and ongoing forms of racial oppression and subordination.[26] Notably, as Myrdal also observed, this white racial frame is often expressed through racist humor, where such joking continues to rely on the use of centuries-old and contemporary racist imagery, slurs, epithets, stereotypes, and the mocking and ridicule of the physical, cultural, and linguistic differences that people of color embody.[27] Consequently, for centuries, this racial frame has served as the dominant lens for understanding racial matters and social life in the United States and has led whites to believe they were innately superior to non-whites. Since white superiority was internalized in this process, it is no surprise that such a worldview also led to pervasive and fully tolerated racist images, stereotypes, notions, and other cultural practices, including jokes. This amused racial contempt that whites have long shared across class backgrounds and social contexts has been both a source of racist pleasure and an everyday endorsement and legitimation of a white racial hierarchy. As a dominant cultural discourse, it has reinforced white superiority and supremacy as the natural order of things—the way the world "is."

These everyday beliefs regarding the natural inferiority of non-whites were fully integrated into America's early entertainment and popular culture industries. In the 19th and early 20th centuries, for example, black-face minstrelsy became extremely popular; it was a form of amused racial contempt that articulated an ideology of white supremacy via a white racial frame. Racial ridicule was normalized on stage, radio, television, and film for the collective pleasure and consumption of white audiences in particular.[28] This kind of white racist humor endured as an ordinary type of cultural expression all the way until the mid-20th century. However, the condemnation of racist humor became more widespread during and after the civil rights period, as people of color mobilized against white supremacy with calls for racial equality and racial democracy. White racist humor came to be viewed as not only "politically incorrect" but as a direct expression of this larger system of racism and racial oppression.

This shift in understanding of such humor was largely due to civil rights groups and cultural critics increasingly challenging amused racial contempt as they "sought positive representations, and demanded that popular culture serve a multiracial democracy."[29] During the second half of the 20th century, non-whites began to publicly challenge such racial ridicule, signaling a turning point in the racist history of the United States and a weakening of a white racial framing of society during this time. People of color began to call for racial democracy and equality,[30] in no small part by advocating to end the practice of white racist jokes. For instance, during the civil rights era, groups like the NAACP protested comedy shows that continued the legacy of blackface minstrelsy, such as the popular comedy show *Amos 'n' Andy*, while organizations such as the Mexican American Anti-Defamation Committee (MAADC) and the Involvement of Mexican Americans in Gainful Endeavors (IMAGE) challenged racist comic portrayals of Latinos as inarticulate buffoons, such as comedian Bill Dana's Latino minstrel character "José Jiménez," a popular brownface minstrel character featured at the 1961 inaugural ball for President John F. Kennedy.[31] As a result of organized public protests against the use of racist humor by whites during and after the civil rights movement, many scholars and writers argued that the social acceptability of white racist humor was declining, and whites began to face condemnation when ridiculing racial and ethnic minorities in public.[32]

This cultural shift in public racetalk in the post–civil rights era contributed to the notion that a new cultural moment had arrived, a shift that conservatives and liberals increasingly described as "political correctness." This trend reflected the fact that how people viewed explicit and offensive racist talk in public by whites also intersected with evolving social and political alliances and larger trajectories of racial politics.[33] For the first time in U.S. society, whites could no longer make use of racist discourse, slurs, and ridicule freely and without opposition and social consequence.[34]

Both ordinary people and those in the media, as well as mainstream humor scholars, began to assume that racism was now in decline and that it was no longer a serious social problem. In turn, they increasingly believed that such humor was disappearing from American culture. However, as this book documents, white racist humor continues to thrive in the United States, and its racial ideologies continue to shape social behavior throughout American life, including public institutions. Today, as I discuss throughout this book, racist joking continues to occur at "all levels of society," both in public and backstage private settings.[35] From private gatherings among friends to the political arena, racist joking continues to play an important role in maintaining a "white racial framing" of U.S. society.

Ethnic Humor Without Racism

As racist humor became less socially acceptable during the second half the 20th century, and as the prevailing assumption emerged that racist humor was declining in significance, the issue of racist humor in general began to receive less attention from scholars and humor theorists. At the same time, a new theoretical framework for understanding humor emerged during the post–civil rights period. This new perspective, the field of ethnic humor studies, was still interested in questions of humor and identity. However, it was not interested in questions of race, racism, and power.

Since the 1980s, the study of ethnic humor has become a vast and influential discipline, receiving widespread attention across the social sciences and humanities. This field has been intent on understanding the prevalence of ethnic jokes and humor at a time when it seemed that racism and racist humor were receding to the social margins. Moreover, in a post–civil rights era, there was a broad effort to no longer view the issue of race and racism as central to the problems affecting modern western societies, as we were fast becoming a *post-racial* society.

According to critical race theorist David Theo Goldberg, the notion of post-racialism, like that of colorblindness, was swiftly embraced by politically conservative pundits, officials, and academics because it articulated the idea that racism was over, that it was a thing of the past, and that it was no longer a problem worth analyzing or discussing. And if racism was finally over and was primarily an issue of earlier historical periods, as post-racialists insisted, they also remained hostile to the idea that racism continued to be a systemic and contemporary social problem. In this way, Goldberg argues, post-racialism became the new racism of the post–civil rights era, in that its proponents sought to ignore the reality and persistence of racism in this new era.[36]

This position—that racism is no longer a serious social problem—was embraced by the burgeoning field of ethnic humor studies during the 1980s and up through the first decade of the new millennium. And it was a perspective that materialized in the work of many ethnic humor scholars and others but was acutely expressed by one of its most distinguished, prolific, and influential proponents: the British sociologist Christie Davies.

Because Davies had such great influence in the empirical and theoretical development of ethnic humor studies, it is worth closely examining his theoretical perspective to see how and why this framework was conceptually and theoretically inadequate for analyzing the persistent problem of racism and racist humor in society, and to understand how these shortcomings by ethnic humor scholars like Davies were tied to an investment in post-racialism.

Davies, highly regarded as one of the most influential ethnic humor scholars in the world, focused much of his scholarship and career on developing a "universal theory of ethnic humor," a field that sidelined and obscured the issue of racist humor in the process. Davies postulated that ethnic humor was a widespread global phenomenon, a "social fact," that was used to assert "distinctive identities" and as a means of reinforcing ethnic and social boundaries. Drawing on the work of sociologist Emile Durkheim, Davies suggested that jokes were "social facts" because they could impact the way individuals and social groups could act, think, and feel about themselves and others, and they could be studied and used to explain characteristics and forms of human interaction.[37] He argued that humor researchers needed to consider the social, historical, cultural, and political contexts in which these particular kinds of "joke themes" emerged and circulated. As Davies noted, "The key question to ask is why this particular set of jokes is in circulation at this particular time in this particular society rather than some other possible set."[38]

His theoretical method consisted of analyzing a large number of jokes "with a common theme." In developing his theory of ethnic humor, Davies collected, analyzed, and compared thousands of ethnic jokes from over thirty countries, from the post-WWII era until the early 21st century. He found that the most common ethnic jokes were ones that targeted a neighboring ethnic group (e.g., geographic, cultural, historic) and their presumed stupidity, canniness, cowardliness, or aggressiveness. He theorized that there was a recurring pattern where ethnic humor was always directed at groups that occupied some sort of peripheral edge or space relative to those who occupied the center or mainstream.[39] Brazilians have stupidity jokes about the Portuguese, the French about the Belgians, the

Swedish about the Finns, Americans about the Polish, and so on, and Davies noted similar patterns in non-western countries. Davies found that stupidity jokes were the most common form of ethnic jokes around the world, and he argued that the proliferation of these jokes correlated with the increasing demands for "rationalization" in modern capitalist societies. The mocking of stupidity and the stupid, he argued, was not about subordinating or oppressing targeted groups, but rather, it illustrated a social desire to expel or relegate "pre-modern irrationality" to the periphery in modern or modernizing industrial societies. Ethnic jokes about the stupidity of rural or migrant ethnic groups, he suggested, often focused on their presumed "inability to comprehend everyday processes."[40]

Davies's ideas on ethnic humor, however, have not been helpful for understanding the relationship between racism and humor, even though he was concerned with the way jokes could reinforce existing social boundaries. This is because he argued that jokes were not connected to issues of power or control; instead, they were primarily ways of distinguishing in-group and out-group in an entertaining and amusing fashion. For Davies, the existence and circulation of such jokes was not due to some underlying conflict, hostility, hatred, or aggression towards peripheral or marginalized ethnic groups. Rather, he argued that ethnic jokes were primarily a form of "play" and "teasing" against these "next-of-kin" groups who were rendered as metaphorical "cousins" or "country cousins" when they became targets of ethnic humor.[41] The joke tellers, Davies assured, "see the people about whom they tell stupidity jokes as a distorted version of themselves, as themselves seen in a fairground distorting mirror."[42]

This assessment of ethnic jokes, which proved to be influential among sociologists and other scholars, poses several dilemmas when contemplating how ethnic humor intersects with racism, in part because Davies did not make a serious effort to focus his analysis on racist humor, past or present. Take his example of Polish jokes in the United States, which he suggested were some of the most common jokes told in the country during the second half of the 20th century.[43] Davies listed several theories about why such jokes were so popular from the post-WWII era until the end of the 20th century, pointing out how they were largely recycled from earlier stupidity jokes targeting the Irish, Italians, Portuguese, and other rural European working-class immigrant groups. He suggested that Polish jokes were ultimately about social class and concluded that such jokes were popular because they were perceived as a harmless source of social fun, teasing, and amusement. "If American ethnic jokes about the Poles were an expression of hostility," Davies argued, "then we would expect there also to exist a significant body of *serious* American folklore about the Poles ascribing negative characteristics to them."[44] The point being, according to Davies, that such a body of negative stereotypes about the Polish did not exist.[45] But Polish Americans and immigrants certainly took the jokes more seriously than Davies did. During the late 1980s and early 1990s, the Polish American Congress, taking the lead from Black and Latino civil rights groups, protested the circulation of "Polack jokes" in media and public discourse, jokes that ridiculed Polish immigrants as "stupid," "crude," and "brutish" people.[46]

In other words, for theorists of ethnic humor like Davies, such jokes were an important subject to study—not because they were symbolic expressions of prejudice connected to systemic forms of inequality, be they class, race, or gender—but because they were merely unserious statements that played with and bent the social rules, norms, and boundaries of public civil discourse. They "are a brief time off from the everyday inhibitions and restrictions" that usually "bind the way we speak," Davies argued, while noting that the targeting of peripheral and low status ethnic groups with such jokes was merely a form of play, social teasing, and group pleasure.[47]

Davies called his theoretical perspective the "center-edge model" of ethnic humor and actively used it to attempt to provide "a clear refutation of the idea that jokes are a product of hostility or conflict or anxiety or threat," while asserting that "the conflict theory of humor is irrelevant."[48] Davies, however, went beyond that claim. He used his academic stature and influence in this field to not only emphasize this point when it came to so-called ethnic humor, but insisted that this was the case for understanding the social function and impact of jokes and humor in general. As he proclaimed, "Jokes have no social consequence for society as a whole. . . .

[They] are entertainment only, a mere laughing matter." And he insisted that those who disagree "must accept the burden of proof" when aiming to illustrate that "such consequences exist."[49]

White Epistemological Ignorance

We can see, then, the theoretical and empirical limitations that a perspective like the one above has on examining the realities of racist humor—how theorists like Davies were conceptually and philosophically inadequate (and opposed) to analyzing the relationship between humor and power during the so called post-racial era. But by fervently adhering to the commonsense notion that ethnic and racial jokes were "just jokes," Davies, among others, ignored how "social facts," as Emile Durkheim had earlier suggested, also impact individual and social behavior by exercising "coercive power" over the ways that people act, think, and feel about themselves and about others.[50]

This theoretical blind spot on the "coercive power" of certain forms of race-based humor is not merely an oversight, but an example of what political philosopher Charles Mills calls "white epistemological ignorance": the resistant logic and practice of "not knowing" that allows whites to minimize knowledge of racial harm, render whiteness and racism invisible, and marginalize the history and memory of white racial domination and its impact on the present, by putting white racism out of sight and out of mind.[51] While certainly not all white theorists reinforce or embrace this epistemological ignorance concerning racist humor, as Myrdal, Feagin, and other scholars illustrate, the notion that jokes are "just jokes" has been the dominant perspective used to reinforce and deny the relationship between racism and humor.

Generally speaking, humor plays a particular role in how groups interact, create meaning, and maintain order among individual members. The example from Chapter 1, of Sergeant Cleon Brown being racially ridiculed by fellow white officers, illustrates the problem associated with this issue in the context of racist humor, even when it targets whites (in Chapter 4, I detail how racist humor is integrated into the culture of law enforcement more broadly). Racist humor, unlike other forms of humor, is fundamentally constructed on social divisions created by historically defined racial ideologies of whiteness and Blackness in particular.

In his book *The Racial Contract*, Mills describes how the division between whites and non-whites, which resulted from the history of European imperialism and colonization of the globe, has remained as a "fundamental conceptual cut" in the development of modern civil society over that last five centuries. In the history and development of western society, non-whites have been continually regarded as "sub-persons" in ways that even marginalized European "ethnic whites" have not. As Mills argues, there are few exceptions where "borderline Europeans" or "off-whites" (e.g., Irish, Jews, Roma) have been subjected to the kind of violent dehumanization that non-whites and Indigenous populations around the world have been historically and continually subjected to (e.g., Nazi Germany). Moreover, today, white ethnic European groups and individuals, including immigrants or religious minorities, enjoy full membership in western society and civilization in ways that non-whites generally do not.[52]

This is a primary reason why describing racist humor as "ethnic humor" is a conceptual problem, because unlike some forms of so-called ethnic humor, which decrease as ethnic groups become more assimilated into whiteness, historic targets of racist humor remain targets of racism even after they gain more civil rights and social status. Indeed, today Polish jokes do not enjoy the same level of social circulation and degree of offense they did some thirty years ago when Davies was putting together his theories on ethnic humor, while the persistence of anti-Black and other forms of racist humor remain a serious problem.[53]

Moreover, another key problem with this framework is that racialized groups are not generally "teased" as metaphorical family members in society—as Davies's theoretical model suggests "ethnic humor" would do among ethnic groups. That is, although Davies concluded that ethnic jokes were harmless because in the end ethnic targets and tellers were rendered "family" or "country cousins" in the process, the fundamental logic of racism and white supremacy is built around the central idea that racialized "others" are *not* family—that they are of some other inferior lineage, origin, or race. Instead, non-white racialized groups are targeted with racist humor through racial ridicule, harassment, and dehumanization in ways that are, when utilized by whites in particular, generally intended to reify a racial ideology and hierarchy of white superiority and dominance.

By approaching the study of racist humor from a post-racial perspective offered by ethnic humor studies, we can also see how the perspective of scholars like Davies is also hostile to the suggestion that racist humor is a subject worthy of serious sociological examination. For instance, in his brief analysis of racist jokes targeting African Americans (e.g., "What did the little Black boy get for Christmas? My bike." "Why did Crimestoppers give the Black lady $50? She had an abortion"),[54] Davies used these kinds of jokes, not in the spirit of further developing his theoretical analysis of humor, but to make a sweeping and ideologically loaded argument to stump "ultra-liberals." He argued that the apparent censorship of jokes targeting African Americans in media and public discourse in the post–civil rights period were merely about "political correctness," while noting that "Poles" (Polish Americans) did not receive the same level of "guilt, concern, or anger on their behalf . . . [from] . . . ultra-liberal elites."[55] He also pointed to the fact that efforts by liberals to censor jokes targeting African Americans were ineffective because such jokes remained popular and in circulation despite political correctness.

The popularity of racist anti-Black jokes at the time Davies was writing is undeniable, particularly when considering those that gained mass public circulation during the early 1980s in the book series *Truly Tasteless Jokes,* published under the pseudonym "Blanche Knott" (e.g., "What do you call a black boy with a bicycle? Thief!" "What's another word for cocoon? N-n*****" "What do you call a black millionaire industrialist? A tycoon" "How do you shoot a black man? Aim for the radio").[56] Following the civil rights movement, which contributed to the cultural changes in the acceptability of public racist discourse, such joke books "landed in force on the nation's bookshelves."[57] In fact, the *Truly Tasteless Jokes* series was so popular it appeared on various national bestseller lists, remaining on the *New York Times* list for over twenty weeks.[58] The books were so popular that writers and publishers began to complain about "being crowded out of the best sellers list" by such joke books, which led to the creation of the "Advice, How-to, & Miscellaneous" category at the *New York Times*.[59] This widely popular book series included hundreds of racist, sexist, and other disturbing jokes during the early part of the so-called post-racial era, jokes that would later appear and be recirculated on numerous white supremacist websites with the emergence of the internet, illustrating the close relationship between popular forms of amused racial contempt and those wielded by racist extremists (as I discuss in Chapter 3).[60]

Early critics of such joke books were concerned with the impact they might have on society. For instance, while some, like Pulitzer Prize–winning historian Barbara W. Tuchman, viewed such jokes as a "breakdown of decency and taste," others were concerned that "bigotry could well be lurking just below the surface" and warned that such "racial jokes could be an invitation to racial hatred."[61] But other critics, including Davies, dismissed such claims and argued that the popularity of such jokes was not the result of racism; they were merely a "rebellious" source of pleasure used to "defy" the censorship efforts by "ultra-liberal elites."[62]

A number of prominent conservative commentators have shared the perspective that such humor should not be examined in terms of its relationship to actual existing racism, but in terms of the unjust "power" used by the liberal establishment trying to censor them. Many complaints from conservative pundits today about political correctness and cancel culture sound very similar to what Davies said about racist jokes when he argued that "a section of the American upper middle class" who, "enjoying a nearly hegemonic control over the mass-media and education, combined with a disproportionate political influence, was able to ban jokes about African Americans from substantial areas of public life."[63] The radio host Rush Limbaugh, for example, pushed similar ideas on his syndicated talk shows, challenging the notion that ridiculing Blacks was unacceptable in the post–civil rights era. As Limbaugh noted, "How come you can't have a little fun about blacks? . . . What protects them? Why are they immune from legitimate forms of humor?"[64] But as we will see in Chapter 5, Limbaugh and other conservatives have used their platforms to advance racist ridicule and rhetoric, particularly during the Obama era.

Leaving aside for the moment the fact that the so-called censorship of racist humor in media and public discourse was not the result of the sensibilities of "ultra-liberal elites" but rather the long and sustained effort by racial justice movements targeting all aspects of racism and white supremacy during the mid-20th century, views of Davies, Limbaugh, and other conservatives illustrate why theories of ethnic humor are conceptually, philosophically, and politically inadequate for examining racist humor in society, past and present. It is this perspective that also bolsters a white epistemological ignorance that is used by many people today to try to explain away racist jokes—as Davies did thirty years ago—as being harmless and nothing more than "just jokes." Developing an alternative framework plays a key role in better understanding the broader mechanisms and impact of racist humor that are documented in the following chapters.

Towards a Theory of Racist Humor

This book looks closely at concrete examples of racist humor in key state and public arenas, as well as among far-right groups, and by doing so reveals how racist humor operates today much as it did in the past, even if it is in subtler and less visible social contexts. To help bring into view how this humor operates, in the following section I discuss some of the conceptual complications for articulating how racist humor works and offer a potential framework for some its key mechanisms.

Developing a theoretical account of racist humor requires drawing from interdisciplinary theoretical insights that account for the ways in which such humor contributes to social affiliation and division, as discussed earlier in this chapter, and in ways that are filtered through the lens of race. What is rendered in the process is not only a theory of racist humor but of a "white sense of humor"—a humor that has played, and continues to play, a significant role in the racial pleasure, subordination, and cultural politics of racism in white-dominated societies that lack multiracial democracy.

It is important to note, however, that it is not only whites who make use of racist humor and that whites can also be targets of racialized discourse and humor, as the example of Sergeant Cleon Brown clearly illustrates. Moreover, there are countless jokes that target and racialize poor and lower-class whites as "white trash," "hillbillies," and "red necks," illustrating the intersections of race and class in the ridicule and dehumanization of poor whites.[65] It is worth noting that the mass reproduction and circulation of these terms that racialize poor whites stem from white-owned mass media and culture industries.[66] But the racial ridicule and mockery of non-whites by whites is different than people of color aiming to ridicule and mock whites and whiteness. The former is often about reinforcing dominant power relations, the latter is often an attempt to resist them. Moreover, racist joking practices generally work to reinforce racism despite the "good intentions" of joke tellers. While a theoretical argument can be made that the use of racist humor in such reciprocal contexts does not necessarily mean that the joke tellers are motivated by racism, cultural theorist Stuart Hall offered a more critical assessment of such joking practices:

> Telling racist jokes across the racial line, in conditions where relations of racial superiority and inferiority prevail, reinforces the difference and reproduces the unequal relations because, in those situations, the point of the joke depends on the existence of racism. Thus they reproduce the categories and relations of racism, even while normalizing them through laughter. To state the good intentions of the joke-makers do not resolve the problem here, because they are not in control of the circumstances—conditions of continuing racism—in which their joke discourse will be read and heard.[67]

Similarly, other critical race theorists have suggested that even in contexts where non-whites engage in the reciprocal use of racist jokes with whites, the use and reliance of conventional racist discourse, imagery, stereotypes and slurs all reflect a type of content that was long ago created by whites, and then perpetuated across generations in ways that maintain and reinforce white racist discourse and ideology—Feagin's "white racial frame."[68]

The insult and ridicule of whites by people of color does not carry the same social, political, and historical *weight* and meaning as it does when whites ridicule non-whites through racialized humor.[69] White racist humor, in other words, is fueled by an element of power and contempt. Attached to this amused racial contempt are the historic and continued inequities that stem from a structured, systemic, and unjust racial hierarchy that produces unequal cultural and social relations.[70] These unequal relations are also often reinforced when non-whites engage in self-deprecation or when non-whites target other racialized groups.[71] In turn, what takes shape through this practice of amused racial contempt is the social and racial ordering of individuals and groups, in ways that are normalized through everyday jokes and laughter that are often framed as innocent, well intended, and just for fun.[72] Such racist joking practices, as Hall suggests, generally work to reinforce racial categories and racism itself despite the "good intentions" of joke tellers.[73]

Racist Humor as a Racial Project

Racist humor, understood this way, can be productively described as a *racial project,* or a process by which this particular form of racial discourse can serve as a mechanism that contributes to the formation of social othering and ordering. Racist humor carries and conveys racial meaning in ways that can inform and reinforce commonsense explanations about how to understand race, in ways that link the concept of race between the macro/structural and the micro/interpersonal level, particularly when circulated within institutions and organizations at the mezzo level. This dynamic contributes to the reproduction and maintenance of what sociologist Victor Ray describes as a "racialized organization."[74] The impact of blackface minstrelsy on the racialization of the entertainment industry and on the development of commonsense race consciousness during the 19th century is a clear example of this process. White blackface performers and entertainers taught white audiences not only how to see and understand Blacks and Blackness, but how to see and understand themselves as whites alongside a racialized hierarchy and social order that was being developed alongside the economic and political development of the United States.[75]

Using racist humor to create race consciousness and foment social identity, division, and social order more generally has not disappeared from

American culture, even though explicit racial ridicule, such as blackface, is no longer considered socially acceptable. This type of race consciousness and its relationship to social identity is deeply embedded in a long history of racial and social affiliation in the United States, and humor continues to be used for "teaching" social affiliation and social ordering through race.[76]

Using the concept of "racial formation," race theorists Michael Omi and Howard Winant have also written at length on the topic of "race making," or how race came to be, how it has changed, and how it has impacted our society, past and present.[77] Referring to specific elements of the social and political construction of race, or racial projects, Omi and Winant have highlighted how race and racism have been formed through powerful social forces, structures and institutions like the state, imperialism, capitalist development, religion, science, and the law. Cultural institutions and practices have also played a significant role in forming race, and the close relationship between humor, racism, and social affiliation suggests that for as long as race has been central in forming and ordering society, so too has racist humor as a mode of reproducing racial boundaries and hierarchies.

Some scholars have begun to turn their attention to this issue. Sociologist Simon Weaver, for example, has demonstrated how racist humor operates through language and communication as a rhetorical or "persuasive" discourse and how humor can rhetorically impact and support an exclusionary logic of "othering" in general. Weaver identified several typologies of different forms of racist humor—including "embodied racist humor," "cultural racist humor," and "post-modern racist humor"—which can rhetorically contribute to the maintenance of a racial order in modern and late-modern western societies, and potentially support far-right and racist ideology.[78]

While Weaver does not explicitly link his scholarship to race theorists like Omi and Winant, his framework on the rhetorical impact of racist humor can be used productively to advance a theory of racist humor as a racial project and to show how humor contributes to racial formation. His rhetorical approach to racist humor can also be linked to the affective, or socio-emotional, model of humor that I lay out here, what I call *amused racial contempt*, in order to illustrate that it is not solely the rhetorical capacity of humor that creates and contributes to social alignment and affiliation. Because humor is generally connected to individual and social emotions, such emotions are also racialized, contribute to social "alignment" and "alienation," and play a central role in the formation of race and racism.

The Forbidden Pleasure of Racism

During the mid-20th century, the civil rights movement changed the social and political conditions for humor in the United States. The social and institutional changes that occurred at this time, including civil rights legislation and anti-discrimination laws, helped push the idea that racist language in public was now unacceptable. Since that time, researchers have noted the decline of overt and explicit racist discourse in public and across social and institutional settings and contexts.[79] Humor scholars also observed that following the civil rights movement, white racist humor (e.g., blackface) was no longer socially accepted as a form of entertainment.[80]

While racist ideology and discourse did not disappear in this new context, the new stigma of racism did make it more challenging for such notions to be publicly expressed. However, in contrast to Jim Crow era racism, in this new post-racial and colorblind era, overt racist discourse began to be minimized, leading whites, as sociologist Eduardo Bonilla-Silva has noted, to continue to "enunciate positions that safeguard their racial interests without sounding 'racist.'"[81] This shift, however, between prior modes of racist expression, which were often explicit, and current ones, which are implicit or minimized, is important to keep in mind, as it suggests that many of the historical studies and approaches to understanding more explicit forms of racist humor (e.g., blackface minstrelsy) are insufficient for understanding newer mechanisms and social functions of racist humor in the post–civil rights and ostensibly colorblind era.

More recent approaches for understanding contemporary racism do offer valuable theoretical tools for analyzing racist humor today. Theories of colorblind racism, for instance—which consider the ways racist ideologies, practices, and discourses have changed in the aftermath of the civil rights movement—provide a useful framework for helping us think about the way that, for example, racist humor has come to be enjoyed as a "forbidden pleasure" that allows for the expression and enjoyment of repressed racist notions and sentiments. But there is still more work to be done for understanding how racist humor has emerged and operates in the current era, something that this book is intended to address.

By bridging theories of colorblind racism with Freud's analysis of jokes and their relations to repressed individual and social sentiments, we gain a productive framework to better understand the forbidden pleasure of racist humor in contemporary U.S. society. In his book *Jokes and Their Relation to the Unconscious*, Freud pointed to the ways that civil society— to curb the overt use of aggression, hostility, violence, sexual fulfilment, and related discourse—has produced social norms that repress these "instincts" or urges. Jokes, he argued, are a pleasurable means of circumventing these social norms to express repressed urges or tendencies. As Freud observed, "[Jokes] make possible the satisfaction of an instinct (whether lustful or hostile) in the face of an obstacle that stands in its way."[82] This forbidden pleasure, however, was not enjoyed solely by the individual. Because of the social nature of humor, Freud noted that hostile or "tendentious" jokes were also a "pleasurable bribe" used to form an "alliance" between the joke teller and the listener, against a third party who was the target of the joke.[83] Connecting this insight to Sara Ahmed's perspective on social alignment and alienation in the cultural politics of emotions, and Du Bois's notion of the psychological wages of whiteness, we can see that in a seemingly post-racial and colorblind society, racist jokes are a forbidden pleasure that potentially offer emotional alignment and unity between the joke teller and listener against the racialized target.

In our current so-called colorblind and "politically correct" era, humor continues to play a key role in the way racist notions proliferate among American social groups. Racist joking allows joke tellers to "gain pleasure from expressing feelings and views that are normally repressed because of social pressure," where "just beneath its apparently joking and unserious surface" jokers often signal more serious racial feelings and/or views that they may harbor.[84] In this way, racist joking in a so-called colorblind society allows joke tellers to share and test the waters of racial sentiments in seemingly benign or unserious ways, as "just a joke."

Moreover, the idea that racist humor is "just a joke" works to minimize "charges of racism."[85] Because many cultures have strong "cultural expectation that individuals 'go along' with jokes," this cultural expectation regarding humor "generates a normative response of silence, inaction or engagement with the joke."[86] This dominant cultural practice regarding the interpretation of humor, including racist humor, works to strengthen colorblind and post-racial ideologies, including the notion that racism is less significant today than it was in the past. In turn, the continued prevalence of racist humor, and the denial that such humor is racist, including among revered scholars, works to simultaneously deepen and reveal the prevalence of amused racial contempt in a society where overt and explicit racism is ostensibly unacceptable or in decline.

But this myth was in many ways shattered during the Obama and Trump presidencies over the last decade. The election of Obama, in particular, served to embolden racist discourse in the public arena, particularly in the form of racial ridicule and insult targeted against the first Black president, as I will examine in Chapter 5.[87] In turn, these changes in public racial discourse following the civil rights movement are ones in which, as Moon-Kie Jung put it, "whites conceded the importance of racism" as a "temporary" rather than "permanent shift" in U.S. society.[88] Racist humor, via direct expression and debate around its social (un)acceptability, has played a crucial role in the (re)legitimation of serious racism.

Applying a Theory of Amused Racial Contempt

As described earlier, my concept of *amused racial contempt* links the intersection of racial fun and amusement alongside the emotional, structural, and interactional dimensions of race and racism. I began applying this framework to racist humor within the entertainment industry and later expanded my analysis to contexts beyond entertainment to find that racist humor has functioned—and continues to function—as a powerful racialization mechanism over the last two centuries.[89]

W. E. B. Du Bois's prescient essay "The Souls of White Folk," discussed in Chapter 1, was one of the first to theorize whiteness as a social and political construct based on a feeling of superiority over racialized others—a kind of racial contempt. Here I extend Du Bois's insights to the study of humor, connecting theories of racial formation to parallel ideas about the social power of humor. By critically synthesizing scholarship on race, humor, and emotions, I argue that humor functions to produce racial alienation, dehumanization, exclusion, and even violence. Rather than being harmless fun, this form of humor plays a central role in reinforcing and mobilizing racist ideology and power relations under the guise of amusement, while foregrounding the central role of emotion and humor in racial formation and white racial dominance. From this synthesis, I show that racism is not only about ignorance or hate, but about reproducing a pleasurable racial solidarity. And this approach can help us refocus our attention and understanding about what white supremacy is and why it persists. By tracing the development of amused racial contempt throughout American history and into the present, I demonstrate that this is not a new phenomenon, despite the new ways in which it manifests.

In the examination of racist humor in three contexts—among the far right, in law enforcement, and in the political arena—amused racial contempt is an everyday practice that has proliferated since the civil rights era. I chose to focus on these contexts for two important reasons. First, much contemporary research on racial and ethnic humor tends to focus on the uses of such humor in entertainment in general, and comedy in particular. But the use and impact of racist humor within other social settings remains largely under-theorized and under-examined.[90]

Second, there is a lack of research on the use of racist humor in social institutional settings that wield social influence and power in everyday life. This is not to suggest that cultural industries like comedy are not influential or powerful in society, as was discussed earlier. However, when we find law enforcement officers routinely sharing racist jokes within their ranks while the racial abuse of Black and Brown communities continues as a widespread problem; when white supremacists are deliberately using racist humor to engage political discourse, spread racist and fascist propaganda, and increasingly engage in violence; and when we see political candidates, elected officials, and local and global leaders being targets of, and trading in, racial insults to gain political influence, I believe such settings are in urgent need of theoretical and critical attention.

CHAPTER 3

HIDING IN PLAIN SIGHT
The Violent Racist Humor of the Far Right

"We like to use humor and satire like anyone else does. . . . We always like to use things that we think are funny."

Tom Metzger, *White Aryan Resistance*

"Most people are not comfortable with material that comes across as vitriolic, raging, non-ironic hatred. . . . The unindoctrinated should not be able to tell if we are joking or not. . . . There should be a conscious agenda to dehumanize the enemy, to the point where people are ready to laugh at their deaths. So it isn't clear that we are doing this—as that would be a turnoff to most normal people—we rely on lulz."

Andrew Anglin, The Daily Stormer

RACIST HUMOR IN AMERICAN CULTURE and society remains systemic and deeply rooted. It also continues to evolve as new political and moral systems emerge. In the so-called colorblind society of the post–civil rights era, racist humor has taken on new rhetorical and political forms, while recent innovations in technology and social media have altered the means by which this humor reproduces and reinvents racist ideologies for the 21st century. This chapter looks at humor among the far right and discusses how amused racial contempt has been incorporated into the language and discourse of people with explicit racist agendas.

Far-right racist humor has long played a particularly insidious role in propagating racist ideologies in the United States, and today it is no different. However, since the civil rights movement, it has been evolving, and social media and the internet have introduced new mediums for this humor to circulate and carry over from white supremacist leaders of the past. But while this effort has been going on for decades, it appears that Americans are only recently beginning to take notice.

One evening in late summer of 2019, Joanna Schroeder, a mother of teenage boys in Los Angeles, went online and proceeded to write on her Twitter feed: "Do you have white teenage boys?" She then continued, "Listen up," and, in a series of viral tweets, described how she had recently found on her young teenage boys' social media accounts a stream of racist, sexist, homophobic, and anti-Semitic memes and videos veiled with humor, irreverence, and "edginess."

"I saw the memes that came across my kids' timelines, and once I started clicking on those and seeking this material out, then it became clear what was really happening," she wrote. While combing through her kids' social media feeds, Schroeder noticed that these racist and sexist jokes and memes soon led to more serious white supremacist propaganda. "I've been watching my boys' online behavior & noticed that social media and vloggers are actively laying groundwork in white teens to turn them into alt-right/white supremacists." Schroder encountered tutorials teaching viewers how to "get away with using the n-word" and infographics relaying racist propaganda on Black criminality. "The more I clicked, the more I started to see memes about white supremacy . . . and that's what was really scary."[1] Were these viral tweets merely a partisan moral panic from a liberal white mother, paranoid about the dangers of granting her kids too much screen time in the age of Trump? Or had Schroeder discovered something that we should all be concerned about? As the rest of this chapter illustrates, the evidence suggests the latter.

The Weaponization of Racist Humor by the Alt-Right

Using humor and edginess to spread racist ideas is not a new phenomenon, but it has taken on new forms in today's social media landscape.

Two years before Schroeder wrote these tweets, Ashley Feinberg, a senior reporter for *Huffington Post*, wrote an article discussing a similar kind of outreach effort among members of the nascent alt-right movement. In her essay, Feinberg described a document she discovered from The Daily Stormer,[2] a leading white supremacist website run by neo-Nazi and alt-right propagandist Andrew Anglin. Written in the form of a publisher's formatting style guide for authors wishing to write for The Daily Stormer, the document included suggestions on paragraph length ("between two and three sentences") image size ("at least 618px in width"), vocabulary ("standard 8th grade vocabulary"), and topics of interest ("cover anything that people are talking about"). The document was also explicit about what the primary objective of potential authors writing for them should be: "to spread the message of nationalism and anti-Semitism to the masses."[3] For a white supremacist website, this goal was not much of a revelation. More surprising, however, was one of the key methods suggested in the document for spreading explicit racist ideas and content: *lulz*.

In today's internet jargon, "lulz" is understood as an online form of amusement, fun or laughter that is derived at the expense of someone else, a digital application of the notion of schadenfreude.[4] It has also been described as a "corrupted" form of the earlier internet and text messaging term "lol" for "laugh out loud."[5] Lulz first gained broader visibility as a term used by the online "hacktivist" group Anonymous, a decentralized left-leaning international online activist community organized on the now infamous imageboard website 4chan.[6] Anonymous, as well as later groups like LulzSec, developed a reputation for carrying out international and highly visible pranks and cyberattacks to ridicule and reveal the abuses and hypocrisies of governments, government agencies and officials, corporations, news and media companies, and religious organizations.[7] They were also supportive of broader movements and organizations challenging state and corporate power, such as the Occupy Wall Street movement and WikiLeaks. Members of LulzSec in particular often described their motivation for carrying out these actions as "doing it for the lulz," where "the lulz" was often derived from targeting, exposing, and ridiculing powerful institutions and organizations to a global audience.[8]

Anglin, editor of The Daily Stormer, took note of how these and other online activist groups made use of fun and amusement to draw in participants and gain popular support. He decided to apply this method to the white nationalist movement and the emerging alt-right to make white supremacist ideology more appealing to a broader audience. In some ways, Anglin's approach mirrored key aspects of this form of online discourse, even as he sought to coopt its strategies for his own purposes.

In recent years, Anglin has developed a reputation as a prominent far-right agitator, white supremacist propagandist, and internet troll, and he has become one of the most visible and influential figures in the alt-right movement.[9] He previously ran a far-right website called Total Fascism, which featured long-form essays and content in support of fascism, but he soon realized the limits of this approach. "A lot of people on the Internet prefer to write long essays, which a lot of people don't read, which have a limited audience," Anglin noted in an interview with the Los Angeles Times in 2015, following the mass shooting at a historic Black church in Charleston, South Carolina, by white supremacist terrorist Dylann Roof.[10]

In 2013, Anglin decided to change his format and approach. He abandoned his Total Fascism site and created The Daily Stormer, a new website drawing inspiration from Der Stürmer, the virulent and anti-Semitic Nazi propaganda tabloid founded by Nazi Party member Julius Streicher. Der Stürmer, a paper that was a key part of the Nazi propaganda machine, made regular use of obscene anti-Semitic and racist political cartoons. Such imagery was used to justify racial violence against Jews in particular, through the use of amused racial contempt. Streicher, who made a fortune from the sale of his paper during the rise of Nazi Germany, was later found guilty for "crimes against humanity" during the Nuremburg trials. He was indicted and executed by hanging.[11]

Anglin drew on the legacy of this paper and combined it with today's internet meme culture. "I wanted something punchy and funny and enjoyable to read, and something that anybody can get something out of," Anglin noted at the time.[12] Anglin launched The Daily Stormer around the time George Zimmerman was on trial for the murder of Trayvon Martin, a 17-year-old Black teenager. While the Zimmerman trial was not the main reason Anglin created The Daily Stormer, he exploited the incident, as well as the later shooting by Roof, as an opportunity to gain exposure for himself and his new website. "My ideology is very simple," Anglin noted, while trying to disassociate his ideological beliefs from those of Roof, who frequented and commented on The Daily Stormer website: "I believe white people deserve their own country."[13]

Although current scholars have singled out the alt-right as somehow historically unique in its strategic use of racist humor and amusement,[14] white supremacists like Anglin increasingly package their violent racist ideology in "fun" and "amusing" ways that draw on the methods and racist motivations that have been developed by overt white supremacists over the last century. Indeed, a closer look at the ongoing relationship between humor and racism in the writings and activities of people like Anglin and other individuals in the alt-right suggests that amused racial contempt has long served as a tool to normalize racial dehumanization and advance white supremacist propaganda among far-right groups. White supremacist propagandists continue to use it to rally support for racist ideologies and movements, which are eager to forge and maintain a shared group identity and worldview. These efforts also work to foster solidarity and emotional alignment among far-right supporters and newcomers, while increasing distance and detachment from opponents, perceived enemies, and racialized communities. Moreover, this kind of amused racial contempt is being used to prevent solidarity from forming across racial lines.

Anglin sees himself as a key player in a larger ideological and political struggle over race and nationalism. He points towards the current polarized political moment and is deliberate in his efforts to win white people (and their allies of color) over to the alt-right and the white nationalist movement.[15] "Right now, a divide is happening," Anglin contends. "And there are only going to be two sides. Either you are with the SJWs [social justice warriors] or you are with the Fascists."[16]

As a far-right agitator and propagandist, Anglin's new strategy for attracting young people to the alt-right and white supremacist movement was to normalize racism, anti-Semitism, white supremacy, and fascism in ways that seemed edgy, funny, amusing. The Daily Stormer style guide was offered as a "playbook" on how to disseminate racist content online and highlighted the use of racist humor in particular, in the form of jokes, memes, stories, and slurs.[17] As The Daily Stormer style guide suggests:

". . . when using racial slurs, it should come across as half-joking—like a racist joke that everyone laughs at because it's true. This follows the generally light tone of the site. . . . The reader is at first drawn in by curiosity or the naughty humor, and is slowly awakened to reality by repeatedly reading the same points. We are able to keep these points fresh by applying them to current events."[18]

This strategy has helped Anglin become a leading voice in advising potential alt-right agitators and propagandists on the methods of radicalization, particularly on the question of race. The success of this strategy is seen partly in the fact that The Daily Stormer is now the most visited white supremacist website on the internet, beating out Stormfront, the longest running and largest white supremacist website in the world.[19]

It is worth keeping in mind that the use of racist and politically incorrect humor is not a creation of the alt-right. Racist humor has been a key part of the U.S. cultural landscape for nearly two centuries, as illustrated by the history of blackface minstrelsy, its proliferation and evolution within the entertainment industry, and its perpetuation within public-serving institutions like law enforcement in the post–civil rights era.[20] But Anglin and others in the far right have used racist humor as an intentional pedagogical and outreach tool for the emerging alt-right in an attempt to recruit and create social alignment with their movement. They have seen the current widespread use of such humor across various online platforms and websites, such as 4chan, Reddit, Twitter, and YouTube in recent years.[21] This has led Anglin and other members of the alt-right to believe that many youth are already "naturally aligned" to the alt-right movement. Anglin's strategy has been simply to articulate, encourage, and channel this kind of activity in an effort to reorient the use of amused racial contempt as a tactic aimed at "awakening" or "redpilling" a new generation of white youth towards white nationalism and white supremacist ideology.[22]

The goal of the alt-right movement, for Anglin and others, is to draw in a younger crop of would-be white nationalists and white supremacists to grow the movement and "save the white race."

One of the seeming innovations of the contemporary alt-right movement is to consciously articulate and deploy humor to spread racist propaganda, directly implicating humor as a tool in the larger circulation of racist ideology. The use of internet memes that appropriate online youth culture has been one particularly successful strategy in this regard. For instance, one meme that received much attention during the 2016 presidential election, and that underscores the extraordinary role that humor plays in recent far-right racist strategies, was the transformation of the "Pepe the Frog" meme into an "ironic" anti-Semitic and racist symbol. The original anthropomorphic frog image, with the catchphrase "feels good man," was created by cartoonist Matt Furie in 2005 for his online comic *Boy's Club*. Furie's cartoon, which was not created as a racist symbol, became a popular internet meme that was repurposed by online users as an in-joke on earlier social media platforms and imageboards like My Space, Tumblr, and 4chan. The meme grew in popularity, and by 2010 it was increasingly used by members of the nascent alt-right on anonymous online platforms like 4chan. By 2016, the cartoon meme had been appropriated and weaponized by the alt-right and used to ridicule the Holocaust, celebrate Nazis and candidate Trump, circulate anti-Black images and mock the Black Lives Matter movement, and portray white supremacists and the far right as ironic, fun, and entertaining for the purpose of creating social alignment with their cause.[23]

Anglin is far from a lone culture warrior in this regard, as the strategic use of amused racial contempt has become a deliberate strategy among numerous alt-right writers, bloggers and vloggers, speakers, trolls, and provocateurs in recent years. As George Hawley notes in his recent book *Making Sense of the Alt-Right*, by presenting themselves as a "fun movement," the alt-right "comes across as youthful, light-hearted, and jovial—even as it says the most abhorrent things about racial and religious minorities," in contrast to older white supremacists and white nationalists like the KKK or neo-Nazis who come across as "bitter, reactionary,

Alt-Right Meme Pepe the Frog Branded Hate Symbol by ADL

By **Patrick Young, Esq.** · October 6, 2016   👁 4124   💬 0

FIGURE 3.1. "Pepe the Frog" meme as used by members of the alt-right on anonymous websites like 4chan.

SOURCE: P. Young, Alt-Right Meme Pepe the Frog Branded Hate Symbol by ADL, *Long Island Wins* (October 6, 2016): https://longislandwins.com/news/national/alt-right-meme-pepe-frog-branded-hate-symbol-adl/

and antisocial."[24] As Hawley contends, "whereas earlier white-nationalist movements often claimed the Holocaust never happened, the alt-right typically treats it as a joke."[25]

Scholars like Hawley have begun to highlight such efforts by the alt-right and white nationalists in recent years, pointing out how current white supremacist groups have increasingly made use of humor and ridicule, particularly through memes, to advance and mobilize white supremacist ideologies, notions, and sentiments. These scholars argue that the alt-right is distinct from older generations of white supremacists, like skinheads or the Klan, who are often framed as hate-filled "humorless" racists. As Hawley argues, "Irony and humor—essential to the alt-right—were all but nonexistent in these earlier movements."[26] Although some of these alt-right agitators use modern technology and social media, they also draw directly on historical racist ridicule and humor (e.g., blackface) to develop emotional alignment among whites more broadly.

Today's younger crop of millennial neo-fascists and white supremacists incorporate amused racial contempt in ways that continue to energize racial ideologies for new generations. But its affective politics are rooted in long traditions of far-right racist humor and how such humor was weaponized decades earlier. Despite broader evolutions in the way that race and racism are condemned and discussed in public, this humor continues to allow racist ideologies and their violent consequences to spread in a society that is, officially, against it. A closer look reveals how the use of amused racial contempt has long played a significant role in the ideological and affective politics of the far right, and how the alt-right's use of humor to advance racist ideology shows the central role that humor is playing, and has played, in the broader diffusion of racist ideology in the United States.[27]

The Humor of White Supremacy in the Post–Civil Rights Era

One of the most notorious and influential efforts in using racist humor to advance white supremacist and far-right ideologies and appeal to young white men in the decades following the civil rights movement came in the form of hundreds of vulgar and often violent racist cartoons featured in Tom Metzger's white supremacist newspaper *White Aryan Resistance*, and later website White Aryan Resistance (WAR), which Metzger branded as "the most racist newspaper on earth."[28] With this paper and the steady stream of racist cartoons it featured, Metzger offered a parallel assault to political correctness, colorblindness, and civil rights with a kind of racism that appealed to the irreverent sensibilities of a disaffected and alienated white working-class male youth coming of age in a post–civil rights America. Metzger's efforts to recruit young white men were illustrated in his ability to draw in and mobilize the growing white skinhead movement, the alt-right at the time, in large part by appealing to these alienated white male youth with hundreds of comic images that animated and legitimized their feelings of racial victimhood, resentment, pride, and superiority.

As noted in the previous chapter, during and after the civil rights movement, forms of racist humor that were socially and commercially acceptable before the civil rights era, like blackface minstrelsy, were now deemed racist and socially unacceptable. But new forms of racial comedy and racist humor soon emerged and gained popularity as a source of entertainment.[29] From mass market joke books to the rise of the stand-up comedy industry to comedic television shows and films drawing on racial stereotypes, slurs, and insults in less obvious ways, these new forms of racial comic media and entertainment allowed the cultural production and consumption of the "forbidden fruit" of racism to be indulged by whites and non-whites. This occurred in private (among friends, family, or co-workers), as well as in public settings (movie theaters, comedy clubs), as comedians, humorists, and entertainers were learning how to strategically deliver racist content in seemingly "non-racist" ways in a post–civil rights society.[30]

The emergence of the "equal opportunity offender"—the notion that mocking "everyone" was now a safe and democratic way to engage in racial insult and fun—also arose in this era. But rather than serving some egalitarian principle, this notion allowed white and non-white entertainers and humorists to continue to use racist jokes, slurs, and content, and profit from them, in ways that were supposedly prohibited in this new politically correct context. The idea was swiftly embraced by entertainers, publishers, and network and film producers. Besides the popularity of joke books like *Truly Tasteless Jokes*, this period also saw the proliferation of self-deprecating racial ridicule and comedy across the culture industries, from the Blaxploitation film era and the parodies it inspired in the late 20th century to the rise of Black and other non-white stand-up comedy superstars who made liberal use of racial slurs and stereotypes in their performances. Then, of course, there was the steady stream of films and TV shows, from popular 1980s films like *Sixteen Candles* and *Animal House*, to hit television shows like *All in the Family* and *The Simpsons*, that continued to rely on the use of racist caricatures and stereotypes of non-whites for comic relief. The reproduction and use of racist humor in mainstream American popular culture in the late 20th century, in other words, continually produced a steady diet of pop cultural racism that was a central part of the nation's racial imagination.

Metzger took note of the popularity of this trend and applied it strategically into his white supremacist organizing and propagandizing. As Metzger noted in an interview with the *Los Angeles Times* in the early 1990s, after he was sued for selling T-shirts portraying Bart Simpson as a Nazi, "We like to use humor and satire like anyone else does. . . . We always like to use things that we think are funny."[31] While Metzger's use of racist humor may appear more extreme than its commercial counterpart, and certainly not everyone was reading WAR during the 1980s, Metzger's use of amused racial contempt was readily in alignment with the historic and contemporary uses of racist humor taking place in the film and entertainment industry, in ways that are relevant for understanding the reproduction of racism and white supremacy under the seemingly contradictory racial logic of colorblindness and multicultural inclusion of the period.

From the 1960s through the early 2000s, Metzger would become one of the most visible and influential leaders of the new white supremacist movement. His career and development as a leading figure of the far right carried across various organizations, from earlier participation in the John Birch Society, an anti-communist and anti–civil rights organization, to leading the KKK chapter in California, where Metzger organized vigilante Klan border-watch groups along the U.S.–Mexico border as well as KKK chapters inside the U.S. Marine Corps. In the late 1970s, Metzger also created the White American Political Association, an organization he launched to help him run for various public offices as a Democratic candidate in California.[32] Though unsuccessful, Metzger was able to secure tens of thousands of votes throughout California, which increased his visibility as a new leader in the far-right movement.

But it was Metzger's development of White American Resistance in the early 1980s—soon changed to White Aryan Resistance (WAR) to echo his evolving racial ideology on white supremacy as a global, rather than nationalist, racial political project—that secured his visibility and notoriety as a leading voice of the far right. Throughout the 1980s and 90s, Metzger made use of the WAR movement to advance explicit white supremacist ideology and content at a time when other white supremacist leaders—such as David Duke, the former Grand Wizard of the Ku Klux Klan—were trying to shed their outwardly white supremacist skins and remake their public image to appeal to a more moderate base of white conservative supporters.

Metzger's use of amused racial contempt was purposeful and strategic, as he exploited the contradiction regarding racial discourse in U.S. society at the time: on the one hand racism was now seen as "bad," yet at the same time racist humor remained a popular source of amusement and social pleasure. And it was through the circulation of hundreds of racist cartoons featured in *White Aryan Resistance* that Metzger was able to showcase his distinct brand of in-your-face and irreverent racism and far-right propaganda in U.S. culture. Metzger sought to weaponize and rearticulate racist humor as a critique of the ostensible "power" gained by racial and ethnic minorities at the expense of white males. Multiculturalism, affirmative action, urban unrest and protest, interracial relationships, amnesty for immigrants, and so on—these and other social changes animated (and were the target of) Metzger's use of "satire" and amused racial contempt in hundreds of racist cartoons that he featured in the newspaper.

With the aid of his son John, who ran the Aryan Youth Movement (AYM) for WAR, Metzger used amused racial contempt to appeal to and recruit disaffected white working-class youth, namely the growing white skinhead movement at the time, as well as white right-leaning high school and college students through the development of White Student Unions. WAR's efforts to appeal to white youth often made use of popular culture, such as far-right inspired music festivals and events, as well as the graphic racist cartoon images that became a main staple of the WAR newspaper and later website. These cartoons, in turn, rendered familiar racist depictions of non-whites and the role they have played in white male disempowerment, and they played a key role in garnering widespread attention for the WAR movement among both supporters and critics. As Metzger noted,

"Nothing that WAR prints inflames our critics like these cartoons. Yes, they are simplistic and radical. They go to the root and they are full of brutal truth. Moderates cannot stand unrefined truth."[33]

Under the guise of satire, Metzger used these cartoons to expand *White Aryan Resistance*'s reach and circulation to tens of thousands of readers, including putting it into the hands of white high school students who used the paper as a recruiting tool for White Student Union groups on high school campuses in Southern California.[34]

Metzger's cartoons are a powerful example of the way that amused racial contempt was weaponized by the far right during the early part of the so-called colorblind era. They drew on racist stereotypes of the past, centered them on current events, and immersed them in the cultural discourses and debates surrounding political incorrectness, reverse racism, and anti-affirmative action efforts during this moment to advance and garner support towards the far-right white supremacist movement.

By the early 1990s Metzger's influence and notoriety reached a point where he was regularly invited on various news outlets and talk shows to articulate and defend his organization and far-right racist positions, including the kinds of cartoons that were featured in his paper. The level of interest, controversy, and support that he garnered demonstrates how effective amused racist contempt can be for driving racist ideology in the United States, and for gaining media attention. One notable example, for instance, occurred in 1991 when Tom and John Metzger were invited to appear on *Talk Live*, the CNBC show hosted by the late author and journalist Christopher Hitchens. Early in the interview, Hitchens pointed to a violent racist cartoon featured in *White Aryan Resistance*, which ridiculed and degraded Martin Luther King, Jr.'s iconic "I Have a Dream" speech. In this cartoon, King is depicted with eyes shut in mid-sentence of his famous speech, with a thought bubble floating above his head, as King supposedly fantasizes about his "real dream"—a United States full of naked white women, communism, and Black power. Next to this absurd portrayal of King is an image of a smirking white gunman, holding a smoking sniper rifle, as he looks out of a window and mutters, ". . . yeah, well, I have a little dream of my own, buddy boy . . . only difference is . . . my dream came true."[35]

The punchline in this violent racist cartoon is the celebration of King's assassination by a white supremacist gunman, an image that centers *White*

FIGURE 3.2. Anti-MLK cartoon, originally published in Tom Metzger's *White Aryan Resistance*.

Aryan Resistance's recurring ideological message to followers and potential subscribers and foreshadows our current reckoning with white supremacist gun violence and terrorism: that white men are under attack and losing ground to other racial and ethnic groups and that they need to use violence and fight back. This affective message in these racist comic images is ultimately the primary ideological message that the far right aims to advance and animate. The civil rights movement, the push for racial equality, multiculturalism, affirmative action, and so on, they say, are destroying the status, position, and well-being of white men. The use of amused racial contempt is strategically deployed by WAR and other far-right agitators to advance this underlying affective message, as it allows them to hide their efforts in plain sight, with claims that they are merely joking or exercising their freedom of speech.

As the interview progressed, Hitchens questioned why the Metzgers seemed to refrain from publicly advocating the kind of racial violence they promoted in the paper and asked whether they truly encouraged such racial violence or if it was all simply a sick joke. Before responding, John Metzger quickly plugged the paper's subscription address and placated an annoyed Hitchens by stating that Hitchens should have no problem with him promoting his paper if he was indeed for "free speech." A cornered Hitchens yielded and allowed John to proceed to describe WAR's newspaper to viewers:

> "They can get the most satirical, racist, aggressive, radical, white separatist, whatever term you want to put on it . . . comics, thoughts, ideas . . . and we don't pull punches . . . these cartoons, I didn't write them, but I'm proud . . ."

The conversation soon moved beyond racist and violent cartoons and shifted into a back-and-forth discussion that allowed the Metzgers to frame their calls for racist violence merely as "self-defense."

Hitchens and others have attempted to characterize these and other far-right leaders as tasteless and inconsistent amateur provocateurs who are little more than a joke. But while the Metzgers deny authorship of the hundreds of violent racist cartoons featured in their paper, many of which were signed under a tongue-in-cheek pseudonym, "A. Wyatt Mann,"[36] these cartoons are reflective of the broader ideological, strategic, and discursive aims of WAR as an organization and the influence it has had on contemporary alt-right propagandists. That is, under the guise of satire, free speech, self-defense, and anonymous authorship, while drawing on popular sources of racist humor, *White Aryan Resistance* promoted white supremacist racial violence in a way that liberal and moderate journalists and critics could easily disregard as "unserious," as "just a joke."

"What Will You Do, White Man?"

The way that amused racial contempt can radicalize white men against the various perceived dangers posed by non-whites in a white male-dominated U.S. society is an important example of the nefarious opportunities that racist humor offers. America's history and structural racism provides ample room for this kind of racist humor, and the way that amused racial contempt weaponizes social affiliation and racial resentment through racial ridicule underscores its danger. The Metzgers and their far-right propaganda paper are good examples of this. Their eagerness to exploit social affinities through white power racial ideologies was made clear on the movement's telephone hotline:

"This is WAR hotline. How long, White men, are you going to sit around while these non-White mud races breed you out of existence? They have your jobs, your homes, and your country. Have you stepped outside lately and looked around while these n****** and Mexicans hep and jive to these Africanized rap music? While these Gooks and Flips are buying up the businesses around you? . . . This racial melting pot is more like a garbage pail. Just look at your liquor stores. Most of them are owned by Sand n****** from Iraq, Egypt, or Iran. Most of the apartments are owned by the scum from India, or some other kind of raghead. . . . This here melting pot was spread by the poisonous seeds of Judaism. . . . When you see what these Jews and their white lackeys have done, the gas chambers don't sound like such a bad idea after all. . . . [A]ny of you out there who would like to start a White Student Union on your high school or college campus can write the White Student Union . . ."[37]

While such prerecorded messages made WAR's position of racist contempt for other racial, ethnic, and religious groups clear, it was their steady stream of racist cartoons featured in the paper that provided a regular dose of amused contempt and racial resentment that preyed on the racial anxieties, amusement and fears of its readers.

WAR's propaganda model shows how amused racial contempt can be used to exploit racial anxiety, and the fears and anger of white men, by amplifying narratives and images of disempowered and emasculated white males losing their "rightful" status and power in U.S. society to various inferior and invading "mud races." In rendering and repeating this narrative in hundreds of racist cartoons, *White Aryan Resistance* also provided comic relief and amused racial contempt to these same white men by instilling the notion that this current racial state of affairs could be radically different if they were willing to take some sort of action. Over the course

FIGURE 3.3. Racist WAR cartoon image mocking the phenomenon of white flight in U.S. urban areas, originally published in Tom Metzger's *White Aryan Resistance*.

of two decades, the overarching story provided in hundreds of cartoons is that the "fall from grace" of white working-class men in the post–civil rights United States will be permanent if white men are not willing to regain their position of power and status in U.S. society.

White Aryan Resistance sought to highlight this narrative of white male disempowerment through various self-deprecating images of white masculinity. White men were portrayed as weak, wimpy, and emasculated, often while juxtaposed with racist stereotypical portrayals of harmful or violent non-whites. Numerous images depict white men as fearful, under attack, humiliated, defeated, and subjugated by non-whites, white liberals, and white guilt. Such images were not offered as a means of critical self-reflection, or as a way for white readers to laugh at themselves or at whiteness more broadly. They were used to provoke a sense of shame and humiliation suffered by white men and were intended to echo white supremacist fears and conspiracy theories of the supposed criminalization of whiteness that is leading to white replacement and genocide.[38]

FIGURE 3.4. Cartoon depiction of the alleged reverse racism and discrimination of whites, originally published in Tom Metzger's *White Aryan Resistance*.

FIGURE 3.5. Anti-Black and anti-Semitic cartoon depicting how white nationalists perceive and articulate harm from Blacks and Jews, originally published in Tom Metzger's *White Aryan Resistance.*

However, *White Aryan Resistance*'s popularity and influence as a leading white supremacist paper would not have survived for over two decades if all it offered its subscribers were depictions of weak, humiliated, and powerless white men. The comic incongruity and relief offered by the paper came in the form of an amused racial contempt that juxtaposed the ostensible hardship and unfair treatment of white men alongside racist comic depictions and portraits of non-whites who were presented as inferior, bestial, and ugly using familiar racist stereotypes. Blacks and Jews, for instance, were routinely portrayed with racially exaggerated physical features and were presented as the primary groups harming white males economically and socially. Thus, they were problem groups to be dealt with by white men.

Black men were routinely depicted as violent, criminal, and stupid. They were often drawn as apelike animals who physically endangered white men and lusted after white women. Anti-Semitic cartoons portrayed Jews as large-nosed, greedy, and scheming. Their greed and dominance in banking, media, and real estate industries, according to WAR, harmed the economic and social well-being of white working-class men. Moreover, they were often portrayed as societal manipulators who only advocated for civil rights, race-mixing, and diversity for their own social advantage, by agitating non-whites to support racial equality to the detriment of white Aryan dominance. Such racist images served to ease the racial anxieties and fears of its readers, as these feelings of amused racial contempt worked to remind white men of their natural superiority over these targets of racial ridicule and contempt.

These forms of racist humor are similar to the racist comedic forms offered by blackface minstrelsy during the 19th century. Minstrelsy used exaggerated features of Blackness for the purpose of social affiliation towards whiteness, in a society where white working-class men experienced a sense of economic precariousness and exploitation in early U.S. capitalist development. Amused racial contempt fueled the psychological wages of whiteness. However, in contrast to the 19th and early 20th centuries, where comic racism in the entertainment industry was fully in line with the dominant racial ideologies that cast non-whites, Blacks in particular, as naturally or biologically inferior, the comic racism being used by WAR and others on the far right during the late 20th century was a departure from the normative cultural consensus that had rendered this form of racism as "bad." In this new context, the use of racist humor was not only politically incorrect and misaligned with the emerging colorblind narrative that would become dominant by the turn of the century, but it was now being intentionally used and weaponized as a form of resistance against calls for greater racial equality and democracy in U.S. society.

This can be observed, for instance, when renditions of Blacks and Jews were coupled with a narrative of white racial resentment against the supposed prioritization of resources and rewards for Blacks and other non-whites ahead of white men in the name of diversity and equality. In this

FIGURE 3.6. An example of anti-Semitic conspiracy theories, originally published in Tom Metzger's *White Aryan Resistance*.

way, the WAR movement sought to comically unsettle this new post–civil rights world not only as unjust and unfair towards white men, but as a racial absurdity and nightmare that could only be addressed and corrected by the actions of brave white men. In turn, the newspaper played a significant role in popularizing comic narratives of white racial resentment among the far right, by literally animating the emerging notions of "reverse racism" in the nation, where the belief that white men were now the primary targets of institutional and racial discrimination was gaining steam. Moreover, by offering alternative portrayals of events of racial unrest during the early 1990s—such as the Rodney King beating by the LAPD and the 1992 Los

Angeles uprising—WAR inserted its white supremacist political commentary in ways that re-centered white men and white-dominated institutions, such as law enforcement, as the "real" victims in this new politically correct society that presumed whites and whiteness as guilty regardless of the actions committed by non-whites against whites.

This portrayal of disempowered and emasculated white men was extended to law enforcement itself for its supposed inability to maintain "law

FIGURE 3.7. Cartoon offering white nationalist commentary on the 1992 Los Angeles uprising, following the acquittal of white LAPD officers involved in the Rodney King beating, originally published in Tom Metzger's *White Aryan Resistance*.

...THE FUTURE FACE OF LAW ENFORCEMENT

FIGURE 3.8. Cartoon mocking calls for police reform following the 1992 Los Angeles uprising, originally published in Tom Metzger's *White Aryan Resistance*.

and order" in U.S. society, for fear of being labeled "racist." In turn, the WAR movement sought to exploit these and other high-profile incidents as opportunities to disseminate a white supremacist narrative about the weakness, inability, and unwillingness of institutions, like law enforcement, to put men of color in their place in a liberal and multicultural society.

White Aryan Resistance offered a similar analysis of immigrants and immigration in its cartoons, something that further highlights how racist humor is interwoven into the comprehension and agitation of larger social problems. Immigrants, particularly those from Mexico and Asia, were routinely rendered through familiar racist stereotypes. Mexicans were often portrayed as dirty, criminals, and border crossers bearing too many children, while Asian immigrants were portrayed as backward, unassimilable, untrustworthy, and dog-eating foreigners. The growing presence of these immigrants, especially those from Mexico, presented a major threat to the preservation of a white-dominated U.S. society that would soon be replaced by these intruding, infesting, and overbreeding foreigners. *White*

Aryan Resistance used these cartoons to highlight how immigration and immigrants were harming white American society, and especially white men. By comically dehumanizing immigrants and linking this racial ridicule to the racial anxieties of whites, this effort underscores the centrality of amused racial contempt as a racial mechanism used by white nationalists to advance a more comprehensive racist political perspective and ideology.

The point of these depictions of people of color, especially when portrayed alongside images of white men, was to highlight a clear distinction and separation among the races, both biologically and culturally. The

FIGURE 3.9. An example of a typical anti-immigrant and anti-Mexican cartoon reflecting the anti-immigrant sentiment and politics of the 1990s, originally published in Tom Metzger's *White Aryan Resistance*.

FIGURE 3.10. Cartoon heightening white male fear and anxiety over the changing demographics of the United States, originally published in Tom Metzger's *White Aryan Resistance*.

supposedly natural and inferior predispositions, tendencies, temperaments, and traits of non-whites, as depicted in *White Aryan Resistance* cartoons, posed an inherent threat and danger to white males. The increased presence and ascendency of non-whites—due to civil rights demands, affirmative action, relaxed immigration policies, and reverse discrimination—has, according to WAR, threatened to undermine an entire U.S. society now overrun by "mud people" who are harming the social and economic well-being and status of whites and American society itself.

Moreover, according to WAR, in this new society a culture of political correctness prevents whites from expressing their honest opinions and discontent with this state of affairs for fear of being labeled "racist." Through these racist comic depictions and renditions of various minority groups—all of which drew on familiar physical and cultural exaggerations for comic affect, ridicule, and contempt—WAR sought to capitalize on the "psychological wages" it offered to its white readers with a racist white identity politics that was mobilized by a politically incorrect humor that tapped into the forbidden pleasure of white racism. WAR legitimized white feelings and notions of racial contempt, anger, resentment, and pleasure by expressing and circulating white racist sentiments that had become socially unacceptable. In some ways, racist humor became a more essential ingredient of racism in this new era, as it was now more necessary to cloak racism, vitriol, hatred, and contempt in fun, amusing, and seemingly non-racist ways.[39]

In a broader historical context, *White Aryan Resistance*'s racist cartoons and strategies for creating affiliation and solidarity among specific racial and gender groups (i.e., white men) point to several important aspects of the way racist humor operates and has evolved to effectively spread explicit forms of racist ideology, even as notions of colorblindness, post-raciality, and the idea that race and racism were declining in significance became dominant. Amused racial contempt, as illustrated by WAR, was being used to disrupt, resist, and go against this trend in an effort to advance an explicitly white supremacist ideology in a society that was struggling to move beyond it. In this way, amused racial contempt was a key part of the expressive counterculture resistance movement of the far right in a post–civil rights U.S. society.

"Don't Be a Humble Honky, Be a Mighty Whitey!"

While the humor advanced by Metzger and the *White Aryan Resistance* has a clear connection to far-right white supremacist ideology and movements, earlier studies of such cartoons sought to provide more "nuanced" analysis, illustrating alternative forms of interpretation that downplayed their racist impact. Humor scholar Elliot Oring, for instance, drawing on the theories of sociologist Christie Davies, discussed in the previous chapter, argued that an analysis of the humor produced by organizations such as WAR was better served by moving beyond a "humor and aggression" thesis. As Oring argued, "Only when the marriage between humor and aggression has been annulled will analysts be free to explore the range of motives that inform humor and decipher a variety of messages that these expressions convey."[40]

In his analysis of *White Aryan Resistance* cartoons, Oring was more interested in highlighting the capacity of such humor to forge a "fellowship of laughers," while downplaying the kind of community and fellowship created in the process. Moreover, Oring pointed to the ways such humor allowed the paper to "show there is nothing to fear from liberals, the politically correct and the law," as "[t]hey demonstrate that explicit racist expression is a right protected under the Constitution,"[41] all the while suggesting that the racist and violent messages portrayed in these images could not be taken seriously as the message was diminished when packaged as humor, that it was "just a joke." In other words, by presenting a challenge to the humor and aggression thesis, Oring's own analytic framework, like that of Davies, minimizes the role that humor plays in normalizing and advancing racism, white supremacy, and calls for white racial violence, while it also lessens the social impact of these jokes and cartoons by arguing that such humor is ultimately inconsequential for social behavior.

This argument is problematic for several reasons, most notably because it is this very angle on racist humor—that because it is presented as humorous, people don't need to take it seriously—that enables it to spread racism in the first place. It is in these graphic racist cartoons, offered as satire and as a critique of political correctness, that the violent racist fears and fantasies of WAR and the far right have been shared, archived, and recirculated over and over for the last several decades. Moreover, the purpose of these images is not only to amuse and entertain disaffected whites and members of the far right as a "fellowship and community of laughers," but to advance an entertaining form of political discourse and propaganda used to coax and radicalize white male anger, resentment, and contempt against the notion of multiracial equality and democracy.

Amused racial contempt was one of the key mechanisms that allowed WAR, during a period in U.S. society where colorblindness and political correctness were increasingly perceived as the dominant cultural norms, to routinely advance calls on white men to view the world through a raw and explicit racial lens—the more offensive the lens the better—and to "take action" in order to regain the status and power they believe they had lost to non-whites, by putting non-whites "back in their place." The *White Aryan Resistance* advanced and popularized such calls through comic affect and racialized emotions, presenting its politically incorrect and overtly racist cartoons in ways that were intended to simultaneously amuse, validate, and radicalize its readers and members, in the hopes of ultimately recreating a white male masculinity and subjectivity in the struggle to reassert white male dominance in U.S. society.

WAR's strategic use of racist humor underscores how crucial it is to reject the notion that racism couched in humor somehow lessens the ability of racist jokes to advance dangerous ideological agendas, a position advanced by humor scholars like Oring and Davies. To "analyze" WAR cartoons and the violent racist humor of the far right in the way that these scholars have is, at best, ignorant of the nature of these groups, and at worst, willful denial of the existence of white supremacy as a real social danger. The Metzgers' intentional use of humor enabled the *White Aryan Resistance* to play a central role in advancing and legitimizing calls for white racial violence over the last several decades by deliberately using humor to reach a larger audience and to inspire action. Explicitly using amused racial contempt helped them amplify the notion that the survival and status of whites was ultimately in the hands of "proud" and "brave" white men who would shed their feelings of shame and humiliation only by dealing with non-whites with the kind of racial violence often glorified in its cartoons—a cartoon violence that could be downplayed as "just a joke" by the Metzgers, analysts, and critics alike.

WAR's use of white racial ridicule—a nod to the notion of the equal opportunity offender—also deliberately portrayed emasculated and weak

FIGURE 3.11. An example of the racial agitation used to coax white males to act on racial fears, originally published in Tom Metzger's *White Aryan Resistance*.

white men as objects of ridicule and contempt, in contrast to the violent white men it presented as heroic. In this way, WAR relied on a racist and gendered amused contempt that targeted not only non-whites, but also those white men who were portrayed and rendered as cowards, enemies, and "race traitors." These whites were mocked as unwilling to stand up and defend their self-interests as whites, and thereby the white race—with fearless action, force, and violence. As a so-called vanguard of the white race, WAR offered an ultimatum to these and other white men more generally: you are either with us, or against us.

In other words, as a leading white supremacist voice during the post–civil rights period, WAR was not primarily in the business of ridiculing non-whites, normalizing racist ideas and content, or exercising free speech. Rather, free speech, political incorrectness, and amused racial contempt were strategically weaponized by WAR as a means of political agitation, with the goal of provoking at least some disaffected young white men into violent action. In this way, WAR was intentionally weaponizing amused racial contempt to recreate white masculinity and subjectivity by framing the notion of racial equality and democracy as harmful to the interests and well-being of white men. The punchline in this strategy? Racial equality makes white men effeminate and weak, while white supremacy and white nationalism make white men heroic and strong.

The use of racist humor to achieve these objectives represents an important evolution in the methods and ultimately the goals of racist humor in contemporary U.S. society. During the 19th century and pre–civil rights era, for example, racist humor was an affective and cultural expression of the general dominance that whites had maintained over non-whites as the normative social order. The ridicule of racialized groups, as in the case of blackface minstrelsy, was widely shared as confirmation of the perceived inferiority and place of non-whites in society, which was understood as the natural social and racial order. And while amused racial contempt during the 19th century was also tied to the "psychological wages of whiteness" in a society that also economically exploited white working-class immigrants and citizens, the broader racialized social structure of U.S. society allowed white working classes to rest assured that at least they were white. That whiteness granted them "natural" rank and status in society, while the widespread use of amused racial contempt contributed to their everyday belief that their personal whiteness guaranteed them a place in society above non-whites.

But this "white racial framing" of society was disrupted by the civil rights movement, as calls for greater racial and gender equality, and the implementation of civil rights legislation, publicly outlawed and condemned racial, gender and other forms of discrimination in public and private in-stitutions and organizations. Coupled with the economic dislocation of white men by the forces of capitalist globalization that contributed to their downward economic mobility and stability, the era was in many ways a period in which the place and power of average white men were being questioned, threatened, or lost, when compared to previous times in U.S. history. In this way, the use of amused racial contempt in a colorblind and economically precarious time was now being weaponized by white supremacist groups like WAR to recreate a white male identity resistant to this new era. Racist humor was being used to produce forms of social and racial affiliation among white men that signaled how they were overtly opposed to the cultural and societal shifts that now publicly acknowledged racism and white dominance as wrong and socially unacceptable. Racist humor was now being used as a political weapon for pedagogical outreach by white supremacists who believed this new society was actively working to displace the centrality of the white male in U.S. and western society.

Therefore, it is important, when looking at examples that reference violence in the "joke," to recognize that these images are not merely abstractly calling for violence against the *notion* of racial equality and multiracial democracy, but also for the *physical* racial violence to be en-acted. Oring noted that "For all their concern with violence and exter-mination . . . WAR essays do not encourage specific violent acts. Violence is promoted as an abstract ideological principle, or it is characterized as 'self-defense.'"[42] But this argument downplays the explicit call for racial violence in many of the cartoons, cartoons that seek to incite violence between the races. Take, for example, the image of a white male beating a Black man with a baseball bat as a means of "self-defense." Not only does this image encourage a specific act of racial violence, a baseball bat to a Black man's head, it also correlates with the kind of violence that readers of *White Aryan Resistance* enacted against people of color.

For example, this image is reminiscent of the 1988 murder of Mulugeta Seraw, an Ethiopian immigrant who was beaten to death with a baseball bat by neo-Nazi skinhead and WAR associate Ken Mieske, in Portland, Oregon. Seraw's murder, however, was not an act of self-defense, as Oring

FIGURE 3.12. An example of the circulated and celebrated imagery and messaging of racial violence, originally published in Tom Metzger's *White Aryan Resistance*.

suggests the cartoons imply. On the contrary, it was reflective of trends among white skinheads in Portland and throughout the United States who were increasingly committing acts of violence against racial minorities throughout the 1980s and early 1990s.[43] Metzger took a liking to skinheads and described them as "the new breed of white people who are coming up. They are . . . [angry], disenchanted and ready to fight" and believed they "have a lot of years to contribute to the overall racial struggle."[44] Prior to Seraw's brutal murder, Metzger was working to actively recruit and organize neo-Nazis and skinheads in the Pacific Northwest. Dave Mazzella, one of WAR's key organizers, was sent to Portland to meet with Mieske, who was a member of the skinhead gang East Side White Pride.[45] Mazzella's job was to introduce Mieske and other skinheads "to the ways of WAR," part of which involved "evenings handing out racist leaflets and beating up non-whites."[46] Following Seraw's murder, Tom Metzger recorded a message on the WAR telephone hotline stating that it "Sounds like the Skinheads did a civic duty, and they didn't even realize it."[47] In other words, Metzger was very clear about the kind of violence he encouraged, celebrated, and amplified, and he validated these acts of racial violence by white men across his media platforms, particularly in his use of violent racist cartoons.

Mieske went on to be tried and convicted for Seraw's murder, but the larger question regarding Tom Metzger's responsibility remained. While Metzger tried to dissociate himself from the murder, Morris Dees, a civil rights attorney for the Southern Poverty Law Center, with a proven track record of convicting hate crimes, took on the case in an effort to bankrupt Metzger and WAR. Metzger's connection to Mieske was made clear during the trial, and he was forced to pay $12.5 million in the civil judgment suit to Seraw's family, which effectively bankrupted Metzger. But he would face no jail time for his role, and he would continue to expand his method of political agitation on the World Wide Web for decades to come.

This example helps to make clear that people who engage in weaponizing racist humor and employ amused racial contempt to circulate white racial affiliation against dehumanized targets with calls for racial violence are not merely engaging in fostering "fellowship or community laughter," as Oring and other ethnic humor studies scholars would suggest. They aim to advance and agitate for the violent racist consequences enacted in these so-called cartoons and jokes. These forms of violent affect and rhetoric are interlinked to mobilize white supremacist ideology and action during a period where overt racism is ostensibly disavowed. In this context, white supremacists believe themselves to be on the defensive, rather than on the offensive, and exploit the ambivalent social understanding of humor and speech to legitimize their calls for acts of racial violence.

Today, racist humor and the amused racial contempt employed by *White Aryan Resistance* and other far-right publications continue to enable calls for racial violence to remain hidden in plain sight. Members of the alt-right have actively rediscovered and recirculated these cartoons on social media and other online platforms, inserting their own forms of comic racist propaganda in the current digital age, often in the form of memes. This repurposing reveals how Metzger and WAR's method of political agitation through racist humor has served as somewhat of a blueprint for the current crop of far-right propagandists and agitators. As illustrated at the beginning of this chapter, the current breed of alt-right mouthpieces, like Andrew Anglin and his online platform The Daily Stormer, are modeling and weaponizing the use of racist humor to draw in and radicalize a new generation of disaffected young white men on the internet, in the same fashion that Metzger aimed to do with his paper and media presence.

Metzger's success at becoming one of the most visible and influential leaders of the far right during the post–civil rights era was due, in part, to his ability to appear as a white, defiant, countercultural model to the emerging norms against public expressions of racism in a so-called post-racial and colorblind era. Metzger drew on the forbidden pleasure of racism to weaponize amused racial contempt and free speech to advance and amplify far-right calls for white supremacist racial violence, in ways that could be downplayed as unserious and protected by the First Amendment.

But when the logic of this perspective plays out, and newly radicalized young white men follow through on the calls for action, the outcome is often grotesque and horrific racial violence, as in the case of Seraw. The more recent case of Dylann Roof, the white supremacist teenage gunman who shot and killed nine African Americans in Charleston, South Carolina, in 2015, offers an even more gruesome example. Roof, who shared his own experience of trading racist jokes with classmates in his manifesto, claims to have "self-radicalized" on the internet. While Roof did not explicitly mention Metzger in his manifesto, reading through it reveals the stark parallels in outlook that Roof shares with the overarching narrative drafted in WAR cartoons. Through insulting and describing non-whites in ways that reflect Metzger's racist perspective more generally, Roof noted that he finally felt the urge to "take action" because

"We have no skinheads, no real KKK, no one doing anything but talking on the internet. Well someone has to have the bravery to take it to the real world, and I guess that has to be me."[48]

Roof embraced the kind of "heroic" violent action that Metzger had made visible and accessible to sympathetic whites in his racist cartoons for decades.

These examples illustrate the continuity of the strategic use of racist humor over the last four decades, demonstrating how racist humor has been weaponized by the far right in the aftermath of the civil rights movement. It is used to resist the idea of racial equality and interracial solidarity and to advance calls for more racial violence. These examples show how it is essential to not think of humor as somehow deflecting or minimizing the deeper strands of racial violence and supremacy implicitly and explicitly called for when packaged as humor, because racist humor is never "just a joke": its very foundations are intricately tied to historical and current forces of racial formation, domination, and violence. While the veil of humor conceals this notion in a society that claims to be post-racial or colorblind, white supremacist affect, ideology, and rhetoric have continued to spread over the last half century. Metzger understood this as clearly as anyone. As he noted at a press conference after the Seraw trial,

> "We're embedded now. Don't you understand?. . . We're in your colleges. We're in your armies. We're in your police forces. . . . I have already planted the seeds, they are already in the ground. . . . They have already come to fruition."[49]

But while some will certainly argue that the above examples are extreme, anecdotal, or statistical outliers, it is important to understand that the use and impact of racist humor and its relation to racial violence, while difficult to measure, is not exclusive to the far right. It is a problem that is ultimately also at play in other settings, as the following chapters illustrate.

CHAPTER 4

BLUE HUMOR

The Racist Insults and Injuries of the Police

"[R]emarks made by police, city and court officials . . . shows a number of public servants expressing racist comments or gender discrimination; demonstrating grotesque views and images of African Americans in which they were seen as the 'other'. . . . The content of these communications is unequivocally derogatory, dehumanizing, and demonstrative of impermissible bias."

U.S. Department of Justice, Investigation of the City of Ferguson

"Bigoted jokes are never really jokes at all, so much as a tool by which one sanctifies plunder."

Ta-Nehisi Coates, "The Gangsters of Ferguson"

THE PREVALENCE AND PERSISTENCE of racist humor in the United States is one of the enduring consequences of American racial slavery and the kind of culture and entertainment that it produced. But as this book shows, racist humor is not a phenomenon merely tied to earlier periods in American history when racism and racial domination were explicitly codified and promoted by law or social institutions. It is a phenomenon that shifts and evolves over time, re-inscribing racialized social hierarchies even as overt racist acts and language fall out of favor in public discourse. In the third decade of the 21st century, over sixty years after the civil rights movement, degrading forms of racist humor continue to circulate and reify racial definitions and subjectivities that have been inherited from America's racist past. The previous chapter looked at some of the ways individuals and organizations from the far right make use of amused racial contempt to push explicit racist agendas. But this kind of humor and its violent consequences is not reserved for people with explicit white supremacist ideologies and political agendas. Indeed, the amused racial contempt that underpins much of the racist humor we see today in the United States is also a form of socializing, fraternizing, and social affiliation, a key reason why humor plays such an important role in the spread of racism today. To illustrate the severity of this problem, this chapter looks at the use of racist humor among members of a central and powerful public institution in the United States—American police forces. It highlights some of the ways that amused racial contempt is manifest in social interactions among police officers, even when such humor may not be consciously intended as an explicit project of white supremacy by those using it.

In recent years, numerous police departments throughout the country have come under intense scrutiny over racial abuse and police brutality. Protests arising from these incidents have led to local, federal, and independent investigations of police attitudes, practices, and behaviors. One pattern this trend has revealed is the behind-the-scenes everyday discourse and communication that takes shape within law enforcement organizations across the country.[1] From Department of Justice investigations, to independent reports, to public records requests by media organizations, police officers throughout the United States have been found freely engaging in the routine use of racist (as well as sexist and homophobic) deprecating and derogatory discourse, often in the form of jokes and humor. Traces of such humor are readily found in department electronic communications records and on police officer social media accounts. This amused contempt appears to be a common form of communication within law enforcement and has wide implications for police practice and behavior. It also points to several important insights into the way that racist humor operates today in contexts where explicit racism and white supremacy are officially condemned.

In 2019, Philadelphia lawyer Emily Baker-White and her colleagues at the Plain View Project (PVP) created a database to identify and store racist comments and insults by current and former police officers on their Facebook accounts. The PVP highlighted Facebook posts of nearly 3,000 officers from 8 police departments across the country, as well as posts from 600 retired police from those same departments. Baker-White noted that the initial focus of this research was on "[p]osts that show bias against a certain group of people, posts that use dehumanizing language, calling people animals or savages or subhuman."[2] In the process, the PVP compiled thousands of social media posts and comments "replete with racist imagery and memes" that "appeared to endorse violence, racism and bigotry."[3] Many of these posts were shared in the form of jokes and humor. As the PVP noted, about 20 percent of current active-duty officers in the United States, and about 40 percent of retired officers, have posted or shared public comments on social media "displaying bias, applauding violence, scoffing at due process, or using dehumanizing language."[4] Many of these posts by officers included comments that "mocked Mexicans, women, and black people," and included images that "celebrated the Confederate flag," or targeted Arabs and Muslims such as by showing "a man wearing a kaffiyeh scarf in the crosshairs of a gun."[5] The PVP highlighted such posts in order to illustrate how derogatory comments made by officers "could erode civilian trust and confidence in police," while calling on police departments to "address them immediately."[6]

There is a longstanding myth that police organizations are not plagued with institutional or systemic racism, that its members and staff are largely driven by a commitment to equal protection under the law and to the common good. But this significant effort by the PVP, as well as other similar investigations, are shattering the "only a few bad apples" myth of American police forces.[7] For example, other recent investigations have revealed similar issues and patterns in law enforcement more broadly. Only a few weeks after the release by the PVP database, the nonprofit newsroom ProPublica published an investigative report of a private Facebook group by U.S. Border Patrol agents called "I'm 10–15" ("10–15" is their code for "aliens in custody"). According to ProPublica, the group was comprised of nearly 9,500 current and former agents and was self-described as a forum for "'funny' and 'serious' discussion about work with the patrol."[8] As journalist A. C. Thompson reported, in this private Facebook group,

> current and former Border Patrol agents joked about the deaths of migrants, discussed throwing burritos at Latino members of Congress visiting a detention facility in Texas . . . and posted a vulgar illustration depicting Rep. Alexandria Ocasio-Cortez engaged in oral sex with a detained migrant, according to screenshots of their postings.[9]

These examples further reveal the use of amused racist and sexist contempt as a widespread problem across law enforcement organizations in U.S. society and the role it plays in normalizing racist and dehumanizing organizational cultures, including within institutions that employ a significant number of non-whites, as Latinos currently make up a little over 50 percent of U.S. Border Patrol agents.[10] In other words, non-white officers can also embrace a white racial frame within these organizations and institutions, drawing on and making use of amused racial contempt and behaving accordingly.

But the myth that American police forces are good by nature and design, and that there are just a few "bad apples" within these institutions, endures. As Attorney General Jeff Sessions noted in 2017, in light of growing public scrutiny, protest, and investigations of police misconduct, "you just have individuals within a department that have done wrong."[11] When police racism and misconduct is made public, it is typically relegated to a handful of individual officers, the bad apples, rather than acknowledged or examined as a broader issue reflecting policing culture and institutional racism as a systemic problem in law enforcement. Or it is often framed as *implicit bias*, a theory that suggests that the presence and persistence of racism and racial prejudice is largely due to unconscious behavior rather than explicit motivations or intentions.

But the widespread use of racist humor by police is not a new phenomenon on social media or a discourse engaged in primarily by a few bad apples. It is a decades-long practice that has remained prevalent in shaping the culture of law enforcement organizations, and it reveals the role that humor plays in motivating and animating the racialized worldview of police officers across the chain of command, often in explicit ways. Amused racial contempt is a mechanism that sustains the everyday racist logic of police and law enforcement organizations in the United States and *demonstrates* the powerful role that humor plays in enabling the spread of racist ideologies and emotions in this context.

However, the discursive cover for this type of racism among police forces, like the kind highlighted in the PVP and ProPublica investigations, largely employs the same kind of amused racial contempt that underpins other forms of racist humor, such as among the far right. This type of humor seeks to veil racist humor behind sarcasm and "just a joke" excuses but draws on deeply embedded racist traditions and social hierarchies. As this chapter shows, humor, far from being merely just a tool for laughs, plays a serious role in the transmission of racist culture and its violent consequences.

Racist Blue Humor

Police use humor in the workplace for the same reasons that people in other organizations and settings use humor. Humor is used as a form of fun and amusement against occupational boredom, to strengthen collegial bonds and enhance social and group cohesion, to release work-related stress, and to increase positive group affect and collective pleasure.[12] Police departments, like other organizations, have also strategically used humor to improve the public image of police and enhance police–community relations. For instance, in 2017 the Lawrence Police Department in Kansas received attention and praise for its use of humor on Twitter and social media to inform, educate, and engage with the community.[13] As Officer Drew Fennelly, a member of the Public Affairs Unit of the Lawrence PD noted, "Using humor can be a good way to connect with people and recognize that police officers are humans, too. . . . I think other departments are recognizing that, and it's just an emerging trend in police community relations."[14]

But not all forms of police humor are intended to strengthen police–community relations. Certain kinds of humor, such as racist or sexist humor, can negatively impact police–community relations and organizational culture, as such humor is often reflective of larger and systemic problems within police and other organizations. As in the case of Sergeant Cleon Brown discussed in Chapter 1, such humor can generate conflict and divisions among peers, management, and subordinates, and between police and civilians. However, unlike most other organizations, law enforcement, along with the military, occupies a unique role in not only engaging and serving the public, but in its ability to exercise legal authority and violence against the public. Therefore, because police officers are "violence workers,"[15] understanding the role that amused racial contempt plays, and has played, in the organizational life and culture of law enforcement helps us see how racist police humor shapes racial dynamics and outcomes for officers within police organizations and between police and civilians. It also underscores the need to reevaluate how we think about what humor is, how it works, who it helps, and the risks it poses in a society that encoded race as a path to social organization and domination.

One particularly significant incident during the early 1990s helps to highlight the problem that amused racial contempt poses for American policing, as the presence of such humor is often closely linked to other forms of racial abuse and violence in law enforcement. On March 3, 1991, George Holliday, a 31-year-old immigrant from Argentina, was awakened by a traffic stop across the street from his apartment in Lake View Terrace, a suburban district in the San Fernando Valley area of Los Angeles. From his balcony, Holliday witnessed several LAPD officers brutalizing a Black motorist and quickly reached for his video camera.[16] In the footage Holliday captured that day, three officers were seen violently and repeatedly beating Rodney King with their batons, continually kicking and stomping on him as he lay on the ground and struggled to stand to ward off the dozens of blows he received while trying to shield his body. At least twenty other police officers stood by and watched the beating, none of whom intervened to stop the violence, nor would any of them later report the incident to their superiors.[17]

That video footage would soon be aired on local and national news, and then broadcast around the world. Tens of millions saw the raw and grainy footage of LAPD's sheer brutality on their television screens, in plain view like never before. The outcry was immediate. An angry public demanded that LAPD officers be held accountable for the ruthless actions many saw as racially motivated.

In the wake of this brutal incident and resulting public protest, Mayor Tom Bradley commissioned an independent investigation of the LAPD. The investigation, led by attorney Warren Christopher, was commissioned to "conduct 'a full and fair examination of the structure and operation of the LAPD' including its recruitment and training practices, internal disciplinary system, and citizen complaint system."[18] Moreover, the Christopher Commission Report sought to investigate the problem of racial police violence, in order to recognize and emphasize that "the problem of excessive force in American policing is real"[19] and that "[t]he problem of excessive force is aggravated by racism and bias within the LAPD."[20] The report confirmed what many non-white community members had long suspected and experienced regarding the nature of the LAPD: that a significant number of LAPD officers abused their power and use of force, that such force disproportionately targeted communities of color, that there was little to no oversight of officers regarding such misconduct, and that the weak disciplinary measures set in place were seldom enforced as officers were rarely disciplined or held accountable for their actions.[21]

But the investigation also revealed a much deeper symptom of this culture of abuse and misconduct within the LAPD, one that remained hidden in plain sight: the routine use of violent racist humor by LAPD officers. In conducting a thorough investigation of LAPD culture and practice, investigators collected and analyzed officer communication records to examine the discursive patterns and abusive practices by officers, and their relationship to systemic racial bias and discrimination within the LAPD.

For instance, earlier on the evening of the Rodney King beating, two white police officers who were later involved in the beating, Laurence Powell and Timothy Wind, were recorded sharing racist insults and comments on their mobile data terminal (MDT), a computerized communication device that allows officers to send and receive typed messages and communicate with the central dispatch office and with other police vehicles. Officers Powell and Wind had sent an MDT message describing a prior domestic dispute between an African American couple as a scene "right out of Gorilla's in the Mist." Powell and Wind and other officers were also recorded sharing messages and joking soon after King's beating, with comments like "I haven't beat anyone this bad in a long time," "(laughter) should have known better than run, they are going to pay a price when they do that," and "Oh well . . . I'm sure the lizard didn't deserve it . . . HAHA." The report also noted that at Pacific Hospital, where King was taken for initial treatment, nurses overheard police officers openly joking about how many times King was hit by police.[22]

The kind of jokes that the officers who beat Rodney King were making shows the way that humor, in fact, is directly interwoven into police violence and racism. Racism becomes palatable in many contexts of contemporary society because amused racial contempt provides a vehicle for it to be expressed within the politically correct expectations of today, in ways that continue to animate explicit racist ideologies and emotions in an ostensible post-racial or colorblind society.

Debating the Meaning of Racist Blue Humor

Although racism is widely and publicly condemned as vile, including within law enforcement organizations, there have been some studies on police officers' use of racist humor that have pushed back against the idea that such practices are merely toxic expressions of racist sentiment or that they will necessarily lead to violence. There have only been a few close studies of police humor, and even fewer on racist police humor. But some prior studies have highlighted the importance of police humor in fostering "teamwork" and "solidarity" among colleagues, in shaping the "boundaries of normal policing," as a useful way of "letting off steam," and as an important mechanism for maintaining group morale.[23] Some scholars have also argued against focusing only on the prevalence of racist humor among police forces by pointing out that law enforcement officers engage in many different types of disparaging humor, not just racist humor. Criminologist

Simon Holdaway, for instance, has argued that all sorts physical and cultural markers are subject to police jokes and banter, such as height, weight, as well as religious and ethnic background. But police humor, sometimes called "blue humor," also frequently "[covers] the gamut of racist, sexist, and homophobic speech,"[24] illustrating how police culture also relies on the equal opportunity offender notion in order to legitimize and normalize the acceptability of racism, sexism, and homophobia within this organizational setting.[25] Legal scholar Josephine Chow notes that such humor by police has long been defended, arguing that although police comments are seen as unacceptable when they are directed against private citizens, such disparaging language by police is often framed as a "necessary evil, serving to bond co-workers in the grueling fight against crime."[26]

Many people, including scholars, have tried to defend blue humor as being just a normal part of the job. For instance, criminologist P. A. J. Waddington argues that while many might find this sort of police discourse—or what he calls "canteen sub-culture"—unpalatable, he contends that such discourse is more significant in sustaining police morale than in "actual" police work and behavior—that it is merely banter, rather than an encouragement to future violence. Although the "canteen chatter of police officers is offensive to liberal values," he suggests that researchers need to go "beyond normative condemnation and seek to appreciate even the most offensive behavior" to "*understand* why officers express such views."[27] From this perspective, the racist jokes, stories, insults, slurs, and anecdotes that officers share are primarily "rhetoric that gives meaning to experience and sustains occupational self-esteem."[28]

Other scholars have offered similar analyses of police humor, noting that police officers use humor to test attitudes, feelings, or perceptions with colleagues and to promote social solidarity. They also use humor as a coping strategy to deal with job-related stress and tragedy. Blue humor has been described as primarily a form of "jocular aggression," or a form of humor used to express discontent and dissatisfaction with commanding officers, department policies, or the organization, and also to mock and ridicule peers and civilians. Such humor also allows officers to "test the waters" among colleagues, rather that express sentiments in a serious or direct way, as doing so may be interpreted as insubordination and subject to discipline.[29]

Police officers largely relegate such humorous discourse to private "backstage" settings, away from public view and scrutiny. In unsupervised settings, like the briefing room or late-night gatherings in empty parking lots (or more recently via electronic forms of communication and social media), officers tend to talk in uninhibited ways, in contrast to the professional identity that police are ostensibly expected to display in public "frontstage" settings. Backstage settings are key sites where blue humor facilitates the socialization and social bonding of officers and where joking rituals help police establish friendships, trust, and camaraderie. Through the sharing of jokes, stories, denigrating names, and stereotypes against fellow officers or the public, officers also draw social boundaries, develop and maintain organizational cultural norms, and heighten their own occupational morale. As criminal justice scholars Mark Pogrebin and Eric Poole note in their early study of the strategic uses of humor by police, blue humor works to "promote the police sense of moral superiority and to maintain the dichotomy between police and policed."[30]

But racist blue humor, like the racist humor among the far right, creates solidarity and a sense of moral superiority by directing humor and ridicule at out-groups. It facilitates and legitimizes an Us/Them dichotomy—between "police and policed"—as racist jokes and stereotypes often target non-whites as dangerous—a threat, criminal, and thus subjects to be policed and punished. This poses several serious dilemmas when considering it as a potentially acceptable form of humor to manage occupational stress or boredom. For example, racist blue humor can be used to bolster the mythology of law enforcement's moral superiority and the belief that police are primarily good, crime fighters, and stopping the bad guys. As Waddington suggests, "Policing has historically been transformed from a potential threat to fellow citizens into their protection by ideologically identifying the police with crime-fighting" as "Criminals lie beyond the moral community of society."[31] In this way, the purpose of drawing moral and symbolic boundaries and distinctions between "criminals" and "citizens" on the part of law enforcement "is part of a wider strategy that excludes certain groups from citizenship." And once this is distinction has been achieved, Waddington notes that "the exercise of coercive authority can be conducted almost without restraint."[32]

Racist blue humor works by negatively targeting racial and ethnic minorities with a kind of amused contempt that legitimizes symbolic, cultural, and institutional forms of discrimination and violence against racialized groups. And because law enforcement in the United States has historically been a predominantly white institution that has long engaged in racial exclusion, abuse, and violence, racist humor in law enforcement has played a significant role in maintaining and shaping a culture of racism, dehumanization, and racial abuse in policing.[33]

When non-whites are targeted with racist blue humor, such humor also works as a form of "cultural violence" that potentially primes and legitimizes the use of physical and structural forms of violence against targeted groups. As sociologist and genocide scholar Johan Galtung argues, "cultural violence makes direct and structural violence look, even feel, right—or at least not wrong," by changing the moral character of an action from wrong to right, "or at least . . . acceptable."[34] Racist blue humor is a form of cultural violence that dehumanizes the racialized targets of police who are seen as inherently criminal, thereby potentially facilitating and legitimizing police hostility, abuse, and violence against non-whites. From this perspective, the police involved in the beating of King, as well as the officers who stood by and witnessed the incident, did not see a problem with the events that unfolded. Moreover, because officers are not expected to think critically about the use of racist jokes shared in the workplace, and the role such humor plays in shaping their understanding of police racial violence, the brutal beating that King received was consciously and unconsciously seen as something that was acceptable and that he deserved.

To be sure, telling or hearing a single racist joke by police does not readily lead to police brutality. But the continual and decades-long use of disparaging humor within an organizational setting like law enforcement can work to change the cultural and ethical concerns regarding targeted individuals or groups.[35] Disparaging humor can work to "stretch the bounds" of socially unacceptable behavior, by cueing participants that it is okay to express contempt and hostility toward ridiculed out-groups. And as Waddington puts it, "If the police can persuade themselves that those against whom coercive authority is exercised are contemptible, no moral dilemmas are experienced—the policed section of the population 'deserve it.'"[36]

In the era of political correctness and colorblindness, when racism is otherwise condemned, the amused racial contempt of police nevertheless helps to maintain a racialized social structure and hierarchy, as well as uphold racialized social relations, within the ranks of law enforcement and between police and the broader public. By racially ridiculing civilians and peers, police dehumanize civilians and officers of color, setting the stage for a culture of racial abuse, discrimination, and potential violence. This dehumanization, however, is cloaked in a morally ambiguous rhetoric, allowing officers to create a sense of identity and solidarity by positioning their social camaraderie against historical structures of racial formation, abuse, and violence against racialized groups.

Acknowledging the Harms of Racist Blue Humor

While there has been little scholarship on racist blue humor, the potential harm of such humor has been acknowledged at least since the civil rights period. This is due, in large part, to the broad social, cultural, and political impact of the civil rights movement, which set the stage for the 1964 Civil Rights Act, legislation that outlawed the discrimination of people based on race, color, religion, sex, or national origin.[37] Soon after the passage of this landmark law, organizations, including law enforcement, were forced to draft policies to regulate their own discriminatory practices and discourses, in some cases including humor. This was because people of color, women, and other historically discriminated groups could now legally sue organizations for damages and lean on the federal government to restrict the discrimination that was commonplace, within public and private organizations, in the pre–civil rights era. By the 1980s, numerous organizations, including law enforcement, began to institutionalize policies in efforts to regulate racial and gender discrimination and harassment.[38]

For example, in the 1960s, police departments began to draft organizational policies prohibiting racist speech, including in the form of jokes.[39] Criminologist Jerome Skolnick, in his ethnographic study of a police department in Northern California, noted that as early as the mid-1960s the police chief of the "Westville" police department issued a mandate that strictly forbade the use of the N-word "under any circumstances, including the telling of a joke" by uniformed officers.[40] At the time, the violation of such policies could result in up to a fifteen-day suspension. These efforts arose in a context where law enforcement organizations were attempting to improve police–community relations in the aftermath of the civil rights movement and the rise of the Black Power movement, both of which were mobilized in large part by police racial abuse and violence.

By the late 1980s, similar policies were implemented in police departments around the country. For instance, in 1984 the Wilmington Police Department in North Carolina issued a new departmental policy that focused on what department officials regarded as "unwanted conduct."[41] The Wilmington PD highlighted the use of "racist jokes, insults, cartoons, sexual harassment and religious discrimination" as examples of "unwanted conduct." All department employees were now responsible for reporting such incidents to supervisors in order to "maintain a quality work environment for all members of the Police Department." As Captain J. S. Williams noted, "police departments nationwide are doing what they can to cut down on harassment. This policy reflects the department's desire to stay one step ahead of this kind of problem."[42]

On the opposite side of the country, the Los Angeles Police Department issued a similar departmental policy in the mid-1980s regarding the use of "offensive" discourse, with an emphasis on curbing racist talk in particular. This included the use of racial or ethnic slurs, epithets, terminology, and language "of a derogatory nature." As the LAPD mandate explained, not only was such discourse an inappropriate form of communication, but it was potentially "a destructive wedge in relationships with peers and members of the community." The policy emphasized that such misconduct would "not be tolerated under any circumstances."[43]

As these and other policies illustrate, by the late 1980s there was growing concern and acknowledgment by police departments across the country that racist discourse and other forms of harassment, even in the form of jokes, were socially and organizationally harmful and were now subject to disciplinary action. By recognizing the potential harms of racist blue humor and discourse—to both police organizations and to police–community relations—law enforcement organizations wanted to recast their public image regarding accusations of racism. And by publicly recognizing such policies, at the very minimum police departments appeared to fall in-line with federal civil rights law concerning racial and other forms of discrimination and harassment. But while some police and government officials may have been motivated by the desire to improve race relations in the criminal justice system and believed such policies to be an earnest effort in that direction, the enforcement of such policies was another story altogether.

Between "Unwanted Conduct" and "Acceptable Behavior"

One of the first major scandals involving the use of racist humor by police occurred in the early 1980s. The New York State Police Academy faced numerous complaints from several non-white recruits who stated that they were victims of racial discrimination and harassment. Various Black and Puerto Rican recruits charged that they were routinely targeted with racist jokes and other remarks by white academy instructors and peers. They argued that such discrimination negatively impacted their experiences, training, and retention in the police academy. U.S. Assistant Attorney General William Bradford Reynolds, head of the Civil Rights Division at the time, filed an investigation and emphasized that the racist taunting and ridicule that cadets endured played a significant role in creating an atmosphere of racial discrimination and harassment, which was now a clear civil rights violation.[44]

The federal civil rights report on this incident noted that Black and Latino recruits were frequently the objects of racial ridicule, as white instructors, counselors, and peers routinely and publicly disparaged and mocked the names, dialects, and accents of non-white students; repeatedly cast them as "criminals" in hypothetical situations and exercises; and subjected non-white recruits to racist jokes, insults, and slurs, all in the presence of white cadets. The assistant attorney general argued that this disparate treatment contributed to the lower completion rates among non-white cadets (93.8 percent of white males completed police training, in contrast to 50 percent of Blacks and Latinos). As the government report noted, "The atmosphere established by the academy staff . . . permitted, indeed encouraged, the white recruits to harass the minority recruits and to consistently rate them lower than whites on the peer ratings."[45]

In turn, the U.S. Department of Justice (DOJ) accused New York State Police officials of violating a 1979 non-discrimination order (*United States v. State of New York*), which required New York State Police to increase the presence of non-white recruits. Two key incidents in the 1970s provide some context for understanding the appearance of this non-discrimination order in the State of New York and the push to diversify its police force.

First, this 1979 non-discrimination order came several years after the notorious and brutal response to the Attica Prison uprising in 1971, wherein white New York State Police and correctional officers "jokingly" referred to their police batons as "n***** sticks."[46] The Attica uprising came at a height of Black radicalism and militancy in the nation, two weeks after the killing of Black Panther leader George Jackson at San Quentin State Prison following Jackson's unsuccessful prison escape during which he took several guards hostage.[47]

During this time, Attica was notoriously overcrowded with a largely Black and Brown inner-city population, with Black inmates alone constituting 54 percent of prisoners. Inmates were brutally mistreated, overworked, and living in abysmal conditions. Angry and increasingly radicalized during this period, Attica prisoners forged alliances, rebelled, and took over the prison for four days. Over 500 New York State Police officers, as well as hundreds of deputies, sheriffs, and police from surrounding counties—many of whom removed their identification numbers prior to entering the prison—arrived to violently repress the rebellion. This largely white, suburban, and militarized police force engaged the prisoners with brutal and extreme violence. Racial slurs and taunts of "white power!"

were witnessed by prisoners who were tortured and humiliated by officers who appeared to be amused by the process.[48] A 21-year-old inmate who was shot four times, for instance, observed troopers enjoying themselves as they jammed their rifle butts into his injuries while pouring lime on his body until he lost consciousness. Other prisoners reported that they were made to crawl naked on broken glass, subjected to Russian roulette, and forced to drink officers' urine. By the end of this incident, over 40 people were dead and over 100 others had been shot.[49] Ultimately, the stark and oppressive racial conditions were considered key factors in the clash that served as a critical example of the need to diversify the New York State Police.

The second incident that led to the 1979 non-discrimination order was also a response to an investigation—a 1977 investigation by the U.S. attorney general, against the State of New York and the superintendent of the New York State Police, William G. Connelie. The attorney general argued that there was "a 'pattern or practice' of discriminatory employment practices with respect to blacks, Spanish-surnamed Americans, and women"[50] and that such discriminatory hiring practices were now a constitutional and federal civil rights violation.

In his 1979 ruling on this case, Chief Justice James T. Foley, U.S. district court justice for the State of New York, confirmed that a pattern of racial and gender discrimination was indeed taking place within the New York State Police, where less than 1 percent of the 1977 graduating class was Black, Latino, or female. Judge Foley stressed that this was a "startling and eye-catching statistic" relative to the diverse labor pool in the state. The judge emphasized that such discriminatory hiring practices were an impediment to overcoming the persistence of racism in U.S. society, pointing specifically to "the lengthy and tragic history of our society's treatment of the Negro," while noting that Blacks were "dragged to this country in chains to be sold into slavery" and "marked as inferior by the law." Judge Foley acknowledge that while the legacy of racial and historical injustice "will not be obtained overnight," he would be exerting his legal power and authority to order the State of New York to increase its efforts to recruit minority officers by using "an ongoing affirmative action program to attract members of the minority community."[51]

During these broader discussions on hiring practices and non-discrimination policies in law enforcement, racist humor became a central topic. For example, on behalf of several Black and Puerto Rican members of the 1981 recruiting class who had been the targets of racial ridicule, the DOJ asked the court to hire officers who would have completed their academy training if the 1979 non-discrimination order were enforced, along with retroactive pay and seniority.[52] The DOJ charged that the routine discriminatory and unwelcome discourse, much of it in the form of racial ridicule, reflected an organizational culture hostile towards racial minorities and was in violation of the 1979 non-discrimination order issued by Judge Foley.

But Judge Foley, who was now presiding over the 1981 DOJ case, dismissed these complaints, ruling that the use of racist jokes in this context was not as harmful as the Black and Puerto Rican recruits claimed, and he argued that perhaps the racist jokes could even be useful as a pedagogical tool. While he acknowledged that "racial and ethnic jokes are told at every level of our society" and are sometimes offensive, in his estimation the testimonies brought forward by the non-white recruits, which he treated as anecdotal evidence, had also included "ethnic jokes other than those relating to blacks and hispanics [sic]." Moreover, he believed that use of such humor in a police academy setting

> was to ease tension and to break the monotony of the classroom. I find those purposes acceptable. It must be remembered that the 1981 Academy Class was not comparable to a Sunday School class or the instruction of a group of seminarians.[53]

This judgment is a powerful example of the ways that racist humor, whose racist content was momentarily acknowledged during and after the civil rights movement, is nevertheless set aside in certain social contexts because it is often deemed primarily as a form of amusement, entertainment, and as a mechanism for social cohesion. While earlier forms of racist humor, such as blackface minstrelsy, were now publicly deemed unacceptable, during this early phase of the post–civil rights era we can also see the growing contradiction taking root across social settings and institutions regarding other forms of racist humor: a contradiction that acknowledged racism, racial discrimination, and past forms of racist humor as socially harmful, on the one hand, while other forms of racist humor, although sometimes deemed offensive, were ultimately understood as "just a joke."

By dismissing the harm and impact of racist humor in the context of law enforcement, which Judge Foley had previously ruled was marred by systemic and historic racial discrimination, this new case illustrated how white officials and cadets could be absolved from any wrongdoing or responsibility for reproducing everyday forms of racial discrimination, harassment, and division and how this principle could be applied to law enforcement organizations and institutions more broadly. Moreover, by drawing a false equivalence between the ridicule, insults, and slurs that targeted racialized recruits from historically excluded and oppressed backgrounds alongside other nameless "ethnic targets" who were not the subject of a federal civil rights lawsuit, this case further illustrates the problems involved with folding racist humor into the larger umbrella term "ethnic humor," a category that often works to obscure how racism and racist humor operates in society.

From this perspective, amused racial contempt in this context was socially acceptable because it was believed to be used primarily to stimulate "fun" and "amusement" among peers and potential colleagues, ultimately rendering the racist ridicule, insults, and humiliation that Black and Latino recruits endured as "just jokes," while denying the impact of such discourse as racist and discriminatory in itself. Moreover, as Judge Foley concluded, "these unpleasant episodes must be viewed, if accepted as true, as isolated ones," further subscribing to the "bad apples" myth of policing.

By not carefully considering racial ridicule as a serious form of racial discrimination, harassment, and abuse, this form of discourse is readily and rhetorically dismissed, minimized, and denied the negative impact that it inflicts in creating a racially divisive organizational context, which facilitates the conditions for disparate racial treatment and outcomes. Moreover, by disregarding how racist humor by white instructors and white cadets worked to "align" whites across rank through their collective enjoyment and disparagement of non-white recruits, Judge Foley turned a blind eye to a routine way that a normative culture of racism and racial dehumanization is actively and socially created and constructed in an organizational setting like law enforcement. Far from being "just a joke," such racist practices can work to reproduce and reinforce the "inferior" status of non-whites in a setting historically dominated by white supervisors and peers. It is through these kinds of everyday communication practices that whites can actively create the social conditions for racial discrimination, alienation, and exclusion to become the cultural norm, especially when these forms of communication are allowed to take place within predominantly and historically white organizational institutions.

What this case illustrates is that the policing of racist humor in the post–civil rights era presented a seeming paradox for white liberal elites and decision makers seeking to improve race relations, particularly in the arena of law enforcement. While policies targeting racist discrimination and discourse, including in the form of humor, were being increasingly acknowledged and institutionalized within law enforcement organizations across the country following the 1964 Civil Rights Act (in order to curb the presence of racial discrimination within police departments and improve the public image of police), it soon became evident that the enforcement of such policies was going to be difficult as long as white decisions makers, including liberal-leaning ones such as those justices seemingly invested in advancing racial equality, regarded such discourse as inconsequential to policing behavior, and maybe even constructive for police culture.

But there are serious consequences to racist humor, particularly within policing. As the previous chapter highlighted, there are examples where serious violence has emerged from contexts where racist humor was being used among far-right groups. And as in the case of Rodney King, despite the suggestion that blue humor is potentially permissible or even valuable within police culture, there are also many examples where racist talk and racist action among law enforcement, including in the form of jokes, is connected to physical racial abuse and violence.

Insult and Injury in the LAPD

The beating that Rodney King suffered at the hands of the LAPD took place in 1991, approximately eight years after Judge Foley argued for the "acceptableness" of blue humor. But as the events of that night in Los Angeles underscore, this attitude was not only naïve, but dangerous. Although the video of that event focused on the actual beating, in fact, there was extensive recorded evidence of racist humor that surrounded the event, including evidence of officers "letting off steam" when the incident was over.

According to the commission report's analysis of LAPD electronic communication records of nearly 200 days, from November 1989 to February 1991, officers routinely engaged in disparaging, dehumanizing, and violent discourse, often in the form of violent racist ridicule and jokes.[54] The commission investigating King's beating and racism in the LAPD highlighted the regular use of "remarks [that] describe minorities through animal analogies ("sounds like monkey slapping time"). Often made in the context of discussing pursuits or beating suspects, the offensive remarks cover the spectrum of racial and ethnic minorities in the city ("I would love to drive down Slauson with a flame thrower . . . we would have a barbeque"; "I almost got me a Mexican last night but he dropped the dam gun to quick, lots of wit").[55] Other messages made explicit reference to celebrating the shooting of individuals in pursuit with comments like "Go get em my–man, and shoot him twice for me" and "Everybody you kill in the line of duty becomes a slave in the afterlife."[56]

The officers typing and sending these messages on the LAPD's MDT system had little concern that they would be potentially disciplined for making such remarks. Commanding officers and supervisors generally failed to monitor messages in this system, nor sought to impose any form of discipline for such commentary, even as supervisors themselves were often a source of derogatory comments, the commission report highlighted.[57] Overall, the racist discourse that the recordings captured, much of it in the form of humor, included over 1,400 cases of "objectionable language in the MDT communications," where civilians of color were routinely mocked, disparaged, and described as animals by LAPD officers.[58]

Commission investigators highlighted how casually officers voiced amused racial contempt and condoned violent racist behavior. The report also noted that LAPD officers routinely sent such messages despite policies in place prohibiting this language (e.g., "LAPD Unacceptable Remarks of a Racial Nature," Memorandum, 1987). As the report observed, "The apparent confidence of these officers that nothing would be done about their inflammatory statements suggests a tolerance within the LAPD of attitudes condoning violence against the public."[59] In turn, the use of such racist discourse and humor among LAPD officers in the context of the Rodney King beating was seen as constituting "only a symptom of a larger problem of abuse."[60]

In contrast to those who have argued that police racist humor and talk is disconnected from police action and outcomes, the commission report was clear that these "attitudes of bias and intolerance were translated into unacceptable behavior in the field," as was clearly illustrated prior, during, and after the King beating.[61] The report noted that many LAPD officers routinely employed humiliating and invasive tactics against communities of color in particular, such as frequent and unjustified stops and the overuse of the "prone out" position for minor traffic infractions, which requires a suspect to kneel with arms spread out or to lie flat on his or her stomach with arms behind the back.[62] While the report initially suggested that it was only a minority of officers that engaged in such behavior, interviews with "senior and rank-and-file officers generally stated that a significant number of officers tended to use force excessively, that these problem officers were well known in their divisions, and that the Department did not do enough to control or discipline these officers."[63] Moreover, a survey of nearly 1,000 LAPD officers found that at least 1 out of 4 officers agreed that racist attitudes and prejudice against civilians of color by LAPD officers "contributes to a negative interaction between police and community," while nearly 30 percent of officers surveyed agreed that "an officer's prejudice towards a suspect's race may lead to the use of excessive force."[64] In other words, the commission report highlighted the many ways that LAPD officers routinely disparaged, with violent and dehumanizing racist language and behavior, the multiracial public they were sworn to protect and serve.

These patterns and practices of racial ridicule and abuse among a predominantly white and male police department were not isolated to non-white civilians; they were routinely used against non-white LAPD officers as well. Many Asian, Latino, and African American officers were targeted with racist insults, slurs, jokes, images, and violent racist symbols, such as nooses, by fellow white officers. "A number of racial comments appearing in MDT transcripts . . . were directed at minority officers," the report noted, although the use of racist insults and ridicule targeting non-white officers was not isolated to MTD communications. Most of the minority officers interviewed by commission investigators mentioned that "racially derogatory remarks are made on an on-going basis at roll call and that racist jokes and cartoons appear from time to time on the bulletin boards in the stations' locker rooms."[65]

Officers of color rarely reported such incidents to supervisors, as the report noted that most non-white officers did not believe the problem would be resolved by supervisors and that they did not want to appear "weak" in front of colleagues and commanding officers. "Almost all of the officers said that, while they find such racial slurs and remarks offensive, they endured the name-calling and jokes to avoid the label of being 'thin-skinned' and 'sensitive.'"[66] Moreover, minority officers feared retaliation or harm to their career advancement for speaking out. For instance, one officer interviewed by commission investigators reported that he later found a noose on the station's department telephone from which he called home every morning.[67] Such incidents illustrate just how easily racist jokes can shift towards threats of racist violence when the targets of amused racial contempt are no longer willing to play along with such routine racist harassment and abuse as "just a joke."

Because LAPD management made little effort to discipline such behavior by enforcing existing policy against the use of racial remarks and harassment, the commission report concluded that "the failure to enforce existing policies conveys to minority and non-minority officers alike that such conduct is in practice condoned or tolerated by the Department," despite "its stated policies to the contrary."[68] According to investigators, such behavior was tolerated, in large part, because managerial positions were largely staffed by whites, while officers of color were mostly relegated to entry-level positions:

> Many minority officers cite this white dominance of managerial positions within the Department, even in African American and Latino Areas of the City, as one reason for the Department's tolerance of racially tolerated language and behavior.[69]

Despite the extensive and highly critical commission report (nearly 300 pages), the following year, on April 29, 1992, four LAPD officers involved in King's beating were acquitted from wrongdoing. Within hours of the verdict, Los Angeles exploded with outrage and rioting ensued. Despite the verdict, it was clear that LAPD's racism problem was inescapable and inexcusable. Desperate to regain control and legitimacy, it appeared that finally LAPD began to take its own policies against racial harassment and abuse seriously: the policing of officers' racial discourse, including in the form of jokes, would be routinely monitored and disciplined, for the first time with a "zero-tolerance policy."

Free Speech Society

In the aftermath of the King beating video, the Christopher Commission Report, and the widespread rioting resulting from the acquittal of involved officers, LAPD swiftly embraced the commission's recommendations for a more rigorous screening of officers to weed out "racial bias" from the department. New officers were now required to fill out a 21-page form asking about prior violent or discriminatory behavior. As Pat Patterson, chief of the personnel department's public safety division, noted, recruits were now asked questions like "Have you ever laughed at or told a racial joke?" in follow-up interviews in order to delve into more candid discussions about potential prejudice and discrimination among prospective officers.[70]

While Patterson suggested "there is no absolute bar to somebody because they've either told or listened to a racial joke. . . . What we try to do is determine whether this is indicative of some deep-seated, deep-held beliefs, attitudes, stereotypes." Patterson stated that now "there's just absolute zero tolerance for this type of stuff in the Police Department."[71]

But while it appeared that such forms of racial discrimination and abuse were finally being taken seriously among the LAPD, the screening out of officers based on their use of "offensive humor" was increasingly viewed with skepticism by those who regarded such efforts as not only excessive and unnecessary but as detrimental to the hiring and retention of "qualified" officers and ultimately to the profession of law enforcement itself. An incident in 1996 served as a pivotal case, casting doubt on the regulating of officer racial discourse as an effective means to screen new recruits and discipline LAPD officers.

Randy Mehringer, at the time a 27-year-old San Fernando Valley resident, was on track to becoming a new LAPD officer. A graduate of the University of Arizona and the son of a senior LAPD officer, Bud Mehringer, Randy finished third in his academy class and had already logged over 2,000 hours at the LAPD's Rampart Division as a cadet.[72] According to the *Los Angeles Times*, while Mehringer scored 98 out of 100 on his oral exam and "worked nearly for free for the LAPD for two years without anyone complaining of his attitudes," Mehringer was ultimately rejected by the LAPD after admitting to telling a "bad joke" during his interview. The *Times* reported that Mehringer had previously shared a "racial joke" about the Million Man March. The paper did not repeat the joke in question, only that it "implied that many African Americans are unemployed." The LAPD used this joke to conclude that Mehringer failed to demonstrate "respect for others" through his use of "racially derogatory comments."[73]

Held in Washington, DC, in 1995, the Million Man March was a civil rights demonstration called by Louis Farrakhan, the controversial Black nationalist leader of the Nation of Islam, that was organized by numerous civil rights groups. The purpose of the gathering was to publicly address the persisting issues negatively impacting Black men and the Black

community, such as unemployment and poverty, as well as media stereotypes and images prevalent in the country at the end of the 20th century.
While the gathering was one of the largest civil rights demonstrations held
in DC since the civil rights movement, it was criticized by Black feminist
activists and scholars for its overwhelming patriarchal focus on Black men,
as well as for the anti-Semitic views expressed by Farrakhan, the event
organizer.[74] In other words, the event garnered mixed reaction, making
it easy fodder for criticism and jokes in a context a few decades removed
from the civil rights and Black Power movements of the 1960s and 70s.

Today, racist jokes regarding the Million Man March are easily found
with a quick internet search. It is likely that such jokes originated during
and after the demonstration. There are a few variations of jokes targeting
the Million Man March that continue to circulate today:

"What was the only thing missing from the Million Man March? An
auctioneer."

From "racial joke" threads on Reddit to explicit white supremacist websites like N*****mania.com, this is one of the most common internet
"jokes" related to the Million Man March. Other jokes about the demonstration articulate familiar racist stereotypes about Black men being unemployed, on welfare, or prone to criminality. While the *Los Angeles Times*
did not identify or repeat the specific joke leading to Mehringer's rejection, being that some version of this joke remains in circulation twenty-five
years after the event, it is quite possible that the "racial joke" Mehringer
shared resembled one of these—a joke that mocked one of the largest
demonstrations by African Americans since the civil rights movement with
overt racist stereotypes.

Considering how much racist violence and discourse by the LAPD had
been publicized at this point—including the videotaped beating of Rodney King; the riots that followed the acquittal of the four LAPD officers
involved in 1992; as well as the release of audio recordings of racist slurs
used by Mark Fuhrman, the white LAPD officer involved in the 1995 OJ
Simpson murder case—it is not difficult to see why the LAPD would now

hesitate to hire an officer who admitted using "racial jokes" about African Americans. In more ways than one, it appears that Mehringer's joke suffered from poor timing.

But by the mid-1990s, public cultural norms and the acceptability of racist talk, including in the form of jokes, had shifted, and resistance to these changing discursive norms was growing. Efforts to challenge offensive and harmful language were now mocked and derisively described as "political correctness," the ostensible policing of individual speech (including racist speech), which was now believed to be infringing on individual liberties and the First Amendment.[75]

Nowhere was this infringement seen as most damning and absurd by some conservative figures as in the policing of "racial jokes." As conservative shock jock and radio talk show host Rush Limbaugh noted in the early 1990s, regarding the newfound difficulty among whites in targeting and mocking African Americans in particular, "'How come you can't have a little fun about blacks?' . . . 'What protects them? Why are they immune from legitimate forms of humor?'"[76] Similarly, conservative legal scholar Dan Subotnik, drawing on humor scholar Christie Davies, echoed this critique and offered his own form of amused contempt in his essay titled "The Joke and Critical Race Theory," writing that "the categories of race and gender have been so loaded down by CRATs [critical race theorists] that they work against fair resolution of the joke issue."[77]

It was through such criticism that Mehringer's case increasingly came to symbolize something more than a seemingly well-qualified recruit being rejected because of a tasteless joke. Mehringer became the latest victim in a "free speech society" succumbing to the perils of "political correctness" and the "policing of speech," a problem that was seen as spiraling out of control. Cliff Ruff, the president of the Police Protective League, referred to this incident as

"McCarthyism at its ultimate. We're in the era of being politically correct. . . .There has to be some legitimate quality control as to who may harbor bias and prejudice as opposed to who may have heard or told a joke."[78]

Mehringer's father made a similar plea, noting that

> "There seems to be a problem somewhere if the criteria for selecting
> a police officer is never having told a joke about a protected class. . . .
> We'd better find another labor pool. We'd better go to Venus or Mars,
> because you're not going to find them on this planet. . . . Are we look-
> ing for perfect human beings? Or are we looking for good officers? . . .
> There has to be a balance here."[79]

Los Angeles City Council members appeared to take similar positions on
this issue. For instance, Councilmember Laura Chick, part of the public
safety and personnel committee overlooking this case, stated that "'We
need to be very careful that we're not going overboard . . . that it doesn't
turn into a witch hunt.'" It was now "innocent" police officers, critics of
such policies seemed to suggest, who were the "real victims" of unjust
discrimination and who were being treated unfairly by the enforcement of
these unjust and unrealistic policies. After all, as Chick added,

> "It's part of our national culture that these kinds of jokes are told. . . .
> Until in a much bigger way we take on the task of raising the public's
> consciousness that this is not OK, I'm not sure that it's an effective way
> to screen out for LAPD."[80]

One member of the council, Mark Ridley Thomas, stressed that "one
of the most insidious forms of racism is communicated through humor."
But Thomas appeared to be one of the few political voices calling for
the continued screening of "blue humor," as other seemingly progressive
city officials, like Councilmember Jackie Goldberg, were skeptical of this
process, questioning whether strictly enforcing such policies was a means
of "'dinging people for trivial reasons.'"[81] It did not take long for this
dominant narrative to be reasserted, as the "white racial framing" of such
humor once again rendered racist blue humor as "just jokes."

Soon, opinion pieces and headlines were taking LAPD to task for re-
jecting a seemingly well-qualified recruit for a "bad joke." For instance,

Scott Harris of the *Los Angeles Times* noted that while Mehringer's joke might have been in "bad taste," he questioned whether "such a joke, alone, be enough to torpedo somebody's career?"[82] Bill Boyarsky, also writing for the *Times*, offered a "theory," noting that "you have to understand the bureaucratic mind, and its paranoid fear of the media, to comprehend why Randy Mehringer was denied a job as a police officer because he told a racial joke."[83] Boyarsky condescendingly suspected that LAPD and city bureaucrats were paranoid that Mehringer might one day "beat a black person" and have done nothing to prevent it. In this way, these journalists were displaying their own amused contempt not only for LAPD's policies, but for public reaction and concern over police violence.

The policing of racist blue humor was further complicated when Black and other minority police officers came out in support of Mehringer. Boyarsky, for instance, pointed out that "One of [Randy's] supervisors, Sgt. George Hoopes, an African American, had said he was a 'peer favorite' who 'harbors no hidden animosity for any minority group.'"[84] Similarly, Harris observed that while he received some pushback for his support of Mehringer in his *Times* piece, he also received a letter from Volney E. Hyde, a resident of Van Nuys, who suggested that "'As an African American male I was initially offended when I first read that one of the top recruits of the LAPD had admitted telling an ethnic joke about the "Million Man March". . . What an outrage!'" Hyde then noted that "'Before casting the first stone I had to examine my own glass house. Yes, in the past I've been guilty of telling ethnic jokes.'" Harris asked Hyde whether he believed Mehringer deserved a second chance, to which Hyde responded, "'When they asked this guy if he told any ethnic jokes, he could have said no. At least he was honest. We need that on the force.'"[85]

As political figures, police officials, and journalists increasingly echoed the seeming absurdity of a well-qualified recruit being rejected for a joke, it appeared the stomach for policing racist blue humor was rapidly weakening among LAPD leaders and political officials. In the end, the Mehringer incident seemed to embarrass rather than improve LAPD's community–police relations efforts.

But while regulatory efforts did not appear to be going according to plan in Los Angeles, the national attention and unrest caused by King's videotaped beating prompted the U.S. government to better monitor law enforcement agencies for problems of racial discrimination and excessive force.[86] In the aftermath of the Rodney King beating and the urban rebellion that it incited, the Violent Crime Control and Law Enforcement Act was being promoted under the leadership of Bill Clinton. This 1994 crime bill has received much deserved criticism for its role in exacerbating the current problems of racism in policing and mass incarceration.[87] However, one significant feature of this bill was the purported enhanced role of the Department of Justice's Civil Rights Division in more regularly pursuing "patterns or practices" investigations of law enforcement agencies to determine "whether police departments exhibit patterns of behavior, including excessive force, false arrests, unreasonable searches and seizures, or racial/ethnic discrimination."[88]

Since 1994, over sixty police departments nationwide have been investigated by the DOJ, with over twenty investigations initiated under the Obama administration alone. However, these investigations comprise only a small fraction of the nearly 18,000 federal, state, county, and local law enforcement agencies currently operating in the country. But while the DOJ's Civil Rights Division has been quietly monitoring and investigating dozens of law enforcement agencies over the last twenty-five years—in an ostensible effort to reform policing practices, one department at a time—it was not until a new major incident of racial rebellion that police "patterns and practices," including the use of police racial discourse, was once again regarded as a serious public concern.

Blue Humor and Racial Violence, from Ferguson to Today

Racist humor in law enforcement is a socialization mechanism that enhances solidarity and camaraderie among officers, while simultaneously priming and reinforcing an Us versus Them mentality and work environment, the so-called "thin blue line." These sentiments in law enforcement are not new. They have always been an essential part of the racialized

culture and practice of policing in the United States. And they have remained entrenched in law enforcement even after they were first highlighted during and after the civil rights period, as they are continually
found to be hidden in plain sight. Police departments across the country
have generally tolerated this kind of behavior, in the absence of public
protest or independent public oversight, because the reality is that police
departments in the United States could not function as they do, historically and today, without a culture of ritualized racial dehumanization that
facilitates police racial abuse and violence.

This ongoing "pattern and practice" was revealed in Ferguson, Missouri, in 2014, in light of another major rebellion against police violence.
Following the shooting of Black teenager Michael Brown by white police
officer Darren Wilson on August 9, 2014, protests and unrest escalated in
Ferguson as the presence of a heavily militarized police force occupied this
predominantly poor Black suburb of St. Louis. Black Lives Matter activists
spotlighted these developments and called upon supporters to take to the
streets and demand justice for Michael Brown by holding Ferguson city
officials and police accountable for Brown's death. Over several weeks,
tensions and conflict escalated as angry protestors demanding racial justice
confronted riot police, prompting national and international attention to
the little-known city of Ferguson as it declared a "state of emergency."[89]
Violence and unrest would return to Ferguson on November 24, 2014,
following a grand jury decision not to indict Darren Wilson in the shooting of Michael Brown.[90]

Similar to the investigation that followed the Rodney King beating in
Los Angeles, U.S. Attorney General Eric Holder called upon the Department of Justice to conduct a federal investigation to closely examine the
official communication records and accounts of city officials and police
officers in Ferguson, in order to determine if an underlying pattern and
practice of racial bias had existed in the Ferguson Police Department prior
to Brown's shooting. Holder directed the DOJ to conduct two simultane-
ous federal investigations in Ferguson—one centered on the shooting of
Brown, the other focused on the "patterns and practices" of the Ferguson
PD in general.

On March 4, 2015, the DOJ shared the results of its investigation. The first report supported the jury decision that Darren Wilson shot Michael Brown in "self-defense" and thereby declined to bring criminal charges against Wilson. Understanding that such a result by a federal investigation would do little to calm public anger against the Ferguson PD, the second DOJ investigation was far less forgiving. Here, the DOJ documented and highlighted a pervasive and systemic pattern of racial abuse and "unconstitutional racial bias" taking place within a predominantly white police force policing a city where African Americans comprise 67 percent of the population.

For instance, the report found that between 2012 and 2014, "African Americans account for 85% of vehicle stops, 90% of citations, and 93% of arrests," as well as "nearly 90% of documented force" where "every canine bite incident for which racial information is available, the person bitten was African American."[91] The report also noted that it appeared certain offenses were carried out "almost exclusively against African Americans. For example, from 2011 to 2013, African Americans accounted for 95% of Manner of Walking in Roadway charges, and 94% of all Failure to Comply charges."[92]

This kind of racial abuse within the Ferguson PD was not the result of a department suffering from "unconscious" racial bias; rather, it was carried out by a predominantly white police force that regularly engaged in amused racial contempt for the city's majority Black residents. As Attorney General Eric Holder remarked, there were "a number of public servants expressing racist comments or gender discrimination; demonstrating grotesque views and images of African Americans in which they were seen as the 'other.'"[93] The DOJ highlighted numerous examples of amused racial contempt circulating among police and city officials, some of which targeted then-President Obama as a chimpanzee (see Chapter 5), while others mocked Black civilians with all too familiar anti-Black stereotypes that depicted them as inarticulate, buffoonish, lazy, welfare recipients, and criminals. For instance, a June 2011 email "described a man seeking to obtain 'welfare' for his dogs because they are 'mixed in color, unemployed, lazy, can't speak English and have no frigging clue who their Daddies are.'"[94] Another email that caught the attention of the DOJ and the media was a joke that referred to a Black woman having an abortion as a form of "crime-fighting." The punchline in this particular joke, in other words, was the idea that Black mortality is amusing.

The investigation also found evidence of racially dehumanizing humor in emails sent and shared by Ferguson police, supervisors, and commanders, as well as court officials and supervisors. Such emails were found in official City of Ferguson email accounts, many of which were sent during working hours. These emails gathered by the DOJ illustrated a pattern reflecting the racial ideologies and emotions held by white Ferguson police and officials towards the city's Black residents. These "grotesque views and images" that were shared as "humor" illustrate the widespread use of amused racial contempt by white public servants ostensibly serving a majority Black city. In line with the Christopher Commission Report, which made use of electronic communications records to investigate the presence of racial bias within the LAPD, the DOJ Ferguson report aimed to link the pattern of police racial abuse and violence with the culture and discourse taking place in the police department. As the DOJ report asserted, "The content of these communications is unequivocally derogatory, dehumanizing, and demonstrative of impermissible bias."[95]

Such racist ridicule and dehumanization served to socially bond white Ferguson police and public officials with one another through their shared feelings of amused racial contempt. These everyday rituals of racist bonding also acted as a form of symbolic and cultural violence that worked to prime and reinforce the racial abuse and physical violence carried out by police and court encounters with Black civilians.[96]

As the many examples in this book show, these jokes are an expression of emotional and rhetorical impulses that draw on a deeply rooted history of white supremacy and its methods of achieving and reinforcing social power in America. As Ta-Nehisi Coates observes in his commentary on the DOJ report for *The Atlantic*, "Bigoted jokes are never really jokes at all, so much as a tool by which one sanctifies plunder."[97] Coates argues that jokes mocking Black mortality as a way of fighting crime are not just jokes, but a means through which a pattern and culture of dehumanizing racist ridicule facilitates and legitimizes the practice of police brutality and vio-lence. Moral and legal concerns for how police, as public servants, ought to treat civilians regardless of racial background are abandoned when of-ficers find the death of those who they police laughable, amusing, and worthy of contempt.

This pattern and practice of racial ridicule and abuse was made espe-cially evident in Ferguson, as in the case of the LAPD, by the fact that no

> officer or court clerk engaged in these communications was ever dis-ciplined. Nor did we see a single instance in which a police or court recipient of such an email asked that the sender refrain from send-ing such emails, or any indication that these emails were reported as inappropriate.[98]

The racist jokes of the police are accepted as a normal part of the organi-zational and institutional culture of law enforcement in America.

It was only after the protests and unrest in Ferguson, which brought a national and international spotlight that prompted the DOJ investigation, that Ferguson city officials were finally forced to reckon with the overt racism of its police force. But on the day the DOJ report was released, Fer-guson Mayor James Knowles immediately denounced these emails while insisting that such behavior was not a reflection of the culture and prac-tice of the Ferguson Police Department. "'These actions taken by these individuals are in no way representative of the employees of the city of Ferguson,'" the mayor proclaimed.[99] Knowles's response was familiar and predictable: Condemn this behavior and then isolate it to a few bad apples, rather than acknowledge an institutional and systemic problem of racism in law enforcement.

Many media reports of the Ferguson emails followed a similar script. While the DOJ report did not list the names of Ferguson officials engag-ing in this behavior, public records requests by various media outlets illus-trated that several of these emails were circulated and forwarded by Rick Henke, a former Ferguson police captain; William Mudd, a former police sergeant; and Mary Ann Twitty, a court clerk for Ferguson's municipal

court.[100] These individuals were singled out as being some of the main
culprits circulating racist images and jokes on their City of Ferguson email
accounts. But while it is important to single out those who were specifically involved in these incidents, again the problem is that a broader focus
on an organizational "pattern and practice" is then narrowed and isolated
to just these few "bad apples."

It is worth noting that St. Louis Alderman Antonio French offered a
different interpretation of these emails, stating that these emails show that
a "'culture existed and was allowed to fester in Ferguson municipal government and Ferguson Police Department.'"[101] French noted that these
emails revealed only the surface of a much deeper problem of racism in
law enforcement and suggested that while there were "'a few voluntary
resignations'" in light of the DOJ report, as well as a few individuals fired
or disciplined, there was never "'a full acceptance of responsibility for that
culture that has been allowed to exist in that municipal government.'"
"'Even after the DOJ report,'" French concluded, "'there is still a lot of
work to be done and it still remains to be seen whether the people who
remain in power will be the ones to make the change.'"[102]

In March of 2015, only days after the release of the DOJ's investigation in Ferguson, the San Francisco Police Department made national
headlines for the violent racist and homophobic text messages circulating
there. The media spotlight initially focused on one officer in particular,
Ian Furminger, a white officer who had been named San Francisco Police
Officer of the Year in 2000, but who was now at the center of a federal
corruption investigation and convicted of stealing money and drugs from
dealers. Racist slurs, violent imagery, and white supremacist ideology was
shared in dozens of text messages by Furminger and over a dozen other
officers, including a captain. One text message shared by Furminger "jokingly" described how his family celebrates Kwanza at their school: "'We
burn the cross on the field. Then we celebrate whitemas.'"[103] Furminger
offered a public apology following the revelation of these exchanges, while
downplaying them as mere banter and jokes and stressing his interracial
friendships. "'Those texts are not a reflection of who I am,'" Furminger
pleaded. "'These were supposed to be funny, not to be broadcast on the

news.'" From Furminger's point of view, this was simply a "'rebound reaction to a politically correct environment.'"[104]

Many were shocked by the news of this kind of police behavior taking place in an ostensibly liberal city like San Francisco. Public defender Jeff Adachi stated in response to this revelation:

> "We pride ourselves on being a progressive city, yet we have active officers who are engaging in not only racist banter, but they were talking about killing people, referring to an African American as a 'savage' . . . . A person does not become a racist overnight. These were officers who in some cases had over a decade of service. We need to look at all of them."[105]

But the SFPD incident was also significant because it revealed that it was not only white officers who were engaging in dehumanizing racist and homophobic ridicule. Some officers of color, such as Chinese American officer Jason Lai, were also among those found sharing racist text messages ridiculing and disparaging Blacks, Latinos, and South Asians. These racist messages targeted not only civilians, but fellow officers of color as well.[106]

Whistleblowers within the department faced threats of violence for raising concerns over this kind of behavior on the force. This was the case for an anonymous Muslim officer who reported "witness[ing] blatant misconduct against citizens" and that he was made the target of anti-Muslim jokes and ridicule by fellow SFPD officers. As Evan Sernoffsky reported for the *San Francisco Gate*, "Among the officer's allegations are that co-workers routinely muted their body-worn cameras before making crude comments at crime scenes, and that several expressed support for the white nationalist movement." The anonymous Muslim officer stated that he decided to report this misconduct to the media because his reports to the department's Internal Affairs Bureau and the city's Department of Human Resources were going nowhere; he chose to remain anonymous because he had "'been labeled a rat, singled out by my colleagues, and I now fear for my safety.'"[107]

In other words, the diversification of a police force, or the geographic location of a police department in a liberal-leaning city, appeared to have little impact on an organizational culture steeped in deep and systemic racism. And within this institutional white space of law enforcement, police officers of color either assimilate to the white racial framing and thin blue line of policing or are rendered targets of amused racial contempt and threats of violence themselves.

The early warning signs of this cancerous racist fun was also present in Minneapolis, years before George Floyd's murder. In 2018, only a few years after the fatal police shooting of Jamar Clark, two Minneapolis PD officers were suspended for decorating a Christmas tree with "half-crushed cans of Steel Reserve malt liquor . . . crumpled bags of Takis chips . . . a cup from the fried-chicken joint Popeyes and two packs of Newport cigarettes." At the time, City Councilman Phillipe Cunningham noted that this incident illustrated how Minneapolis police officers view Black people as "'a stereotype to be mocked and . . . reduced to trash in the gutter.'"[108]

By 2019, thousands of active duty and retired police officers from across the country were now being exposed for sharing violent racist jokes, memes, images, and comments in private social media groups, as the Plain View Project, ProPublica, and other investigative and activist media efforts have revealed in recent years.[109] The PVP in particular illustrated that a significant number of police officers routinely engage in derogatory commentary against Black Lives Matter activists, immigrants, Muslims, and other vulnerable civilians that police are paid to "protect and serve." Here, some officers were exposed for joking about brutalizing and choke-holding minority suspects and using cars to run over demonstrators: "WATCH: Car vs. Protesters. Car always wins," a Dallas police officer posted, while another shared a meme containing the phrase "Despite what you've been told, violence does solve problems."[110] Meanwhile, a meme posted by a St. Louis officer showed a policeman at a protest, mid-punch, captioned "I'm going to protect and serve the shit out of you."[111]

This sadism is too often the true face of policing in a nation still grappling with the living history and legacy of entrenched racism and white supremacy. And as the Black Lives Matter protests of 2020 painfully and vividly illustrated, these violent and gruesome jokes are not "just jokes," but were acted out in the tactics used against protesters and those documenting police brutality.

During his presidency, Donald Trump certainly added fuel to this fire. In 2017, he "joked" about police brutality in front of law enforcement officers at Suffolk County Community College on Long Island, suggesting officers should not be so "nice" or concerned with giving head injuries to Central American suspects in custody. The joke, of course, reflected Trump's political strategy of ridiculing and showing amused contempt for people of color to energize his base.[112] "[I]t's not simply a wink and a nod at the old days of unrestrained policing," historian Jelani Cobb said of Trump's comments at the time, but "a foreshadowing of a world he's actively attempting to resurrect."[113] It was no coincidence, therefore, that the International Union of Police Associations—which defended the use of police violence against protestors and journalists during the 2020 protests following the murder of George Floyd by Minneapolis police officers—fully endorsed Trump's 2020 re-election campaign.[114]

Building on the implications of racist humor in advancing racist ideology and white solidarity, as discussed in Chapter 2, and the potential of racist humor to legitimize racist violence among far-right extremists, as discussed in Chapter 3, this chapter explicitly illustrates how the use of amused racial contempt within police forces plays a central role in facilitating the spread of racist ideas as well as fomenting racial violence in the United States. Here, I have highlighted how a publicly funded institution that is legally obligated to grant equal protection under the law routinely privileges the ideology and pleasure of racism, white supremacy, and anti-Blackness above the law.

The amused racial contempt of police, in other words, is a powerful affective and rhetorical discourse that has continually evolved in the United States and has taken firm root in a so-called colorblind or post-racial era. It is a practice that often hides in plain sight because its mechanisms are cloaked in humor and the pleasure of laughter and solidarity among those in on the jokes. But the larger implications and dangers of this kind of practice are consistently overlooked, even when used within spaces regularly wielding institutional and structural violence.

Building on these illustrations of what racist humor *does* in policing and in society, the next chapter looks at how racist humor is manifested as a political discourse more broadly. I underscore the widespread dilemmas that humor poses as a central method of diffusing racist ideologies, emotions, and solidarities in the United States today, and the impact that amused racial contempt has on magnifying political polarization in society.

CHAPTER 5

PRESIDENT CHIMP
The Politics of Amused Racial Contempt

"In anything that white people were likely to read, they wanted to put
their best foot forward, their politely polished and cultural foot, and only
that foot. There was a reason for it of course. They had seen their race
laughed at and caricatured so often."

Langston Hughes

FOR MANY LIBERAL AND CONSERVATIVE pundits alike, the 2008
election of Barack Obama signaled a monumental change in the racial,
political, and social landscape of the United States. Finally, many noted, a
nation built on the backs of enslaved Africans had not only elected a Black
man to the highest office in the land, but his election was a symbolic indi-
cation that we had finally achieved a "post-racial" America. Racism, it was
said, was on its way to becoming a relic of history.[1] Obama's appeal seemed
to be embodied in what many members of the Black intellectual and social
elite had long believed would be the key to earning respect and equality for
African American people in a white-dominated society. As Du Bois himself
observed in his earlier thinking on overcoming racism, "The Negro race,
like all races, is going to be saved by its exceptional men."[2] This aspiration
for exceptionalism, as Langston Hughes suggested, was also rooted in a
desire to overcome centuries of racial denigration and ridicule.[3] As a highly
educated, articulate, and polished Black political leader, with an easygoing
demeanor and a contagious smile, Obama appeared to be the posterchild

for Black exceptionalism. Part of this exceptionalism was Obama's ability to appeal to white voters.[4]

By aiming to present himself as a unifying figure who would be the president for "all Americans," not only Black Americans, Obama sought to serve the nation in as "colorblind" a capacity as possible.[5] And it would be in that capacity, the Obama campaign and administration assured, that Obama would be able to appeal to, and unify, a broad coalition of voters and citizens in general, white Americans in particular, and win back the presidency. Therefore, alongside discussions of the historic significance of the election of the nation's first Black president, and his appeal to white voters, Obama's candidacy and electoral victory also helped strengthen the narrative that racism was finally declining in significance.[6]

Yet, despite the uplifting post-racial narratives engulfing this historic election, the conceptualization of Obama as the "great post-racial unifier" was not sufficient in shielding him from political criticism across the political spectrum. From the Black and multiracial left, Obama was taken to task on a number of fronts: for putting "Wall Street before Main Street" during the aftermath of the 2008 recession; for his inability to take on the prison industrial complex, a system disproportionately afflicting Black and Brown people; for continuing and enhancing the detention and deportation of undocumented immigrants at record levels; for expanding U.S. imperialism and military intervention in the Middle East, including the use of drone warfare. These and other charges represented efforts by Black and other progressives on the left to "speak truth to power," regardless of the president's color or how inconvenient their criticisms were. Beyond "Black faces in high places," such critical voices were unwilling to sit on the sidelines and simply cheerlead the historic and symbolic Obama presidency. They wanted more than *symbolic* racial representation: they were actively demanding structural and institutional change towards *substantive* racial and economic equality, democracy, and justice. It was no coincidence, therefore, that social movements for economic and racial justice, like Occupy Wall Street and Black Lives Matter, would take shape while Obama was in office.

The symbolism of Obama's election, however, remained important for several reasons, and different groups interpreted its meaning in different ways. Although people on the left continued to challenge and push for concrete policy action to advance racial and economic justice, for many on the right, Obama's election symbolized a growing threat to the dominance of whiteness and to the country's longstanding racial hierarchy that this dominance has maintained for centuries. The challenge, for some on the right, was met with a growing resistance to the perceived threat posed by a Black presidency, a threat to the legacy and continuation of the politics of white dominance and rule. This growing political opposition and contempt—from white conservatives in particular—relied less on questioning Obama's political or policy positions and more on delegitimizing his right to the authority of the office itself. Many of the favored tools of this growing resistance involved the same kinds of racialized ridicule, insult, and disrespect that had supposedly disappeared from public view in this new post-racial and colorblind America.[7]

As prior chapters have demonstrated in the context of law enforcement and far-right groups, during and after the Obama election humor continued to provide a mechanism for the circulation of racist ideology. Despite his exceptional "colorblind" qualities, and his efforts to appeal to millions of white American voters, Obama continues to be the target of the very kind of anti-Black racial ridicule that so many on the right claim is a thing of the past yet remains so ingrained and familiar in the white American racial imagination.

N-Word Jokes Without the N-Word

One of the dominant explanations for the persistence of racism in contemporary U.S. society is the notion of *implicit bias*.[8] Research on implicit bias suggests that while racism and racial prejudice remain, this is largely due to unconscious or subconscious forces, rather than explicit motivation or intentions. People don't actually *mean* to be racist, the theory goes, because often they are unaware that they are even *being* racist. Lodged in all our psyches are the centuries-long racial stereotypes that are now unacceptable to utter in public because the civil rights movement showed us that they are morally wrong and bad. But because we are still plagued with "racial smog," these deeply held implicit prejudices can be revealed through sophisticated association tests that illustrate how our biases emerge when confronted with split-second decisions. All of us, this theory suggests, are at least a little bit racist.[9]

An alternative explanation to the implicit bias thesis is that explicit racism has remained all along, but that these sentiments are often hidden from view because of the moral stigma to public racism.[10] As this book illustrates, however, racism frequently continues to be revealed in the private pleasures people consume and share in an array of social and professional contexts in the United States. This suggests that, regardless of whether implicit bias is present, this latter explanation is also likely to be true.

Drawing on Freud's theory of jokes and their relation to the unconscious, former Google data scientist Seth Stephens-Davidowitz points to people's private internet searches as a way to uncover the everyday hidden explicit racism that sophisticated implicit bias association tests or survey data often fail to capture. "There is nothing implicit about searching for 'n***** jokes,'" Stephens-Davidowitz asserts bluntly, pointing to the sharp increase in Google searches for this phrase every time African Americans are in the news. Google searches for the slur average about 7 million per year, with about the same frequency as terms like "economist" or "margarine," Stephens-Davidowitz finds. Twenty percent of searches for the slur include the term "joke." Internet searches for jokes employing the term spiked during Obama's elections, and they accounted for "seventeen times more . . . searches than for 'kike jokes,' 'gook jokes,' 'spic jokes,' 'chink jokes,' and 'fag jokes' combined."[11]

While Stephens-Davidowitz notes that these Google searches take place all over the country, in Democratic- and Republican-leaning areas, and in northern and southern state alike, they occurred at higher rates in districts where Obama underperformed among white voters, an effect that did not predict poor performance for other Democratic candidates. He estimates that the private online consumption of these kinds of explicit anti-Black Google searches cost Obama about 4 percentage points in the 2012 national election, a gap that would tilt in Trump's favor during the 2016 election.[12]

This practice of anti-Black amused racial contempt, therefore, was a key part of, and a contributing factor in, the growing politics of white resentment and nationalism during the tenure of the nation's first Black president. This growth reflects the Southern Poverty Law Center's findings that the membership and number of hate groups increased while Obama was in office.[13] For instance, the leading white supremacist website Stormfront saw their single largest increase in membership ever on November 5, 2008, the day after Obama was elected.[14] Such spaces were breeding grounds for circulating the kinds of racist jokes and far-right humor discussed in Chapter 3. But as the discussion of racist humor among police forces illustrates, racist jokes are not only being shared by those associated with the far right: they are also within institutions responsible for law enforcement in the United States. In other words, while Obama won in 2008 and 2012, and was able to draw in a significant number of white voters, the forbidden fruit of amused racial contempt was steadily being shared and consumed throughout his tenure, in ways not captured by implicit bias tests or surveys on racial attitudes.

Indeed, during and throughout the Obama presidency, anti-Black amused racial contempt was not relegated to private contexts such as conversations in a person's home, nor was it solely shared among those with far-right affiliations. On the contrary, it was expressed in very public contexts, particularly across the internet and in conservative rallies and protests. Although the most public and widespread forms of this amused racial contempt against Obama did not include the use of explicit racial slurs, the racism was nevertheless explicit. For example, memes and internet images resurfaced minstrel tropes that spread familiar anti-Black images ridiculing the notion of Black competence, leadership, and governance. Conservatives also spread depictions of Obama as a foreigner and outsider (e.g., tribal witch doctor, Muslim terrorist), someone who was fundamentally "un-American" and "dangerous," during anti-Obama protests. These public forms of racially ridiculing Obama relied less on overt racial slurs, while essentially conveying the same idea. These were N-word jokes without N-words.

One of the most widespread forms of racial ridicule aimed towards Obama, particularly during his first term, appeared in the form of the centuries-long racist and dehumanizing notion that people of African ancestry are "closer to the animal kingdom" than to humanity. This notion, of comparing and portraying Black people to apes, is rooted in the historical development of European colonialism and white supremacy. Its re-emergence as a form of public anti-Black racist ridicule increased during the Obama election and presidency, something that underscores the role humor plays as a driving political force in the diffusion of racist ideology in the 21st century

It is important to keep in mind that although these racist portrayals focused on ridiculing and dehumanizing Obama, they were not aimed solely at the nation's first Black president. Rather, this anti-Black amused racial contempt was aimed at what the Obama election and presidency represented, as symbolized in the imagined anxieties of an angry white populace fearing losing status and power in a demographically changing America. This fear, hostility, and anger were often expressed, and relieved, through the politics of amused racial contempt.

Birth of an Insult

The use of animal imagery as a racist trope has been around for centuries. From Eurocentric Christianity and theology to racial science and western political thought, and across popular culture, from literature to film and cinema, the comparison of non-white racial groups to animals continues to endure as a central notion grounded in the ideology of white supremacy.[15] In the 19th and early 20th centuries, the field of "racial science" inspired by Darwin's theory of evolution, offered legitimacy to this form of racism. Throughout this period, various descriptions, theories, and illustrations depicting and juxtaposing Africans as closer in proximity to apes were used to elevate whiteness as the highest stage of human evolution, development, and civilization, in contrast to the "primitive" and stagnant development of non-whites, those of African origin and ancestry in particular.[16]

Fig. 339. — Apollo Belvidere.

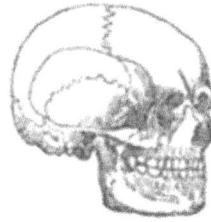

Fig. 340.

Greek.

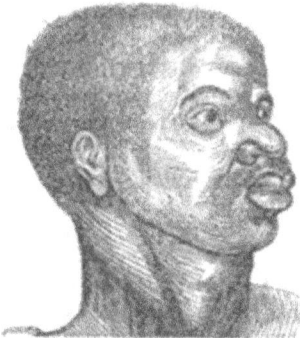

Fig. 341. — Negro.

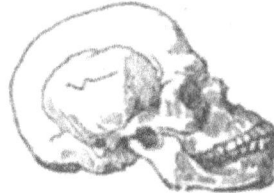

Fig. 342.

Creole Negro.

Fig. 343. — Young Chimpanzee.

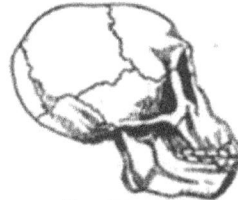

Fig. 344.

Young Chimpanzee.

(458)

FIGURE 5.1. Graphic illustration of scientific racism published in the influential book *Types of Mankind* in 1854.

SOURCE: J. C. Nott, *Types of Mankind: Or, Ethnological Researches, Based upon the Ancient Monuments, Paintings, Sculptures, and Crania of Races, and upon Their Natural, Geographical, Philological, and Biblical History.* Lippincott, 1854, 458.

As Du Bois recalled, "I remember once in a museum, coming face to face with a demonstration: a series of skeletons arranged from a little monkey to a tall well-developed white man, with a Negro barely outranking a chimpanzee."[17]

Political philosopher Charles Mills calls this particular form of anti-Black racial dehumanization *simianization,* or the process of articulating the supposed "natural" racial inferiority of those of African origin by approximating their likeness to apes.[18] "Scientific" notions of race existed as early as the mid-18th century, but when combined with Darwinian theories of the evolution of the "races of mankind" in the late 19th and early 20th centuries, the idea of a natural racial hierarchy gained strength. These theories of scientific and biological racism, in turn, were used to defend European colonialism and the brutal treatment of Black, Indigenous, and non-white peoples around the world, while offering a rationale and justification to the prior era of imperialism and racial slavery.[19]

Dehumanizing animalistic and bestial comparisons of other racialized groups have long existed in the historical development of colonial and biological racism. Colonized European ethnic groups, like the Irish, were also targeted with animalistic depictions, some of which included simian comparisons, challenging the position held by ethnic humor scholars like Christie Davies, which argues that such humor is not connected to colonial racism.[20] But the portrayal of Black people to apes, as Mills notes, signified something more than a dehumanizing insult. In the formation of a white Eurocentric racialized modernity, the African/simian comparison, now backed by racial science, was offered as "scientific proof" of a natural racial order and hierarchy of the world. This biological racism not only secularized the dehumanization of Blacks but legitimized the existing racial order that placed whites above non-whites in the natural order of things, as if it was inherently "the way it should be," illustrating the role that science and "rationality" played in supporting and maintaining white supremacy. Popular culture—from the World's Fair and national museum exhibits of the era, to literature and films such as *King Kong*—would then help to spread and normalize this notion in the global racial imagination, thereby closing the gap between western elites and those in the streets and their racial understanding of the world.

Since the civil rights movement of the 1960s, this idea of race being rooted in science and biology has been strongly challenged and condemned. The scientific community has roundly dismissed this racist and dangerous idea. Nevertheless, even when contemporary literal connections of Black people to apes are routinely downplayed as "innocent satirical comparisons," this pernicious racist notion continues to exist with a "semiotic aura" that reanimates and perpetuates the enduring racist trope over the centuries, across generations, and into the present.[21] This racist notion was revitalized and circulated widely during the election of the nation's first Black president.

President Chimp

Given the long history of this racist image, and the deeply engrained bigotry in American society, it should come as no surprise that this image would be used to target the first African American president of the United States. But it is important to note that Obama was not the first U.S. president to be depicted as an ape, and it is worth looking at some of these examples a little more closely.

Abraham Lincoln, the "Great Emancipator," was also depicted as an ape during his presidency. Following his Emancipation Proclamation on January 1, 1863, David H. Strother, illustrator at *Harper's Weekly*, drew an image of Lincoln as a smirking monkey sitting on a chair. The monkey was holding a copy of the Emancipation Proclamation, with what appeared to be a slave jumping up to try to grasp ahold of the document.

By employing a trope long used to dehumanize Africans and thus justify their enslavement, this cartoon sought to connect Lincoln with the interests of a denigrated population of Black "inhuman" slaves (also depicted here as animals) and disassociate him from the cultivated culture of whites and whiteness. As critical race studies scholar Philip S. S. Howard has pointed out, behind this kind of cartoon is the argument that by seeking to advance the freedom of slaves, Lincoln had "compromised

FIGURE 5.2. Cartoon depiction of President Abraham Lincoln as a monkey, holding a copy of the Emancipation Proclamation.

SOURCE: D. H. Strother [attributed], *Harper's Weekly* (January 4, 1963): https://collections.libraries .indiana.edu/lilly/exhibitions_legacy/cartoon/monkey.html

his whiteness . . . and exposed him[self] to the kind of antiblack racist iconography to which the simian trope belongs." Moreover, Lincoln was disparaged with the use of this racist trope because he was "perceived to have disrupted the racial order and transgressed the color line by betraying white interests."[22]

But while the depiction of Lincoln as an ape may indicate the presence of anti-Black racism in this reading, this mockery of Lincoln was intended to denigrate and dehumanize Lincoln alone for ostensibly crossing the racial boundary, not all whites, nor all northerners or Republicans by extension. In other words, the depiction of Lincoln as an ape was not offered as a form of anti-white racism, something that underscores an important element in the way that racist humor in America operates and further weakens the notion that racist humor is ever "just a joke." Racist humor is inherently structured around the historical marking of whiteness with normality, and Blackness and non-whites as sub-human. Consequently, humor today continues to provide a key mechanism for the propagation of this persistent anti-Black racist ideology.

There are more recent examples that highlight the differences between this kind of racist humor depending on whether it is targeting white or non-white elected officials. For example, prior to Obama's election, George W. Bush was routinely portrayed as a chimpanzee throughout his presidency. The portrayal of Bush as an ape began soon after he defeated the Democratic candidate Al Gore, who won the popular vote, in the 2000 presidential election. Bush quickly became a target for liberals who saw his presidency as illegitimate. Candidate and President Bush, the son of a previous Republican president and a member of one of the most influential political dynasties in the country, presented himself as an "everyman" to distance himself from his elite background and appear more relatable to white working-class voters—despite being a Yale graduate from a wealthy and politically powerful family. Bush didn't do himself any favors among liberals when he boasted of being an average student during his time at Yale, joking that "C students" can still manage to be president of the United States.[23] Bush's presumed mediocrity, incompetence, and mannerisms would become a target of ridicule for liberal satirists and cartoonists who increasingly mocked him as an unintelligent buffoon who came to power on his father's coattails, assisted by a corrupt Electoral College system.

This early and persistent ridicule of Bush as dumb quickly evolved into depictions of him as an ape. As political cartoonist Steve Bell noted:

> I first drew Bush as a monkey after his installation by the Supreme Court. . . . It was by accident. . . . I had been trying to depict him as a turkey, because Bush's reputation for uselessness was growing as we got to know him, and (barring underpants) there is no better symbol of uselessness than that poor, maligned bird. But no amount of drawing him as a turkey would ever make him look like a turkey.[24]

Political satirists and cartoonists often depict political leaders in non-human ways in an effort to scale down their distance and power, and do so in ways that they believe will resonate more broadly through mockery and contempt.[25] And this depiction, according to Bell, is one that the satirist needs to find fitting and amusing to achieve the greatest effect. Bell noted that he decided to depict Bush as a monkey after watching multiple televised interviews and focusing on mannerisms that stood out to him:

> There was something about the way he held his arms as he walked up; then, as he faced the cameras, his mouth formed into a distinct pout. He moved like a chimp, walked like a chimp and even talked like a chimp. This was no play acting; George Bush actually was a chimp.[26]

One early illustration captured Bush arriving in Spain in 2001 on his first trip to Europe as president. Bell satirized the incident of Bush descending from Air Force One.

Bell's detailed account of how and why he chose to depict Bush as an ape illustrates the kind of anti-Bush humor that took root soon after his inauguration in 2001. While the depiction of Bush was certainly an effort to mock his intelligence and undermine his leadership, the Bush ape depictions were not just personal insults. Rather, they were intended to

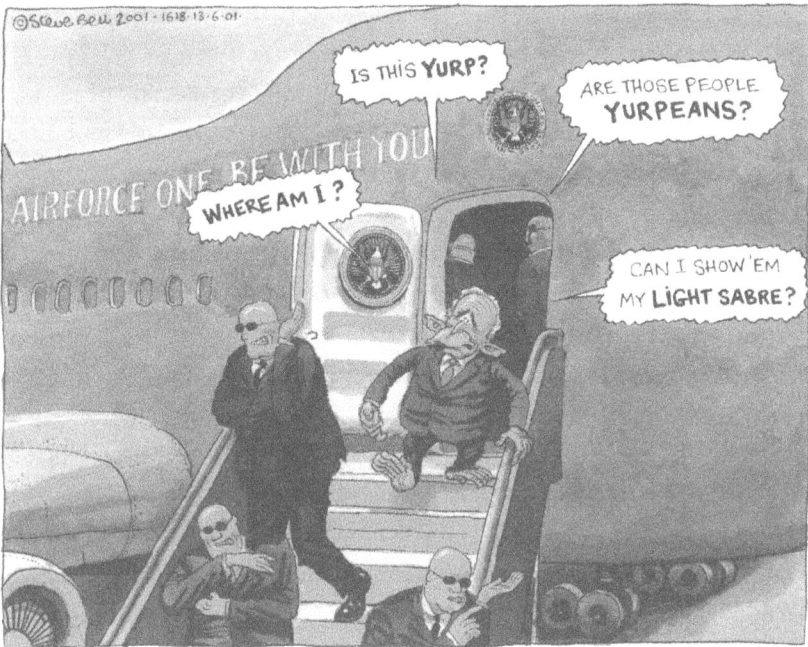

FIGURE 5.3. Cartoon depiction of President George W. Bush as an ape, published in *The Guardian* in 2001 by political cartoonist Steve Bell.

SOURCE: S. Bell, *The Guardian* (2001): https://www.theguardian.com/cartoons/stevebell/0,7371 ,519655,00.html

characterize, perhaps by extension, Republicans and conservatives more broadly. The punchline? Bush and conservatives are stupid.

But while this particular ape depiction is certainly an insulting one, it was not issued or interpreted as racist or as anti-white propaganda. This is because such an interpretation is not consistent with the history of racism in the United States or around the world. The ape depiction of Bush continued throughout his presidency. And while cartoonists like Bell were criticized for offering an image seen as disrespectful, they usually didn't change their position. As Bell noted after receiving complaints for his depiction of Bush as an ape, "I would be failing in my duty if I refused to acknowledge his unique qualities as a chimpanzee, for how often does a leader of the free world come along who resembles a monkey in every particular?"[27]

There is an argument to be made that because Republicans had to endure eight years of ape depictions of Bush, conservatives might have felt justified in returning the gesture in kind following the election of Obama. But such an argument ignores the discursive, historical, and moral difference in depicting a white president or political figure as an ape, in contrast to ridiculing any Black person as an ape. This is because in the history of slavery and colonialism—and the continuation of structural, systemic, and discursive forms of racism—the depiction of those of African descent as primates remains an anti-Black racist signifier.

As the new energetic face of the Democratic Party, Obama captivated liberal Democratic voters with campaign slogans built around hope and change. But at the same time he sparked the ire and racial contempt of a white Republican and conservative opposition that was immediately hostile to his popularity, election, and leadership. Dehumanizing depictions of Obama and his family as apes and monkeys were immediately circulated by white conservatives, in particular across various social settings and contexts, on the internet, in right-wing media and protests, and among elected officials and citizens alike.

White conservatives would routinely plead ignorance when confronted for partaking in these racial transgressions. But it was clear that white conservatives consciously and/or unconsciously understood the gravity of depicting Obama as an ape—despite rehearsed denials that their "intentions" were not motivated by racism. Indeed, when the use of primate imagery in cartoons about Obama first began, white conservatives expressed trepidation and seemingly acknowledged that such an association was, in fact, problematic and racist. Despite this initial apprehension, the racial dehumanizing of Obama would soon evolve into more widespread and aggressive forms of amused racial contempt, something that would directly embolden white resistance to the first Black president, highlighting the key role of humor in conveying modern racist political discourse.

A Kinder, Gentler Anti-Black Racism?

One of the first public associations of Obama with primate imagery occurred in early 2008 on conservative radio host Rush Limbaugh's show.

In a discussion of presidential candidates for the 2008 election, a female caller shared that her 12-year-old daughter allegedly thought that then Senator Obama looked like a beloved children's cartoon monkey character.[28] The caller claimed that her daughter didn't care "what the guy's middle name is" but that "he looks like Curious George." Limbaugh, a white conservative shock jock known for expressing racist and derogatory commentary on his show, initially found the comment amusing. But during the exchange, Limbaugh appeared to grasp the potential issue at hand, while acknowledging the caller's and his audience's sentiment about Obama. "You're going to have to be very careful," he added, apparently referencing the historically racist trope the caller was presenting. "You don't have to disabuse Republicans of Obama, Tammy. Everybody's on the same page with you about Obama."[29] But even Limbaugh was caught off guard by the very public use of this racist imagery. Rather than continue this discussion with the caller, Limbaugh cut to a commercial break and took a moment to figure out how to respond to a caller associating candidate Obama with a cartoon monkey.

When this exchange occurred in early 2008, there was already growing hostility towards candidate Obama among white conservative politicians, media personalities, and voters, a hostility exemplified by Sarah Palin, that year's Republican vice-presidential candidate. After being chosen as John McCain's running mate, Palin rose to political stardom by presenting herself as a "folksy" anti-elitist who did not bother with polite political discourse and decorum. She preferred a personal style of "country" frankness and lingo, including showing contempt towards other candidates, Obama in particular.[30] This hostility would later provide space for openly racist sentiments towards Obama to emerge on the internet and in the media by Palin and other conservative officials and commentators.[31]

But in the first part of 2008, months before Obama's election, there was still an expectation that media figures like Limbaugh would avoid circulating racist humor and racist language. For example, just the previous year in 2007, long-time CBS shock jock Don Imus was fired for "jokingly" referring to the Black female basketball players at Rutgers University as "nappy-headed hos."[32] Imus's firing illustrated the unacceptability of public racial insult in the nation at the time, an unacceptability routinely challenged as political correctness and as an attack on free speech by conservative commentators.

Perhaps with Imus's recent firing in mind, soon after the commercial break Limbaugh issued what appeared to be an apology for the racial transgression on his show:

"I need to apologize to both Senator Obama and to Senator McCain. We had a caller, the last caller of the hour, her name was Tammy, is that right? We were talking about Hillary and Obama and that race with her, right? Obama's qualifications. And she told me what her 12 year old's reaction to Obama was. The little 12 year old thought Obama looked like Curious George, and I chuckled and we went to a break. I'd never heard of Curious George. Only now have staffers sent me little pictures of Curious George. . . . I had no idea Curious George was a monkey."[33]

At this point, Limbaugh seemed to acknowledge the problem with associating Obama with an ape, and he attempted to distance himself from the caller's comments by implausibly claiming that he was unaware that Curious George was a cartoon monkey. Limbaugh then gave a longwinded explanation for why he allegedly did not know that Curious George was an ape, before continuing with his apology:

"So I wish to apologize. . . . It was not my intent to bring dishonor and guttural utterances into this campaign. It happened, I laughed about it. . . . I was laughing because I was being polite, but I'd never heard of Curious George. I still don't know what the deal is. I see the pictures of Curious George now, but I have no clue what Curious George does. I don't know. And Dawn, stunned me, 'Curious George was around when you were growing up.' Well, this is the first I have heard. In fact, I can tell you, I have never seen a cartoon starring a monkey, unless there was one on the Flintstones, but I think those were dinosaurs and alligators."[34]

Although it is difficult to imagine that Limbaugh was unfamiliar with one of the most popular children's book characters of the 20th century, he was trying to deny any racial intent or harm on his part with a plea to racial ignorance.[35] And while the error may or may not have been genuine on Limbaugh's part, his excuse was clearly an attempt to hedge against condemnation for diffusing racism against a Black presidential candidate on his show.

By swiftly pivoting to a rant against political correctness, which was one of the frequent targets on the show, Limbaugh helped lay the groundwork for what would become, in the coming months, a broader turn among conservatives in the media and in public discourse toward the use of racist humor, particularly in relation to Obama:

"So, at any rate, we have fired the caller, Tammy. We're not going to put up with this on this program. We're not going to tolerate this kind of stuff on the program, and I do officially apologize to both Senator Obama and to Senator McCain. Why aren't you apologizing to Hillary? Well, she's probably happy it happened. I guess I better apologize for saying that. You see, ladies and gentlemen, I'm doing this as an illustration for you of how really uptight and tense everybody is going to be with any kind of criticism of Barack Obama on the Republican side. I think we may set a record in this upcoming campaign. If Obama is the nominee, we may set a record for the number of apologies to him and his campaign by various Republicans and so forth."[36]

Limbaugh's "apology," in other words, was intended as a "teachable moment" for the millions of listeners on one of the most popular radio shows in the country. Limbaugh used the racial transgression on his show to teach his audience about the threat posed by liberals and political correctness to conservative and Republican free expression. He used the incident to issue a warning to the audience: if they thought political correctness was already out of control, it was going to get worse under Obama. With a Black nominee, Limbaugh grumbled, Republicans and conservatives would be forced to "bite their tongue" and "walk on eggshells" on all racial matters and commentary, leading to greater constraint on the "free speech" of white conservatives and their ability to voice their displeasure, criticism, and true feelings about Obama. As Limbaugh noted, "there is a big sensitivity to this. This is why I say the race business is only going to get bigger with Obama's election"[37]—a business that white conservative figures like Limbaugh were eager to exploit and profit from.

Limbaugh would continue to advance amused racial contempt towards Obama on his show in various ways under the guise of satire and pushback against so-called political correctness. In early 2007, for instance, Limbaugh aired a parody of the song "Puff the Magic Dragon" titled "Barack the Magic Negro" by conservative comedian Paul Shanklin. The song was in reference to a 2007 *Los Angeles Times* article titled "Obama the 'Magic Negro,'" in which columnist David Ehrenstein suggested that white liberals were supporting Obama as a "magical Negro," a recurring figure in the white American imagination and cinema, who would "assuage [their] white 'guilt' . . . over the role of slavery and racial segregation in American history" by embracing their "desire for a noble, healing Negro" who would save them.[38] Shanklin, who is white, drew on this column to skewer Obama and his white liberal supporters in his song parody by impersonating Al Sharpton, the Black civil rights leader, as envious of Obama's popularity ("They'll vote for him, and not for me, 'cause he's not from da 'hood"), using a comedic trope harking back to the era of blackface minstrelsy.[39]

Limbaugh, who was criticized as racist for airing this song, understood the social and political stakes of a white conservative taking the first Black president to task in this new era and quickly realized he would need to modify his approach to Obama. As a leading conservative "culture warrior," he was determined to figure out how do so. Prior to Obama's nomination, Limbaugh noted that he hadn't yet "figured . . . out exactly" his strategy and tactics for how to bash Obama. But soon enough, he began to reveal his new approach to his listeners:

> "Ladies and gentlemen, I had a conversation with a friend Wednesday afternoon after the program, and he said, 'Nobody's criticizing

Obama. How are you going to do this? How are you going to handle criticizing the first black American to run for president?' I said: 'I'm going to do it the way I always do it. First, at the top of the list, I'm going to do it fearlessly. I'm not going to bow to political correctness. I'm going to do it with humor."[40]

Limbaugh emphasized the role that humor and "satire" would play in his political criticism of Obama, while seemingly stressing that he would do so in a "colorblind" way. "'I'm going to focus on the issues. I'm going to react to what he says,'" Limbaugh declared to his listeners. "'I'm going to do it just like it were any other case . . . he's a man, right? He's a liberal. How do I criticize liberals? I criticize them.'"[41]

But Limbaugh was clearly aware that as a white male conservative commentator, he could not freely criticize Obama, a leading Black candidate, particularly on racial matters. So he developed a different approach, strategy, and voice for getting his racial commentary across in this new so-called post-racial moment:

"I have devised, ladies and gentlemen, an even more creative way of criticizing Obama. I have, just this morning, named a new position here on the staff that is the Official Obama Criticizer. The E.I.B. Network now has an Official Obama Criticizer. He is Bo Snerdly."[42]

By enlisting Snerdly (James Golden), the Black phone operator on his show, as the "Official Obama Criticizer," Limbaugh suggested that he had found a new way to advance his political criticism of Obama. Snerdly, a conservative, played his part on Limbaugh's show by introducing himself as an "African-American-in-good-standing-and-certified-black-enough-to-criticize-Obama guy" while declaring that he was now speaking "on behalf of our E.I.B. brothers and sisters in the hood."[43] With Snerdly, Limbaugh was able to simultaneously minimize accusations of racism while seemingly appealing to Black conservatives. But by exploiting Snerdly's Blackness to advance his own racist commentary and amused racial contempt towards Obama—for the amusement, political, and emotional alignment of his millions of white listeners—Limbaugh's approach was neither novel nor colorblind. It relied on the same racist strategies and tropes from the minstrelsy era, a strategy also used and abused by white liberal comedians and shock jocks, such as the New York radio personality Howard Stern.[44]

Limbaugh's use of amused racial contempt to push back against political correctness and to criticize and ridicule a leading Black presidential candidate highlights the role that racist humor continues to play in American society, as a form of discourse that aids in political and social affiliation and movement building among white conservatives. As the conservative Israeli author and commentator Zev Chafets noted, "The bit was typical Limbaugh confrontational, deliberately insensitive and funny," while suggesting that "It was also a declaration of independence" by Limbaugh from the Republican Party and presidential nominee. "Whatever special courtesies John McCain might plan to extend to Barack Obama," Chafets observed, "Limbaugh is going to conduct his air war, as he always has, by his own rules of engagement."[45]

These examples also tie into the larger discussion of how humor continues to play a central role in diffusing racist ideology in the United States under the guise of the humor, free speech, and challenge to political correctness, in ways that are also often embraced more broadly beyond the arena of entertainment, as the previous chapters illustrate. Only weeks after the Curious George incident on Limbaugh's show, a bar owner in Georgia made headlines for selling T-shirts with an image of Curious George eating a banana captioned "Obama in 08."[46] Following protests outside his business, owner Mike Norman stated that the T-shirts, which were sold out, were "not meant to be racist." "I saw the cartoon on TV," Norman claimed, "and I looked, and this [sic] was the ears and the hairline, and the big smile, and Obama has all three." While Norman alleged that he got the idea for the T-shirt after watching the character on television, it is likely that Norman, described as an "ultra conservative," made a note after listening to Limbaugh's show a few weeks earlier and decided to market the idea. Soon, civil rights groups, like the regional Anti-Defamation League, were condemning Norman's statement as "disingenuous," "offensive," and "a demeaning stereotype used to insult African-Americans." But while

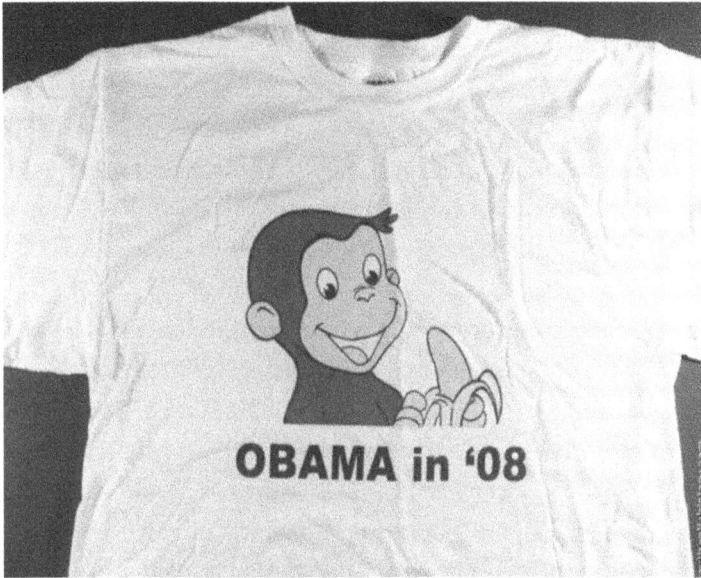

FIGURE 5.4. Anti-Obama T-shirt produced and sold by Georgia bar owner Mike Norman during the 2008 presidential election.

SOURCE: The Coon Caricature: Blacks as Monkeys (2012): https://www.historyonthenet.com/ authentichistory/diversity/african/3-coon/6-monkey/

the ADL denounced Norman's actions as "inappropriate" and "hateful," it held that Norman's activity was "protected speech."[47]

The Boston-based publisher, Houghton Mifflin Harcourt, also took issue with the unsolicited use of the character and issued a public statement criticizing Norman, noting that it would never authorize nor approve of such use of the Curious George character, and that it would consider legal action.[48] Norman claimed that he was not trying to profit from the sale of the T-shirts and that he planned to donate the proceeds to the Muscular Dystrophy Association. The MDA issued a public statement soon after stating that it was unaware of Norman's intended donations and that the association did not want his money.[49]

Despite the reactions by specific companies and groups seeking to distance themselves from this kind of racist humor, there was plenty of interest in the humor itself as a vehicle for mobilizing political identity and affiliation. The T-shirts sold out, and the publicity helped increase popularity. As the image circulated, it further gained traction, revealing how racist humor, in the post–civil rights era, can still be used effectively to generate social and political cohesion among those on the right. This practice also illustrates that amused racial contempt in an ostensibly colorblind or post-racial society is actively being used to signal a form of white political resistance, not only to the idea of political correctness but to multiracial democracy.

This ape depiction of Obama would continue to circulate well into the 2008 election season. Only weeks before the election, a smirking middle-aged white male was spotted carrying a stuffed animal version of the character with an Obama bumper sticker over its head at a Sarah Palin rally in Johnstown, Pennsylvania. The crowds at Republican rallies for John McCain and Sarah Palin had become increasingly hostile and angry over the course of the campaign.[50] Palin made openly insulting remarks against Democratic candidates during and after the campaign, something that spurred on her aggressive and vocal conservative followers. She took special aim at Obama, insisting that he was a "radical Muslim" planning to instill "shariah law" to "destroy America." She would also help spread the birther conspiracy theory that claimed Obama was not born in the United States.[51]

By the end of the 2008 election cycle, this seemingly innocuous comment from a caller on a radio show had morphed into a full-blown racist symbol exploited by white Republican voters at conservative rallies. While it is true that much more aggressive and virulent anti-Obama racist rhetoric and imagery was being circulated on the internet and in private, and that the insistence by Palin and others that Obama was a radical Muslim was illustrative of the Islamophobia that had been normalized in post–9/11 America, by comparison this seemingly gentle racist association of Obama with a cartoon ape was one of the first overt forms of amused racial contempt to be used against the nation's soon-to-be first Black president. The image was far from benign. It created an entry point for more overt and aggressive forms of amused racial contempt to circulate following the election of Obama, even as white conservatives denied that such forms of humor had any racist intent.

Kill the Ape

A few weeks after Obama was inaugurated in 2009, and almost a year into the Limbaugh and Curious George incident appeared in national headlines, the *New York Post*, a conservative tabloid owned by billionaire Rupert Murdoch and NewsCorp, published a cartoon of an ape being shot to death by a white police officer, captioned "They'll have to find someone else to write the next stimulus bill." The cartoon would set off a round of national and international headlines debating whether the image was indeed racist.

The cartoon was produced by Sean Delonas, a conservative political cartoonist with a history of publishing racist, homophobic, and derogatory images.[52] The context surrounding this cartoon centered on two events. The first was the stimulus bill mentioned in the captioned image. Delonas was referring to the $787 billion economic stimulus bill that Obama signed during the 2008 financial crisis, also known as the American Recovery and Reinvestment Act of 2009.[53] The bill was pitched as trying to salvage and create jobs during the Great Recession, modeled in part on Keynesian economic theory and the need to increase public investment and spending during periods of economic recession and depression. While the $787 billion figure was much higher than the initial $150 billion that Obama mentioned on the campaign trail, it was much lower than what many economists believed was necessary to stimulate the economy given the severity of the economic crisis at the time.[54]

Although the stimulus bill was strongly opposed by Republicans and conservatives, as illustrated by Delonas's editorial cartoon, the dollar amount was similar to the $700 billion emergency funds signed by Bush in 2008, the Emergency Economic Stabilization Act, also known as the "bank bailout." This earlier government action was not aimed at public spending, public investment, or job creation. It went exclusively into the hands of the very corporate entities that were responsible for the economic crisis to begin with.[55] Nevertheless, a majority of both Republicans and Democrats supported the bank bailout. But when it came to supporting Obama's proposed economic relief effort, much like everything else Obama would propose throughout his tenure, conservatives resoundingly opposed and rejected these efforts as "socialism."[56]

Although conservatives would claim that Delonas's jab was aimed squarely at Obama's economic bill, in fact the cartoon clearly drew from another recent news event—one that involved a real-life ape and violence against a white person—that was not at all related to the needed economic recovery. On February 16, 2009, the day before Obama signed the economic stimulus bill, a white woman named Charla Nash was mauled nearly to death in Stamford, Connecticut, by "Travis," her wealthy employer's celebrity pet chimpanzee. That afternoon, the ape's owner Sandra Harold watched in horror as her 200-pound chimp ripped off Nash's nose, lips, eyelids, and hands before being shot by a police officer on her driveway.[57] The horrific mauling incident made national headlines and became fertile comic material for Delonas to make a racist partisan political statement, aimed ostensibly at Obama's proposed stimulus bill. Delonas merged the two news events to produce a cartoon image that kicked off an international racial spectacle, one that appeared as a veiled call for Obama's assassination (downplayed as "just a joke") only weeks after Obama's inauguration and amid the most severe economic crisis since the Great Depression (at the time).[58]

The publication of the cartoon, however, is not necessarily that remarkable when one considers the importance that anti-Black racist humor continues to play in American society, particularly among conservatives and those on the far right. The image, as overtly racist and disgusting as it was, nevertheless exemplified important ways that notions of colorblindness ("it wasn't about Obama or race") provided the rhetorical space for racist depictions to emerge, and be defended, in ways that would not have made sense or been necessary prior to the colorblind era.

After the cartoon was published, the charges of racism came quick, as did the attempts to downplay the gravity of the violent racist imagery. Reverend Al Sharpton called the cartoon "'troubling at best, given the

THE POLITICS OF AMUSED RACIAL CONTEMPT 147

FIGURE 5.5. Controversial anti-Obama cartoon published in the *New York Post* in early 2009 by political cartoonist Sean Delonas.

SOURCE: S. Delonas, *New York Post* (February 18, 2009).

historic racist attacks [on] African-Americans as being synonymous with monkeys.'" Sharpton and other Black leaders would lead a demonstration in front of the *New York Post* headquarters to demand an explanation, removal of the cartoon, and a reprimand for the cartoonist.[59] Numerous other voices rallied around protesting the racist image and aligned it with the history of anti-Black racism and amused racial contempt in the United States. As Barbara Ciara, president of the National Association of Black Journalists, stated "'How could The Post let this cartoon pass as satire? . . . To compare the nation's first African-American commander-in-chief to a dead chimpanzee is nothing short of racist drivel.'"[60] "'[A]nyone with an iota of sense knows the close association of black people and the primate imagery,'" historian Jelani Cobb stated sharply, adding that "'there was no getting around the implications of it.'"[61]

In response to mounting pressure and protest, the *New York Post* chief editor, Col Allan, issued a public comment downplaying the racist cartoon while blasting critics and protestors. According to Allan, the cartoon was nothing more than "'a clear parody of a current news event . . . the shooting of a violent chimp in Connecticut,'" while mocking "'Washington's efforts to revive the economy.'" Allan denied that the ape in the cartoon was a reference to Obama and took a jab at Sharpton as "'nothing more than a publicity opportunist.'"[62]

Ted Rall, president of the Association of American Editorial Cartoonists, offered a less aggressive defense of Delonas. "'He was trying to jam two stories together,'" Rall insisted. "'The comparison he had in mind: The guy who wrote the package wasn't Obama; it was a bunch of white economic advisers, and he wasn't thinking about Obama.'"[63] Delonas, who initially tried to steer clear of the controversy, soon came to his own defense:

> "It's absolutely friggin ridiculous. Do you really think I'm saying Obama should be shot? I didn't see that in the cartoon. The chimpanzee was a major story in the Post. Every paper in New York, except The New York Times, covered the chimpanzee story. It's just ridiculous. It's about the economic stimulus bill. If you're going to make that about anybody, it would be [House Speaker Nancy] Pelosi, which it's not."[64]

But as political protests continued to escalate, the issue became more than just the cartoonist and his image. The increasing pressure on the *Post* and owner Rupert Murdoch culminated in public statements and apologies, a rare move for Murdoch. But the nature of these apologies was now following a familiar pattern and tone, and in many ways echoed Limbaugh's approach to the issue. By the end of the week, the *New York Post* published a statement on its website that was essentially a carbon copy of Allan's initial statement. While restating that the cartoon was intended to ridicule the "'ineptly written stimulus bill,'" and seemingly acknowledged critics' concerns that the image was "'a thinly veiled expression of racism'" aimed at Obama, the *Post* maintained that "'This most certainly was not its intent'" before apologizing "'to those who were offended by the image.'" However, the statement then declared that "'no apology is due'" to those who "'see the incident as an opportunity for payback.'" Like Allan's take, the *Post* referred to these critics as mere "'opportunists [who] seek to make it something else'" before concluding that "'Sometimes a cartoon is just a cartoon.'"[65]

Delonas, his defenders, and the paper's editors and owners sought to dissociate the cartoon from any racial meaning or harm by downplaying and insisting that it was merely humorous commentary on the headlines and proclaiming that the artistic and editorial process is one of creative freedom and expression. It was "just a cartoon." Yet, it is not difficult to see the centuries-long racist genealogy and the anti-Black racist symbolism in this image, as well as the veiled call for racial violence that is reminiscent of the kind of images published in Tom Metzger's *White Aryan Resistance*. Both kinds of images, whether appearing in white supremacist pamphlets or in mainstream conservative newspapers, were used for the purpose of advancing racist ideologies and propaganda, while hiding behind the banner of "free speech" and "just a joke." Moreover, this frequent pattern of offense/apology/non-apology arising from the use of amused racial contempt was not an accident; it was the direct result of underlying social behaviors that were trying to preserve a white racist hierarchy and resist multiracial democracy, while using racist humor as a model of agitation and self-promotion.

Despite the denials of racist intent, the publication of a cartoon that drew directly on a historical trope of anti-Blackness in one of the most widely circulated conservative newspapers in the country also coincided with a growing number of death threats and assassination attempts aimed at the first Black president.[66] As the *Washington Post* reported in 2014, Obama faced an average of three times as many death threats as previous presidents, averaging thirty per day during the first year of his presidency, and more than four times that of his predecessor George W. Bush.[67] The number of far-right white supremacist militia groups, as well as the number of hate crimes, also increased under the Obama presidency.[68] Combined with the escalation of police racial discourse and violence under the Obama era, as discussed in the previous chapter, and at a time when the FBI was pointing to the increased presence and infiltration of white supremacists in law enforcement,[69] it appears that this cartoon image featured in the *New York Post* was much more than "just a cartoon." Rather, it was a form of amused racial contempt that was contributing to the growing white nationalist backlash that was building up against the symbolic threat posed by the election of the first Black president.

Republicans Sharing a Racist Laugh

The widespread condemnation against Delonas's racist cartoon seemed to suggest that this form of amused racial contempt against Obama would not be tolerated in public discourse. As noted above, many compared Delonas's cartoon to the kinds of racist images and commentary that were more commonly found circulating in white supremacist and far-right on-line spaces. In such corners of the internet, it was no surprise to find vulgar racist images and insults aimed at Obama and non-whites more generally. But to have this kind of material out in the open in what was purportedly a colorblind and post-racial era did not fit the narrative being crafted by both liberals and conservatives. Therefore, to distance themselves from such views, it appeared that conservative leaders and officials were publicly in agreement that such forms of racial animus, even under the guise of a joke, were unacceptable.[70]

But while conservative leaders publicly denounced this behavior, in private the forbidden pleasure of racist joking was too tempting to resist. This was illustrated, for instance, by the Republican National Committee Chairman, Chip Saltsman from Tennessee, who only weeks after the 2008 election, and before the Christmas holiday, mailed fellow RNC committee members a CD with songs like "Barack the Magic Negro" and "The Star Spanglish Banner" on a disc titled "We Hate the USA" as a holiday "joke." "'I think most people recognize political satire when they see it. . . . I think RNC members understand that,'" Saltsman told CNN at the time.[71] Republican officials continued to share such materials in private throughout Obama's first term.

Only a week after the controversy surrounding Delonas's cartoon, Republican Mayor Dean Grose (white male) of Los Alamitos in Orange County, California, was found emailing a photoshopped image of the White House with a watermelon patch on the front lawn with the title

"No Easter egg hunt this year."[72] Mayor Grose sent the image on his private email account to a list of supporters, as a "joke." One of the recipients included Keyanus Price, a local Black businesswoman and fellow board member of the Los Alamitos Youth Center alongside Grose. "'I was horrified when I read that e-mail,'" Price told the *Orange County Register,* which broke the story.[73] "'I honestly don't even understand where he was coming from, sending this to me,'" she stated in shock following the incident. Price noted that she had been exposed to her share of "'chicken and watermelon and all those kinds of jokes'" throughout her life, but that "'[a]s a black person receiving something like this from the city freakin' mayor,'" left her in disbelief.[74]

Price's shock soon turned to anger. "'What I'm concerned about is how can this person send an e-mail out like this and think it is OK?'"[75] she said. Price shared the email with her supervisor, John Bryant, who reached out to Mayor Grose to request that he apologize to Price, which he attempted to do.

But by then the news was out, and the spotlight was now focused on the mayor of a small city in what was still Republican-dominated Orange County. Grose initially sought to plead racial ignorance by claiming that he did not know that associating watermelon imagery with Black people was "offensive," even though he believed the idea was comical and suggested that given "'the way things are today, you gotta laugh every now and then.'" Grose ultimately acknowledge that he used poor judgment in sending the email and that he didn't intend to cause Price any pain, before minimizing and trivializing his actions by adding that "'It was not sent to a whole bunch of people. . . . People e-mail things all the time.'"[76]

Local residents were split between condemning and supporting Grose. Tom Stretz, executive director of the youth center, called Grose's actions shameful and "'totally contrary to our organizational values of respect and celebration of cultural and racial diversity,'" while Marjorie McDowall, a 74-year-old resident of the neighboring city of Tustin, noted that the incident reminded her of the casual racism she witnessed during her youth. "'All the filthy jokes . . . about blacks,'" she noted, "'It's really offensive. I thought we were beyond that. I really did.'" Supporters of Grose believed

FIGURE 5.6. Emailed image of the White House following Obama's election, sent by Republican Mayor Dean Grose of Los Alamitos, California, in 2009.

SOURCE: J. L. Fletcher, Mayor Is Criticized for White House Watermelon Patch E-Mail, *Orange County Register* (February 24, 2009): https://www.ocregister.com/2009/02/24/mayor-is-criticized-for-white-house-watermelon-patch-e-mail/

the media attention the incident was receiving was extreme and exaggerated. Katey McDonnell, a 31-year-old resident of Placentia, believed that while Grose used poor judgment in sending the email, the incident had "'been blown way out of proportion.'" Anonymous readers on the *OC Register*'s comments section echoed her sentiment, adding that the email wasn't racist at all and that Grose had no reason to apologize.[77]

But after receiving widespread media attention, hundreds of complaints, and public pressure on his (mis)leadership, Grose decided to step down as mayor. He believed the incident and the media attention it created had mischaracterized him, although he claimed to recognize his mistake by taking "'steps to make sure this is never repeated.'"[78] Although Grose resigned as mayor, he retained his seat on the Los Alamitos City Council after the incident.

White male Republican leaders were not the only ones ridiculing Obama; white conservative women would also advance amused racial contempt for the first Black president. Just a few months before the incident in Los Alamitos, the Chaffey Community Republican Women, a largely white women's group in nearby Rancho Cucamonga, California, sent out a mailing with an image of a fictitious food stamp bill labeled "Obama Bucks" and "United States Food Stamps." The image included a picture of a smiling Obama with a donkey body centered alongside images of KFC fried chicken, ribs, the Kool-Aid man, and a slice of watermelon.[79]

Sheila Raines, an African American member of the club, was deeply offended by the image and was the first to complain to the group's president, Diane Fedele, about the newsletter. "'I'm really hurt. I cried for 45 minutes,'" she noted. Raines, of nearby San Bernardino, a far less white and less affluent city in the region, had been working to recruit other Black voters to join the women's group and the Republican Party. "'This is what keeps African-Americans from joining the Republican Party,'" Raines stated, feeling betrayed by the group. Fedele's explanation of racist denial followed a predictable pattern. "'I didn't see it the way that it's being taken,'" Fedele pleaded. "'It was just food to me. It didn't mean anything

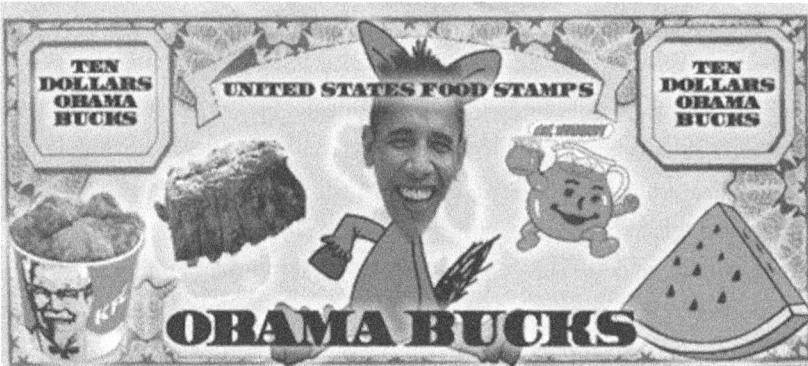

FIGURE 5.7. Mailing sent by the Chaffey Community Republican Women, a white conservative women's group in Rancho Cucamonga, California, in 2008.

SOURCE: G. Gardner, GOP Mailing Depicts Obama on Food Stamps, Not Dollar Bill, *NPR* (October 16, 2008): https://www.npr.org/sections/newsandviews/2008/10/gop_mailing_is_mouth_watering.html

else.'" Fedele added that the image "wasn't intended" as a racist insult against Obama, but as a way to mock a comment that Obama had made earlier in the summer about how as an African American he "'doesn't look like all those other presidents on the dollar bills.'"[80]

One would think that, after the frequent public embarrassment of white conservatives and their failed attempts at satirical commentary that veered toward blatant racism, Republican officials would think twice before sending or forwarding an email with questionable racial content—especially if such incidents had recently been in the news. But with the growing frequency of these racial media controversies, and the entrenched denial and claims of racial ignorance by white conservatives in the spotlight, it appeared that the more negative attention these and other incidents received, the more support white conservative officials and personalities would earn from their predominantly white conservative base.

This was the case for Marilyn Davenport, a member of the Republican Central Committee of Orange County, and a Tea Party supporter. In 2011, Davenport emailed an image of a family of clothed apes that included a photo of Obama's face superimposed on the infant chimp. "Now you know why no birth certificate," was the tagline included in the email. The image was being circulated among Tea Party supporters in the middle of the growing birther movement, a conspiracy theory spread during Obama's first term that claimed he was not a native-born U.S. citizen, but born in Kenya, and therefore an illegitimate president.

Davenport, who supported Grose during his controversy two years earlier, was now in the headlines for spreading a racist birther image that she found amusing. "'It struck me as just political satire with all that's going on with the birth certificate,'" she said.[81] But after her email was made public, on cue, Davenport denied any racist intent and pleaded racial innocence. "'Oh, come on! Everybody who knows me knows that I am not a racist,'" Davenport implored. "It was a joke. I have friends who are black. Besides, I only sent it to a few people—mostly people I didn't think would be upset by it.'"[82]

Davenport's predictable response to charges of racism was too much even for some fellow Republicans to swallow. Scott Baugh, the chairman of

FIGURE 5.8. Image circulated by Marilyn Davenport, a member of the Republican Central Committee of Orange County, in 2011.

SOURCE: R. S. Moxley, Racist Orange County Republican Email: President Obama and His Parents Are Apes, *OC Weekly* (April 21, 2011): https://www.ocweekly.com/updated-ktla-gets-davenport-scoop-racist-orange-county-republican-email-president-obama-and-his-parents-are-apes-6471201/?sfw=pass1605035150

the Orange County Republican Party at the time, called Davenport's email "'despicable'" and "'dripping with racism.'"[83] Baugh emphasized that "'The email is without question extremely racist'" because the depiction of "'African Americans as monkeys is a longtime, well-known and particularly offensive slur because it denies them their basic humanity.'"[84] Baugh further added that this kind of behavior by Davenport and others "'undermines everything we are doing to reach out to ethnic communities.'"[85]

Baugh, among other Republican officials, condemned Davenport's racist actions because they believed she was hurting the party's image and outreach, and they pressured her to apologize and resign. Davenport soon issued a public apology but refused to be ousted from her post.[86] Davenport, serving her fourth elected term during this incident, aimed to appear sincere and remorseful for engaging in the racist ridicule that was putting numerous white conservatives in the spotlight throughout Obama's first term in office, just like Limbaugh had predicted. "'I wasn't wise in sending the email out. I shouldn't have done it,'" Davenport stated. "'I really wasn't thinking when I did it. I had poor judgment,'" she noted, echoing Grose's reply from the still-fresh Los Alamitos incident. Davenport sought to deny and minimize her racism with a now familiar pattern of racial ignorance. "'I think it's only racist when the intent in my heart is to make it that way, and that was not the intent of my heart,'" she pleaded.[87] But as calls for her resignation grew, including from members of her own party as well as civil rights groups, Davenport remained steadfast that she would not cave to the pressure. "'I'm not going to resign,'" Davenport stated firmly. "'I really have no plans to do so. My constituents have told me not to resign, and I'm very happy with their support. Everybody who knows me says they can't believe people are calling me a racist. I am not a racist.'"[88]

The use of racist tropes by right-wing politicians to ridicule Barack Obama are examples of the way humor is continuing to shape American racial discourse and politics today. Over the course of the first Obama term, amused racial contempt by white conservatives continued to advance political and social alignment, objectives, and ideologies. These examples underscore the value of racist humor as a tool for building social cohesion in America, and they point to the way people continue to turn to racial tropes as a source of racist pleasure and social bonding.

The use of anti-Black racist humor during the 2008 campaign and throughout Obama's presidency was not solely about Obama. It was a collective expression to reassert a racial order and hierarchy that, from the point of view of white conservatives, appeared to be slipping away.[89] These examples highlight how fundamental humor is as a means of circulating racist ideas in the 21st century. Understood this way, the point of racially dehumanizing and ridiculing Obama was not only for the purpose of denigrating and mocking the Black president. Rather, it was a discursive effort to elevate and strengthen a collective sense of whiteness and white rule by those threatened by and opposed to a multiracial democracy. In turn, the widespread amused racial contempt of Obama—along with the debates, controversies, and divisions that unfolded—played a significant role in animating the politics of whiteness and white nationalism during and after the Obama presidency.

By paying close attention to the affective politics of amused racial contempt during the Obama era, we can also see that the politics of white resentment and white nationalism did not emerge during the Trump era. These trends were well underway before Trump entered the political scene. And they were being publicly activated, in part, by the widespread use of amused racial contempt towards a Black president, a symbol of the demographic changes threatening white dominance and rule. This cultural practice during the Obama era echoed the long history of white supremacy that never went away in U.S. society. It was now being unleashed in ways that facilitated the expansion of a racial populism that relied on weaponizing racial humor, ridicule, and insult as tools for political mobilization particularly among white conservatives.

The circulation of amused racial contempt in contemporary American society is often explained away as "just a joke." Obama himself, when asked about being racially ridiculed by conservative commentators like Rush Limbaugh, downplayed this racist commentary as mere entertainment. "'I'm not one of these people who, who takes myself so seriously that I get offended by . . . every comment made about me,'" Obama noted, adding that "'I don't mind folks poking fun at me. . . . That's part of the job.'"[90] Obama, of course, took the opportunity to respond with his own form of amused contempt against Trump and his supporters in his much-celebrated White House Correspondents' Dinner in 2011, an event where Obama publicly ridiculed Trump in front of the nation's power elites. Many have speculated that this public humiliation emboldened Trump to run for public office.[91] This example illustrates the uneven and unequal terrain in the politics of amused contempt.

These examples, and the subsequent pattern of racial denial and excuses of ignorance and innocence, are part of a larger discursive commentary that illustrates the way humor and "just a joke" rationalizations are being used to propagate a racist culture. These actions actively resist post–civil rights cultural norms that framed public racist discourse as wrong. More-over, the use of racist humor in this new post-racial era that the election of Obama was supposed to have ushered in shows how racist ideology and affect can be advanced and shaped by forms of humor, in ways that are both similar to and distinct from earlier periods of U.S. history.

The racist depictions of Obama as an ape or minstrel character hark back to an era where the normative culture of white supremacy was ex-plicitly and publicly encoded into every facet of American culture. But in a post–civil rights United States, such depictions are publicly condemned as racist, or have been relegated to the dustbin of history, or are seen as extremist discourse embraced solely by the far right. Yet, as this book highlights, amused racial contempt continues today as a form of racist pleasure—whether by the new breed of far-right agitators, among police officers and law enforcement officials, or among mainstream white con-servatives and elected officials—to advance racist ideologies and maintain white racial solidarity under the guise of a "politically incorrect" humor, a humor that is being exploited to advance a racist understanding of society.

RACIST HUMOR AND THE CULT(URE) OF WHITENESS

"The time may come when [non-whites] and whites can tell jokes about each other in ways which do not reproduce racial categories of the world in which they are told. The time . . . is certainly not yet arrived."

Stuart Hall, "Racist Ideologies and the Media"

OVER THE LAST TWO CENTURIES in the United States, the practice and politics of amused racial contempt has played a significant role in shaping a racist understanding of society. It has played this role across different eras of racial history—from slavery to post-emancipation, Reconstruction, and Jim Crow and from the so-called colorblind and post-racial era that emerged after the civil rights movement of the mid-20th century and into the present day. Amused racial contempt is a significant, and often overlooked, social and affective mechanism that works to link individual, cultural, and structural dimensions of racism and white supremacy. It is used as an affective pedagogical tool that aligns and reproduces the ideologies and cultural emotions of whiteness, white supremacy, and anti-Blackness across societal contexts, social settings, classes, and generations. It is used not only by white people but also by non-whites who aspire towards the social power of whiteness and its class privileges.[1] It is a key feature in the everyday formation of whiteness and racism via a "white racial framing" of society. In the current era, racist humor has also served to unite a broad swath of conservatism and white nationalism, in an ostensibly colorblind and post-racial society, by playing a significant role in recreating whiteness as a resistant racial identity and ideology that is openly hostile to the notion of multiracial egalitarianism, solidarity, and democracy.

The cases and incidents explored in this book illustrate that amused racial contempt is a pervasive feature of contemporary social life in the United States. It is a practice that connects the emotional, cultural, and structural processes of racial formation and domination, in ways that are often minimized as "just a joke," even among the most esteemed scholars of humor. The examples this book highlights are not meant to be exhaustive, nor should they be perceived as a problem exclusive to the United States. They are but a brief exploration into the prevalent use of a ritualized and racialized discourse that is deeply invested in the affective maintenance and reproduction of structural racism and white supremacy, in the nation and around the world. The relationship between the ridicule and treatment of Indigenous communities, Africans, Asians, Muslims, and immigrants in European and other western societies, for example, are cases that could be productively explored and analyzed along these lines. These examples show how amused racial contempt continues to shape the emotional, socio-psychological, and cultural ways that racism, white solidarity, and white supremacy are maintained and reproduced over the centuries and across the globe. This *white schadenfreude* or the racist pleasure in feeling superior to racialized groups—who are seen as inferior objects of amused contempt and who are believed to be worthy of racial control, punishment, and violence by both individuals and the state—has contributed to the affective and emotional maintenance of whiteness as a dominant and resistant racial order. It is a worldview that is opposed to seeing the shared humanity of all racialized groups and targets.

The continued circulation of racist humor, with its underlying ideology of racism, anti-Blackness, and white supremacy, has been facilitated by the increasing cultural resistance to so-called political correctness. This resistance not only helps provide space for engaging in racist humor among entertainers, politicians, and commentators, but it also encourages others to engage in it, as if by doing so they are self-righteously standing up for free speech and fighting the political correctness and the cancel culture of

the left. Among a vocal faction of Republicans and conservatives—including figures like Rush Limbaugh, commentators on Fox News, and other
right-wing media pundits and personalities in the digital age—resistance
to progressives' condemnation of racism and racist humor is increasingly
reframed as a battle with the so-called liberal media and liberal elites in an
ongoing culture war. If they are going to win the culture war, this argument goes, they are going to have to stand their ground.

Among the most significant recent examples of people using this kind
of discourse to gain social and political power is, of course, Donald Trump.
Trump, early on dubbed "America's Insult Comic in Chief,"[2] exploited the
politics of amused contempt and much of this political rhetoric throughout Obama's second term in office. Trump took the reins of the birther
conspiracy and the Tea Party energy, and he won the strong support from
the far right/alt-right and the police unions, funneling this momentum
into his 2016 presidential campaign. Trump understood that by taking
aim at political correctness and leading with insults and amused contempt
against political opponents and marginalized groups (e.g., Blacks, women,
immigrants, disabled people)—a strategy that similarly elevated conservative figures like Rush Limbaugh and Sarah Palin to national political
stardom among white conservatives—he might be able to ride this wave
into the White House. As Trump stated during the first Republican debate
in 2015,

"I think the big problem this country has is being politically correct. . . . I've been challenged by so many people, and I don't frankly
have time for total political correctness. And to be honest with you,
this country doesn't have time either. This country is in big trouble.
We don't win anymore. We lose to China. We lose to Mexico both in
trade and at the border. We lose to everybody."[3]

By centering a narrative of national victimhood, while simultaneously
taking aim at the specter of political correctness and Obama during the
Obama presidency and beyond, Trump and his supporters were able to
use this phantom threat to rally a white conservative base to support him:

an overtly crude and vulgar racist billionaire who made his political de-
but by questioning Obama's birth certificate; lobbing insults at racialized
groups, women, and political opponents; and appearing to offer a forceful
rebuke to the notion of political correctness and the liberal elites who enable it. In doing so, Trump was able to energize majority support from
working-, middle-, and upper-class white conservatives, as well as support
from conservatives of color, by presenting himself as an individual who
was unafraid to say what was on his mind about whatever and whomever
he wanted, whenever he wanted. No restraint. No apologies. In this way,
Trump's unfiltered and unrestrained use of amused contempt articulated
a sentiment that captivated millions of white and non-white conservative supporters, by appearing to confront the cultural constraints that so-
called political correctness was infringing on their freedom of expression
as "real Americans." Trump's political incorrectness, therefore, embodied
a "strong man" fantasy that white conservatives were more than eager to
embrace, after feeling the loss of social and political power witnessed by
the election of Obama.

The core issue revealed by this widespread problem, however, is not
only that such discourse is offensive to liberal ears and sensibilities, but
that the politics of amused racial contempt also works to legitimize calls
for more racial abuse and violence. The horrific events that occurred in Atlanta, Georgia, have further crystalized this point. Only two months after
the storming of the Capitol on January 6, 2021, by a mob of thousands
of angry white Americans who believed the 2020 election was stolen, on
March 16 a 21-year-old white gunman targeted an Asian immigrant community with murderous racial violence, in a pandemic year that witnessed
the sharp rise of anti-Asian racism and violence.[4]

The shooter in this incident, Robert Aaron Long, was another violent
young white male who would have been celebrated by the white supremacist leader Tom Metzger, who died in 2020. In a move that appeared to
conform to the colorblind racial logic of the era, Long swiftly denied that
his murderous rampage was racially motivated. Instead, he claimed that
his violent shooting spree of a string of Korean-owned spas that killed six
Asian women was due to the shame induced by his religious beliefs, which

conflicted with his sexual addiction.[5] Following Long's arrest, white police officials in Atlanta uncritically echoed Long's testimony to the media, while also denying that the incident was racially motivated.[6] Moreover, Captain Jay Baker, the initial spokesman for the Cherokee County Sheriff's Office, also appeared to demonstrate a degree of sympathy with the white male shooter by stating that the gunman was having "a really bad day."[7] Captain Baker, in other words, was asking the public to sympathize with Long and to not lose sight of his humanity.

Baker, of course, was promptly criticized for comments that seemed to show more empathy with a white mass shooter than with the victims of this appalling murder spree. But within a day of this horrifying incident, it was revealed that Baker himself had previously engaged in amused racial contempt against Asians on social media, despite having an adopted Vietnamese brother, by echoing the racist contempt aimed at Asians during the 2020 global coronavirus outbreak. Asian American elected officials, scholars, and activists pointed to an image that Baker circulated a few months earlier, of a T-shirt he found amusing, which referred to COVID-19 as the "Chy-Na" virus.[8] This sentiment was continually echoed in Trump's routine engagement in the politics of amused racial contempt against Asians throughout the 2020 election year, by incessantly referring to the coronavirus as the "China virus" as well as the "Kung Flu," terms his supporters found amusing.[9]

Trump's use of amused racial contempt towards China over the course of his presidency had a significant impact on legitimizing anti-Asian racism and violence during the pandemic. A June 2020 Pew survey, for instance, found that over 30 percent of Asian Americans had been on the receiving end of racist insults, slurs, and jokes since the start of the coronavirus outbreak.[10] Moreover, a study by the Center for the Study of Hate and Extremism found that between 2019 and 2020 anti-Asian violence increased by nearly 150 percent in major cities across the United States.[11]

Of course, anti-Asian racism did not start or end with Trump's presidency. The long history of "yellow peril" narratives, which include countless insulting racist images and cartoons, coupled with anti-Asian violence committed by Americans both at home and abroad (from mass lynchings and hate crimes to violent genocidal wars committed throughout Asia by the U.S. military), illustrates the link between anti-Asian racism, amused racial contempt, and organized racial violence. Then there is Hollywood's role in relentlessly reproducing amused racial contempt for Asians and Asian Americans, as well as the ongoing political fearmongering, rhetoric, and propaganda concerning China's rise as a global economic power among both liberal and conservative media and politicians, which further normalizes the dehumanization of Asians and the "forever foreign" racist narrative of exclusion, marginalization, and contempt. This is all part of the legacy of white supremacist racist contempt and violence committed against Asians in the United States and globally. As author Viet Thanh Nguyen observed following the events in Atlanta, "The acceptability of microaggressions, racist jokes, casual sexual fetishisation lays the groundwork for an explosion of racist and sexist violence that can be literally murderous."[12]

The toxic mixture of amused racist and sexist contempt, and its relationship to the politics and fantasies of white nationalism, only appears to be gaining traction among Republicans. This was clearly illustrated in November 2021, during a congressional debate regarding an animated video produced and circulated by Republican Representative Paul Gosar's staff as a "joke." The video sent by Gosar's office was a rendition of the intro for the Japanese anime series *Attack on Titan*, a show depicting a world in which humans are under constant attack by giant cannibalistic invaders (Titans). The humans fight back with an elite flying force of Titan hunters. In the altered video, Gosar is shown as the hero, while clips of "invading" immigrants and refugees are spliced into it. Gosar battles invaders with superimposed faces of Democratic officials, including Alexandria Ocasio-Cortez, whom Gosar has described as "representative of the plague of illegal immigration."[13] The video then shows Gosar slicing the giant's neck, alluding to him "symbolically killing" Ocasio-Cortez in a battle to "defend" America from "illegal immigrants," a graphic illustration reminiscent of the 2019 massacre in El Paso, Texas, by another white male gunman, 21-year-old Patrick Crusius.[14]

"It is a cartoon intended to be entertaining," Gosar noted in an open letter on his official government website, after a slim majority of House members (223–207) voted to censure him and strip him of committee assignments.[15] Only two Republican officials voted in favor of disciplining Gosar. As if taking a cue from white supremacist Tom Metzger and the alt-right playbook, Gosar stressed that the use of this "cartoon" was merely an effort to appeal to young people and anime fans, by "making a point that the open borders our country suffers is an evil that plagues the land."[16]

The refusal of Gosar and the vast majority of Republican officials to publicly condemn the video illustrates how the strategy of amused racist and sexist contempt has been more openly embraced by the Republican Party since Trump, in ways that have shifted even more to the far right. While Trump "strongly condemned" doctored images of him killing political opponents and media critics (in a video his administration claimed it did not produce but that was shown at a conference for his supporters),[17] Gosar and the GOP appear to be standing firm behind this *Attack on Titan* incident. This approach—of hiding behind the tiring claim that it was "just a joke"—only further normalizes calls for racial and political violence, according to political philosopher Jason Stanley, author of *How Fascism Works*. "'It's legitimating political violence explicitly by saying America is under mortal threat,'" Stanley told *Los Angeles Times* columnist Jean Guerrero. "'He places killing AOC [Ocasio-Cortez] in a framework that legitimates killing her. She's an enemy officer of an invading army. And white America is what's being invaded.'"[18]

It's worth noting that it's not just male Republican officials engaging in this kind of violent rhetoric and posturing. In September 2020, a year before the Gosar incident, Georgia Republican congressional candidate Marjorie Taylor Greene posted an image of herself on Facebook holding a gun, alongside images of Ocasio-Cortez and Representatives Ilhan Omar and Rashida Tlaib, captioned "We need strong conservative Christians to go on the offense against these socialists who want to rip our country apart."[19] While Greene denied that this stunt was an effort to incite racial violence against these progressive women of color, noting that it was "just a meme," Representative Omar highlighted that they were already receiving "death threats in response to this post."[20] Greene would go on to win Georgia's 14th Congressional District two months after this incident.

In contrast to Obama's colorblind approach to being the target of amused racist contempt, Alexandria Ocasio-Cortez stressed the peril of this kind of rhetoric, which normalizes calls for political and racial violence. "What is so hard about saying that this is wrong,"[21] Ocasio-Cortez asked during the House deliberation over Gosar's behavior:

> "I've seen other members of this party advance the argument, including Representative Gosar himself . . . that this was just a joke, that what we say and what we do does not matter so long as we claim a lack of meaning. I am here . . . to say that it does. . . . As leaders in this country, when we incite violence with depictions against our colleagues, that trickles down into violence in this country. . . ."[22]

Racism and white supremacy, in other words, are not only mobilized by racial hatred and ignorance, but by a pleasurable solidarity that highlights the central role that racialized emotions and humor play in white racial dominance. Amused racial contempt is not an anecdotal, peripheral, or anachronistic form of racism. It does not exist in some bygone past or merely at the social margins. It is not "just a joke." It is a widespread form of racist pleasure that is used in both private and public contexts, among laypeople, co-workers, family members, entertainers, political leaders, and extremists—and it is routinely wielded by those who enjoy social, political, and legal power. These racist joking practices are "everyday mechanisms"[23] that contribute to legitimizing, strengthening, and advancing "common-sense" notions of race and racism and the legitimation of racial violence. This is because the history and legacy of racist humor is intimately connected to the continuity of white supremacy through the use and spread of racialized emotions and ideologies.

In this way, racist humor is always an open invitation to white supremacy and racist ideology in all its forms. It is a racist pleasure that invites participants to share and enjoy in the uncritical amused contempt of racialized targets, regardless of their historic and continued experiences of systemic, structural, and cultural oppression, abuse, and violence. Regardless of past or present circumstances, amused racial contempt is a racial pleasure that denies racialized targets their humanity and leaves them open to both individual and structural contempt, abuse, and violence.

Decolonizing the Sense of Humor

The history and legacy of amused racial contempt, and the ways in which this form of humor has been deployed and understood among the general public, as well as among esteemed scholars, is rooted in the historical development of colonialism, white supremacy, and racial capitalism. Racist humor comes from a racialized system of valuation and extraction. It is part of a system that, as Du Bois pointed out over a century ago, is designed to produce difference, division, hierarchy, and the concentration of wealth, privilege, and power, on the one hand, while rechanneling aggression, hostility, conflict, and contempt away from white political and economic elites and towards racialized masses and public figures, on the other. Racist humor is the humor of white supremacy and racial capitalism: it is the colonial sense of humor.

This book reveals the larger historical trajectories and social impact of this kind of cultural practice. A "humorous" event that was previously allowed to be explicit (blackface during slavery and the Jim Crow era) helped normalize and cultivate white supremacy as a racial commonsense and dominant racial order. It then became increasingly disavowed in the second half of the 20th century, after the civil rights movement challenged the widespread use of amused racial contempt. But during the so-called colorblind and post-racial era that has developed in recent decades, this practice has continued to serve as a weapon for fueling racialized emotions and solidarities in a society where social hierarchies continue to be defined and organized by race. Moreover, in this current era, white resistant identities, and their non-white counterparts, are increasingly making use of an "antipolitical correctness" discourse in an effort to create the moral space to once again normalize the use of racist humor and contempt by increasingly drawing on the language and politics of nationalism, liberty, and free expression.

In this moment that is increasingly calling for the decolonization of the institutions of knowledge production, and for the racial "diversification" and "inclusion" of all organizations and institutions that have historically excluded racialized groups, there is an opportunity to radically reimagine and decolonize how we understand the *sense of humor*. Decolonizing the sense of humor means challenging the humor of white supremacy and how we understand and conceptualize the sense of humor, which is largely based on the flawed perspectives of white, conservative and liberal, Euro-centric academics and thinkers. Decolonizing the sense of humor means developing a critical reassessment of what humor is supposed to do in a "good society." This effort allows us to imagine and practice alternative forms of collective joy and pleasure, as Sara Ahmed suggests, in ways that do not seek to reproduce and maintain hierarchies of racial power and domination.

But it appears that commonsense notions of the sense of humor are still deeply rooted, even among so-called radical thinkers. The Slovenian philosopher Slavoj Žižek, in his critique of "political correctness," suggests that one way to reduce social animosity and increase genuine communica-tion and exchange between individuals is to allow for the free exchange of "dirty jokes." Rather than trying to cover up social tensions with "nice words," which do little to alleviate the social problems and inequalities that underlie the surface of polite civil society, Žižek suggests that by laugh-ing at one another's differences "in the right way," the free flow of "dirty jokes" can contribute to forging solidarity with "others":

> "Let's say I'm an Indian and you're an African American. We are tell-ing all the time dirty jokes to each other, about each other, about ourselves, but in such a way that we just laugh and the more we are telling them the more we are friends. Why? Because in this way we really resolved the tension of racism."[24]

Žižek's example is an interesting one to consider. Certainly, friend-ships have been forged and maintained using this approach, and some of the most famous and wealthiest comedians in the world have made their fortunes by engaging in this very process, the so-called equal opportunity offender. But the notion of the equal opportunity offender only works in an equal context. When and where the social context is radically unequal, there is no such thing as equal opportunity offending. While the equal opportunity offender thesis has been challenged to some extent in this book and elsewhere,[25] there is another major flaw in this illustration. Žižek is most certainly a humorous, engaging, and often insightful Marxist public intellectual. But he is not Indian. How does Žižek's argument change if he acknowledges his own whiteness in this example? The fact that he chose to present himself as non-white in order to emphasize his criticism of political correctness is revealing of his overall position on the issues and how he understands the "sense of humor." Žižek, a white European scholar, is still subscribing to the "ethnic humor" thesis proposed decades ago by the conservative and influential British sociologist, Christie Davies. Žižek is correct that a so-called political correctness that merely "tries to conceal racism and sexism, but does not address the underlying causes of the problems," will be ultimately ineffective in resolving the tension of racism and sexism in society. This is certainly not a perspective advanced or advocated in this book. But the suggestion that a libertarian approach to dirty jokes could serve as a tool to forge broader social unity and solidarity is misguided.

Unless there is already an existing social and material foundation grounded in unity, radical empathy, and "thick solidarity," as Roseann Liu and Savannah Shange have described it, a libertarian approach to "dirty jokes" threatens to do more harm than good. A *thick solidarity*, Liu and Shange contend, is a kind of solidarity that "mobilizes empathy in ways that do not gloss over" differences or inequalities and is "based on a radical belief in the inherent value of each other's lives despite never being able to fully understand or fully share in the experience of those lives." This radical empathy, they contend, is rooted in an effort to link the "personal and affective dimension" of social life to egalitarian "political commitments."[26]

A libertarian approach to race or gender-based humor does not center such a position, because this perspective focuses on the pursuit of amusement and pleasure above all else. But in the wake of the recurring number of police shootings of unarmed Black men, violent racist attacks against Asian, Latinx, and other communities of color, and the continued abuse of migrants by white vigilantes and the state, white liberal comedy icons, from Sarah Silverman to Jay Leno, have finally begun to recoil from this libertarian position on humor and have publicly recognized, apologized, walked back, or renounced their prior reliance on amused racial contempt in their work.[27]

But this is not the first time celebrated white comedians have policed their own racial discourse. In the early 1970s comedian George Carlin, perhaps the most celebrated white "libertarian" comedian of the last half century, expressed his position and refusal to perform jokes that targeted racial and ethnic groups. "'There isn't a lot that outrages me . . . except racial jokes, ethnic jokes. I find nothing funny about that— just tasteless,'" Carlin stated.[28] By 1990, Carlin echoed this perspective in an interview with CNN host Larry King, during a conversation about the notorious comedian Andrew Dice Clay, the first comedian to sell out Madison Square Garden. Clay's style of comedy is deliberately racist, misogynistic, vulgar, and offensive, and reminiscent of Trump's use of amused contempt in the political arena. "'His targets are underdogs,'" Carlin observed, "'Women and gays and immigrants . . . to my way of thinking, are underdogs.'" In the exchange, Carlin offered a hunch about what made Clay's comedy so entertaining and to whom his comedy was appealing:

> "I think his core audience are young, white males who are threatened by these groups. A lot of these guys aren't sure about their manhood . . . and women who assert themselves and are competent are a threat to these men, and so are immigrants in terms of jobs . . . and I think that is what is at the core that takes place in these arenas. There is a certain . . . sharing of anger and rage at these groups and at these targets."[29]

While "anger and rage" are certainly connected to the cultural and emotional politics of racism, so are fun and amusement, as I have tried to demonstrate in this book. This enduring aspect of systemic racism, and its relationship to the politics of amused contempt, has led some critical scholars, activists, and artists to continue to be skeptical of the notion that we have reached a point in time where whites and non-whites can freely trade in racist or dirty jokes without reinforcing the dominant and existing racial, classed, or gendered categories, ideologies, and divides upon which such humor is based. As Stuart Hall noted, given the continuity of existing racial conditions, such humor ultimately works to reproduce and maintain the racial categories and inequalities of the world, rather than subvert them.[30]

While whites are certainly not the only ones who engage in the use of amused racial contempt, racist humor stems from the white racial and colonial imagination. It is a colonial humor tied to the history and legacy of racial slavery, genocide, and empire, and its racist logic and affective motivations remain the same today when shared by white nationalists, police officers, or political leaders who actively and derisively oppose racial equality and the advancement of a multiracial democracy. Therefore, the ongoing struggle against racism and white supremacy is a struggle that must necessarily be waged on many fronts: in the political arena, in the streets, in the workplace, in the universities, on our screens, and in our jokes.

Some will certainly argue that such a critical emphasis on the sense of humor will only fuel the so-called culture war and that it is a distraction from the more "serious" and pressing material need to forge broader social or class-based unity and solidarity. But the politics of amused racial contempt has an intimate and centuries-long relationship with the politics of racism, whiteness, and white supremacy, a politics of "divide and conquer," that is rooted in the development and evolution of racial and colonial capitalism. The continuity and acceptability of this practice presents a significant roadblock to forging cross-racial and class-based solidarity. Building and maintaining solidarity is always easier said than done, and forging a cross-racial and class-based solidarity is hard work. It is made more difficult by pretending that racist humor is insignificant, inconsequential, and that it is "just a joke." These "just a joke" claims are generally hostile to critical analysis and are inherently anti-sociological, even when articulated by esteemed sociologists. They deny a fundamental sociological premise—that context and history matters. A critical sociological examination of humor emphasizes that humor is *not* context free. It is deeply and inextricably tied to social, historical, and political contexts and social inequalities.

Perhaps once the preconditions of structural, racial, and economic equality and democracy are materialized in society at large, we may freely joke across racial lines without consequence or concern for potentially reinforcing social division and harm, in the ways that such humor so often does in our current racially unequal society. But perhaps at that point we won't need race-based jokes any longer. In a society where economic, social, and political equality have been met, we will have also envisioned alternative forms of social pleasure, joy, and happiness.

But in the meantime, we need to decolonize our understanding of the sense of humor and imagine alternative forms of collective joy and pleasure that are not rooted in values, ideologies, and emotions of social and racial division and contempt but in an urgent desire for a social and material reality that elevates social and racial egalitarianism as a core principle of unity, solidarity, and shared well-being. We should push for and work towards building and advancing a multiracial and economic democracy for everyone, while not losing sight that racism and all other forms of oppression, including in the form of jokes, are barriers to getting there.

The point of challenging the humor of white supremacy, therefore, is to undo the normative and dominant sensibilities we have about the relationship between the sense of humor, race, and society, a relationship that is complicit in the history and legacy of structural and systemic racism and white supremacy. These dominant sensibilities have produced commonsense understandings and forms of amusement that have largely been in the service of entrenched social and racial hierarchies and power relations. A decolonizing approach to the sense of humor is one that reveals the structural and affective power that humor has in reproducing, maintaining, and normalizing forms of inequality and domination. But a decolonizing approach does not mean a sense of humor that is joyless, puritanical, or ascetic. A decolonizing humor is one that challenges all forms of structural and cultural power relations and inequalities, by centering not only the struggles of the oppressed but the joy and laughter *of* the oppressed and *with* the oppressed, rather than *at* the oppressed. It is a sense of humor with a sense of justice.

ACKNOWLEDGMENTS

This book was made possible because of the generous support from numerous colleagues, scholars, editors, institutions, research centers, and loving family members and friends. This project has been over a decade in the making, and it is the result of countless conversations, presentations, publications, debates, and discussions on the topic of humor and racism in society, all of which have contributed to my evolving perspective on this issue. I was fortunate enough to have been introduced to Marcela Maxfield at Stanford University Press by Nina Bandelj a few years ago at the American Sociological Association's annual conference in New York City. Marcela and the team at SUP—including Sunna Juhn, Emily Smith, and Jennifer Gordon—have been incredibly patient and encouraging every step of the way. I am also indebted to the careful editorial guidance provided by Chris Lura.

The seeds of this project began to germinate when I was an undergraduate at the University of California, Irvine. David J. Frank and Sam Gilmore were some of the first to take an interest in my undertaking. Their early mentorship provided the tools and reassurance I needed to keep this project going and to pursue it as a graduate student. David continued to be one of my most devoted advocates and mentors throughout my time in graduate school—a sounding board to help me think through my ideas more clearly and a supportive reader and critic of my work every step of the way. Thank you, David, for your continued encouragement.

Belinda Robnett and Ann Hironaka also played a significant role throughout my time at Irvine, and I am extraordinarily grateful for the mentorship and support they provided, particularly through their leadership in the Race Research Workshop. This was an intellectually nurturing environment that allowed me to think more deeply and seriously about my work and about myself as a scholar. Many thanks to the various students who took part in this workshop and who have continued to offer valuable feedback, including Yader Lanuza, Jonathan Calvillo, Jessica Kizer, Dana Nakano, Edelina Burciaga, and Matt Rafalow. I would also like to recognize the importance of the friendships I developed at UC Irvine with Chuck O'Connell, Dennis López, Fernando Chirino, Sheila Xiao, Wai Kit Choi, and the Worker Student Alliance crew. Our study groups, political discussions, and organizing work have been foundational in helping me maintain a critical analysis of the interrelationship of racism, white supremacy, and capitalism. These insights were reinforced through the mentorship provided by Raúl Fernández and Gilbert González. Other colleagues and faculty at UC Irvine played a part in my thinking and analysis: Rudy Torres, Belinda Campos, David Snow, Francesca Polletta, Rubén Rumbaut, Geoff Ward, Frank Wilderson, David Theo Goldberg, Mark Villegas, Teishan Latner, Héctor Martínez, Andrew Penner, Jacob Avery, Charles Ragin, Rocío Rosales, Keith Murphy, and Susan Coutin. I am also grateful for the support provided by the UC Irvine Center in Law, Society, and Culture.

The University of California more broadly has provided me with various opportunities to enlarge the scope of my project. The University of California Center for New Racial Studies, under the direction of Howard Winant at UC Santa Barbara, provided funding and an early platform to share some of my early work with leading race scholars across the UC system. The opportunity to work with faculty at other UC campuses was an invaluable experience. Mike Davis's creative writing course at UC Riverside was vital and helped me expand my political and expressive imagination in my thinking and writing. Otto Santa Ana at UCLA created multiple opportunities to share my work and provided me with advice and feedback over the last several years. Chon Noriega in the Chicano Studies Research Center at UCLA provided resources and space to work on my project, and I am grateful to Laura Gómez for making this connection possible. I am also thankful for the feedback and support I've received over the years from France Winddance Twine at UCSB and Tanya Golash-Boza at UC Merced. And thanks to Tanya for reading and commenting on an earlier version of this book.

My time at the University of Denver also allowed me to further advance my work. I am especially thankful to Lisa Martínez, Hava Gordon, Deb Ortega, and Nancy Wadsworth for their generosity, kindness, and support during my time there. Thanks as well to my colleagues in the Department of Sociology and Criminology—Jared Del Rosso, Tate Steidley, Jeff Lin, Nancy Reichman, and Paul Colomy. Tom Romero graciously provided ample resources and space during his leadership at IRISE. The Graduate School of Social Work's Catalyst Series for Social Justice gave me a platform to share my work with the broader Denver community, for which I am grateful. I am especially thankful for the friendships I established during my time at DU—in particular with Armond Towns, Aaron Schneider, and Daniel Olmos—and I greatly appreciate the anti-racism and solidarity work we helped to cultivate on campus and beyond. Shout out to Armond and Danny for the feedback they provided on earlier portions of this manuscript.

Further thanks go to Roberta Waldbaum, the Italian Studies Department, and the Maglione-Sie faculty fellowship at DU, which allowed me to spend some time at John Cabot University in Rome, where I could expand the scope of my project and share my research. I am especially thankful for the generosity of the faculty and staff in Rome, in particular Mary Merva, Anna Colella, Gina Marie Spinelli, Federigo Argentieri, Peter Sarram, Pamela Harris, and Paola Cascinelli.

Colleagues and staff at my current position at the University of La Verne have also played an important role in helping me finalize this project. Thanks to Roy Kwon, Joseph Cabrera, Sharon Davis, Margaret Gough, Nick Athey, Glenn Goodwin, Ally Brantley, Alma Martínez, Andréa

Minkoff, Stephanie Abundiz, Kristin Howland, and Shannon Mathews. And I am especially grateful to Jason Neidleman for reading through an early version of this manuscript and providing invaluable feedback.

Earlier aspects of this project have been presented at various associations and conferences over the years: American Sociological Association; Society for the Study of Social Problems; Pacific Sociological Association; American Studies Association; Working-Class Studies Association; Association for Humanist Sociology; International Society for Humor Studies; New Directions in Critical Race and Ethnic Studies Conference at the University of Tennessee, Knoxville; and Notre Dame Institute for Advanced Study. Numerous other scholars have also continued to support my work in various ways, including Eduardo Bonilla-Silva, Woody Doane, David Brunsma, James M. Thomas, Victor Ray, Ellen Berrey, Corey Dolgon, Joe Feagin, Eli Anderson, Charles Gallagher, Meghan Burke, Jennifer Mueller, Kasey Henricks, Brandon Manning, Maggie Hennefeld, Matthew Hughey, Viveca Greene, Giselinde Kuipers, Ugo Corte, Simon Weaver, Gary A. Fine, Claudia Leeb, Sharon Quinsaat, Teun van Dijk, Tariq Modood, James McKeever, Khayyam Qidwai, José Quintana, and Pete Kunze.

Two recent opportunities have helped me finish up writing this book. I am very thankful for the generous funding and time provided by the Woodrow Wilson Career Enhancement Fellowship. This fellowship gave me the time and space I needed to think more critically and deeply about the kind of book I wanted to write. And the M. Thomas Inge First Book Workshop, sponsored by the American Humor Studies Association and led by the wonderful Beck Krefting, was an invaluable experience. The advice and feedback provided by colleagues in this generous space greatly improved my writing and my critical thinking as I finalized the details of the project.

And last, but certainly not least, I want to give a special thank you to my family. I would like to thank my son Lucca, and my partner Linda, for enduring the everyday challenges and frustrations of dealing with an academic writing a book—an experience made more painful and grueling during the pandemic—and for their patience, love, support, joy, and encouragement all along the way. Thanks also to my parents—Tere, Raúl, Luis—my siblings—Mayra, Enrique, and Luis Ángel—and all of my extended family members and friends who have continued to nourish my spirit and well-being, especially during a time of pandemic where we lost several cherished loved ones.

NOTES

Chapter 1

1. Here, and throughout, I do not use racial categories to connote that they are "real" in a biological sense. They are social and political constructions that emerged out of European colonialism and have had disparate social consequences for racialized groups and individuals over the last five centuries. See, for instance, R. Sussman, *The Myth of Race: The Troubling Persistence of an Unscientific Idea*. Harvard University Press, 2016.

2. J. Eligon, A Sergeant Who Learned He's Part Black Says He Faced Racist Taunts at Work, *New York Times* (May 12, 2017): https://www.nytimes.com/2017/05/12/us/cleon-brown-black-lawsuit.html

3. DNA tests do not illustrate the biological nature of race, and their accuracy and findings are often misunderstood and misinterpreted. For extended discussions on race and DNA, and racial science more broadly, see A. Nelson, *The Social Life of DNA: Race, Reparations, and Reconciliation After the Genome*. Beacon Press, 2016; T. Duster, Ancestry Testing and DNA: Uses, Limits–and Caveat Emptor, in *Genetics as Social Practice* (pp. 75–88). Routledge, 2016; D. E. Roberts, *Fatal Invention: How Science, Politics, and Big Business Re-Create Race in the Twenty-First Century*. New Press, 2011; D. A. Bolnick, et al., The Science and Business of Genetic Ancestry Testing, *Science*, vol. 318, no. 5849 (October 19, 2007): 399–400.

4. J. R. Miller, Cop: I Was Taunted After Genetic Test Revealed I Am Part Black, *New York Post* (May 12, 2017): https://nypost.com/2017/05/12/cop-i-was-taunted-after-genetic-test-revealed-i-am-part-black/

5. Eligon, Sergeant Who Learned He's Part Black.

6. N. Rojas, White Police Officer Receives $65,000 Settlement from City in Racial Discrimination Suit, *Newsweek* (August 1, 2018): https://www.newsweek

.com/cleon-brown-hastings-police-michigan-racial-discrimination-settlement
-1052977

7. R. Pérez, Racism Without Hatred? Racist Humor and the Myth of "Color-blindness," *Sociological Perspectives*, vol. 60, no. 5 (2017): 956–974; R. Pérez and G. Ward, From Insult to Estrangement and Injury: The Violence of Racist Police Jokes, *American Behavioral Scientist*, vol. 63, no. 13 (2019): 1810–1829.

8. Eligon, Sergeant Who Learned He's Part Black.

9. See E. Anderson, The White Space, *Sociology of Race and Ethnicity*, vol. 1, no. 1 (2015): 10–21.

10. E. Anderson, *The Cosmopolitan Canopy: Race and Civility in Everyday Life*. Norton, 2011, 253.

11. See, for instance, T. Yosso, et al., Critical Race Theory, Racial Microaggressions, and Campus Racial Climate for Latina/o Undergraduates, *Harvard Educational Review*, vol. 79, no. 4 (2009): 659–691; S. A. Harwood, et al., Racial Microaggressions in the Residence Halls: Experiences of Students of Color at a Predominantly White University, *Journal of Diversity in Higher Education*, vol. 5, no. 3 (2012): 159–173.

12. M. Omi and H. Winant, *Racial Formation in the United States*. Routledge, 2014.

13. W. E. B. Du Bois, The Souls of White Folk, in *Darkwater: Voices from Within the Veil*, ed. H. L. Gates, Jr. Oxford University Press, 2007.

14. See A. Morris, The Souls of White Folk, *Sociology of Race and Ethnicity*, vol. 4, no. 1 (2018): 158–159.

15. W. E. B. Du Bois, *Black Reconstruction in America: 1860–1880*. Free Press, 2017, 700. See also D. R. Roediger, *The Wages of Whiteness: Race and the Making of the American Working Class*. Verso, 2007.

16. T. Piketty, *Capital in the Twenty-First Century*, trans. A. Goldhammer. Belknap Press/Harvard University Press, 2017; T. M. Shapiro, *Toxic Inequality: How America's Wealth Gap Destroys Mobility, Deepens the Racial Divide, and Threatens Our Future*. Basic Books, 2017.

17. A. Morris, *The Scholar Denied: W. E. B. Du Bois and the Birth of Modern Sociology*. University of California Press, 2015.

18. W. E. B. Du Bois, *The Souls of Black Folk: Essays and Sketches*. Dover Publications, 1903, 2–3. Emphasis added.

19. A. P. Farley, The Black Body as Fetish Object, *Oregon Law Review*, vol. 76 (1997): 457.

20. J. Morreall, *Comic Relief: A Comprehensive Philosophy of Humor* (vol. 27). John Wiley & Sons, 2011.

21. E. Bonilla-Silva, Feeling Race: Theorizing the Racial Economy of Emotions, *American Sociological Review*, vol. 84, no 1 (2019): 1–25.

22. J. H. Turner, The Sociology of Emotions: Basic Theoretical Arguments, *Emotion Review*, vol. 1, no 4 (2009): 340–354, at 342.

23. E. Bericat, The Sociology of Emotions: Four Decades of Progress, *Current Sociology*, vol. 64, no. 3 (2016): 491–513.

24. E. Bonilla-Silva, Rethinking Racism: Toward a Structural Interpretation, *American Sociological Review*, vol. 62, no. 3 (1997):465–480.

25   26 Bonilla-Silva, Feeling Race.

26. P. Ioanide, *The Emotional Politics of Racism: How Feelings Trump Facts in an Era of Colorblindness*. Stanford University Press, 2015, 1.

27. S. Ahmed, Affective Economies, *Social Text*, vol. 22, no. 2 (2004): 119. Emphasis in original.

28. S. Ahmed, Happy Objects, in *The Affect Theory Reader*, eds. M. Gregg and G. J. Seigworth. Duke University Press, 2010, 34.

29. S. Ahmed, *The Promise of Happiness*. Duke University Press, 2010, 41.

30. Ibid., 38.

31. See, for instance, M. M. Hurley, D. C. Dennett, and R. B. Adams, Jr., *Inside Jokes: Using Humor to Reverse-Engineer the Mind*. MIT Press, 2011; R. R. Provine, *Laughter: A Scientific Investigation*. Penguin, 2001; R. A. Martin and T. Ford, *The Psychology of Humor: An Integrative Approach*. Academic Press, 2018.

32. S. Lockyer and M. Pickering, eds., *Beyond a Joke: The Limits of Humour*. Springer, 2005.

33. Ahmed, Happy Objects, 37.

34. C. Cooper, Elucidating the Bonds of Workplace Humor: A Relational Process Model, *Human Relations*, vol. 61, no. 8 (2008): 1087–1115.

35. Ibid., 1101.

36. Ahmed, Affective Economies.

37. Pérez, Racism Without Hatred?

38. See, for instance, M. Billig, *Laughter and Ridicule: Towards a Social Critique of Humour*. Sage, 2005; T. E. Ford, et al., Not All Groups Are Equal: Differential Vulnerability of Social Groups to the Prejudice-Releasing Effects of Disparagement Humor, *Group Processes & Intergroup Relations*, vol. 17, no 2 (2014): 178–199; J. C. Meyer, Humor as a Double-Edged Sword: Four Functions of Humor in Communication, *Communication Theory*, vol. 10, no. 3 (2000): 310–331.

39. T. Dwyer, Humor, Power, and Change in Organizations, *Human Relations*, vol. 44, no. 1 (1991): 1–19.

40. J. R. Feagin, *The White Racial Frame: Centuries of Racial Framing and Counter-Framing*. Routledge, 2010.

41. Ibid., 126.

42. J. Feagin, *Systemic Racism: A Theory of Oppression*. Routledge, 2013.

43. A. Tchekmedyian and C. Chang, Top L.A. County Sheriff's Official Resigns over Emails Mocking Muslims and Others, *Los Angeles Times* (May 1, 2016): http://www.latimes.com/local/lanow/la-me-ln-sheriff-aid-tom-angel-resigns-emails-20160501-story.html

44. Pérez and Ward, From Insult to Estrangement and Injury.

45. See, for instance, J. Boskin, *Sambo: The Rise and Demise of an American Jester*. Oxford University Press, 1988; E. Lott, *Love & Theft: Blackface Minstrelsy and the American Working Class*. Oxford University Press, 2013; A. Saxton, Blackface Minstrelsy and Jacksonian Ideology, *American Quarterly*, vol. 27, no. 1 (1975): 3–28.

46. F. Douglass, The Hutchinson Family—Hunkerism, *North Star* (October 27, 1848): http://utc.iath.virginia.edu/minstrel/miar03bt.html

47. See Boskin, *Sambo*, on the struggle to dismantle blackface minstrelsy.

48. See ibid.; Lott, *Love & Theft*; Roediger, *Wages of Whiteness*.

49. R. Pérez, Brownface Minstrelsy: "José Jiménez," the Civil Rights Movement, and the Legacy of Racist Comedy, *Ethnicities*, vol. 26, no. 1 (2016): 40–67.

50. M. Pickering, *Blackface Minstrelsy in Britain*. Routledge, 2017; Boskin, *Sambo*.

51. W. T. Lhamon, *Raising Cain: Blackface Performance from Jim Crow to Hip Hop*. Harvard University Press, 1998.

52. M. Riggs, director, and E. Rolle, narrator, Ethnic Notions, *California Newsreel*, 1987. http://newsreel.org/video/ethnic-notions

53. Lott, *Love & Theft*, 142.

54. K. Sotiropoulos, *Staging Race: Black Performers in Turn of the Century America*. Harvard University Press, 2006, 21.

55. Lott, *Love & Theft*, 143.

56. Saxon, Blackface Minstrelsy and Jacksonian Ideology, 3–4.

57. P. H. Collins, *Black Feminist Thought: Knowledge, Consciousness, and the Politics of Empowerment*. Routledge, 2000, 69.

58. S. V. Hartman, *Scenes of Subjection: Terror, Slavery, and Self-Making in Nineteenth-Century America*. Oxford University Press, 1997.

59. D. A. Jones, *The Captive Stage: Performance and the Proslavery Imagination of the Antebellum North*. University of Michigan Press, 2014.

60. See J. Boskin and J. Dorinson, Ethnic Humor: Subversion and Survival, *American Quarterly*, vol. 37, no. 1 (1985): 81–97, at 93.

61. Roediger, *Wages of Whiteness*, 127.

62. Ibid., 13.

63. E. Durkheim, *The Elementary Forms of the Religious Life*. Free Press, 2008, 212.

64. Pérez, Brownface Minstrelsy.

65. Billig, *Laughter and Ridicule.*

66. See, for instance, C. Davies, *Ethnic Humor Around the World: A Comparative Analysis.* Indiana University Press, 1990; D. Subotnik, The Joke in Critical Race Theory: De Gustibus Disputandum Est? *Touro Law Review,* vol. 15 (1998): 105–122; P. A. Waddington, Police (Canteen) Sub-Culture. An Appreciation, *British Journal of Criminology,* vol. 39, no. 2 (1999): 287–309.

67. See, for instance, Davies, *Ethnic Humor Around the World*; J. Lowe, Theories of Ethnic Humor: How to Enter, Laughing, *American Quarterly,* vol. 38, no. 3 (1986): 439–460; D. Gillota, *Ethnic Humor in Multiethnic America.* Rutgers University Press, 2013.

68. C. Davies, *Jokes and Targets.* Indiana University Press, 2011.

69. See, for instance, B. Haggins, *Laughing Mad: The Black Comic Persona in Post-Soul America.* Rutgers University Press, 2007; J. P. Rossing, Deconstructing Postracialism: Humor as a Critical, Cultural Project, *Journal of Communication Inquiry,* vol. 36, no. 1 (2012): 44–61.

70. Ioanide, *The Emotional Politics of Racism..*

71. M. E. Hayden, Southern Poverty Law Center Says Pepe the Frog Meme Was "Hijacked" by Racists. *ABC News* (September 28, 2016): https://abcnews.go .com/Politics/southern-poverty-law-center-pepe-frog-meme-hijacked/story?id= 42419782

72. S. Stephens-Davidowitz, The Cost of Racial Animus on a Black Candidate: Evidence Using Google Search Data, *Journal of Public Economics,* vol. 118 (2014): 26–40.

73. Davies, *Jokes and Targets.*

74. Ahmed, Happy Objects, 50.

Chapter 2

1. M. Billig, *Laughter and Ridicule: Towards a Social Critique of Humour.* Sage, 2005; J. Morreall, *Comic Relief: A Comprehensive Philosophy of Humor* (vol. 27). John Wiley & Sons, 2011.

2. S. Ahmed, Affective Economies, *Social Text,* vol. 22, no. 2 (2004): 119.

3. See, for instance, R. L. Coser, Some Social Functions of Laughter: A Study of Humor in a Hospital Setting, *Human Relations,* vol. 12, no. 2 (1959): 171–182; R. L. Coser, Laughter Colleagues, *Psychiatry,* vol. 23, no. 1 (1960): 81–95; M. Douglas, The Social Control of Cognition: Some Factors in Joke Perception, *Man,* vol. 3, no. 3 (1968): 361–376; G. A. Fine, Sociological Approaches to the Study of Humor, in *Handbook of Humor Research* (pp. 159–181). Springer, 1983; Morreall, *Comic Relief.*

184   NOTES TO CHAPTER 2

4. Coser, Social Functions of Laughter, 172; G. A. Fine and M. De Soucey, Joking Cultures: Humor Themes as Social Regulation in Group Life, *Humor*, vol. 18, no. 1 (2005): 1–22.

5. M. Gervais and D. S. Wilson, The Evolution and Functions of Laughter and Humor: A Synthetic Approach, *Quarterly Review of Biology*, vol. 80, no. 4 (2005): 395–430, at 402.

6. S. Manninen, et al., Social Laughter Triggers Endogenous Opioid Release in Humans, *Journal of Neuroscience*, vol. 37, no. 25 (2017): 6125–6131; F. Caruana, Laughter as a Neurochemical Mechanism Aimed at Reinforcing Social Bonds: Integrating Evidence from Opioidergic Activity and Brain Stimulation, *Journal of Neuroscience*, vol. 37, no. 36 (2017): 8581–8582.

7. J. Gorman, Scientists Hint at Why Laughter Feels So Good, *New York Times* (September 13, 2011): https://www.nytimes.com/2011/09/14/science/14laughter.html

8. See R. R. Provine, *Laughter: A Scientific Investigation*. Penguin, 2001; M. M. Hurley, D. C. Dennett, and R. B. Adams, Jr., *Inside Jokes: Using Humor to Reverse-Engineer the Mind*. MIT Press, 2011; J. Morreall, Humor as Cognitive Play, *JLT Articles*, vol. 3, no. 2 (2010).

9. C. Darwin, *The Expression of the Emotions in Man and Animals*. University of Chicago Press, 2015 [1872].

10. G. Dezecache and R. I. Dunbar, Sharing the Joke: The Size of Natural Laughter Groups, *Evolution and Human Behavior*, vol. 33, no. 6 (2012): 775–779.

11. Morreall, *Comic Relief*; J. Morreall, J. (2012). Philosophy of Humor, *Stanford Encyclopedia of Philosophy*. Stanford University, 2012 (substantive rev. 2020): https://plato.stanford.edu/entries/humor/?#HumPlaLauPlaSig

12. A. Ziv, The Social Function of Humor in Interpersonal Relationships, *Society*, vol. 47, no. 1 (2010): 11–18; Fine and De Soucey, Joking Cultures; M. Smith, Humor, Unlaughter, and Boundary Maintenance, *Journal of American Folklore*, vol. 122, no. 484 (2009):148–171.

13. Fine and De Soucey, Joking Cultures; A. R. Radcliffe-Brown, On Joking Relationships, *Africa*, vol. 13, no. 3 (1940): 195–210; D. Roy, "Banana Time": Job Satisfaction and Informal Interaction, *Human Organization*, vol. 18, no. 4 (1959): 158–168; S. Linstead, Jokers Wild: The Importance of Humour in the Maintenance of Organizational Culture, *Sociological Review*, vol. 33, no. 4 (1985): 741–767; M. A. Seckman and C. J. Couch, Jocularity, Sarcasm, and Relationships: An Empirical Study, *Journal of Contemporary Ethnography*, vol. 18, no. 3 (1989): 327–344.

14. R. Pérez, Racist Humor: Then and Now, *Sociology Compass*, vol. 10, no. 10 (2016): 928–938; R. Pérez, Racism Without Hatred? Racist Humor and the Myth of "Colorblindness," *Sociological Perspectives*, vol. 60, no. 5 (2017): 956–974.

15. J. C. Meyer, Humor as a Double-Edged Sword: Four Functions of Humor in Communication, *Communication Theory*, vol. 10, no. 3 (2000): 310–331.

16. Billig, *Laughter and Ridicule;* M. Abedinifard, Ridicule, Gender Hegemony, and the Disciplinary Function of Mainstream Gender Humour, *Social Semiotics*, vol. 26, no. 3 (2016): 234–249; S. Lockyer and M. Pickering, eds., *Beyond a Joke: The Limits of Humour*. Springer, 2005.

17. Billig, *Laughter and Ridicule*, 31.

18. R. Martin, Sense of Humor, in *Positive Psychological Assessment: A Handbook of Models and Measures* (p. 313). American Psychological Association, 2003.

19. Ibid., 314.

20. S. Meer, *Uncle Tom Mania: Slavery, Minstrelsy, and Transatlantic Culture in the 1850s*. University of Georgia Press, 2005; M. Pickering, *Blackface Minstrelsy in Britain*. Routledge, 2017; E. Lott, *Love & Theft: Blackface Minstrelsy and the American Working Class*. Oxford University Press, 2013.

21. T. Odumosu, *Africans in English Caricature, 1769–1819: Black Jokes, White Humour*. Harvey Miller Publishers, 2017, 39.

22. G. Myrdal, *An American Dilemma: The Negro Problem and Modern Democracy* (vol. 1). Routledge, 2017. Originally published in 1944. The chapter opening quote is from p. 38.

23. Pérez, Racist Humor; J. Boskin, *Sambo: The Rise and Demise of an American Jester*. Oxford University Press, 1988; M. Riggs, director, and E. Rolle, narrator, Ethnic Notions, *California Newsreel*, 1987. http://newsreel.org/video/ethnic-notions

24. J. R. Feagin, *The White Racial Frame: Centuries of Racial Framing and Counter-Framing*. Routledge, 2010.

25. J. R. Feagin, *Racist America: Roots, Current Realities, and Future Reparations*. Routledge, 2014, 26.

26. Ibid.

27. Feagin, *White Racial Frame*, 126–129.

28. In addition to Lott, *Love & Theft*, see S. V. Hartman, *Scenes of Subjection: Terror, Slavery, and Self-Making in Nineteenth-Century America*. Oxford University Press, 1997.

29. M. A. Kibler, *Censoring Racial Ridicule: Irish, Jewish, and African American Struggles over Race and Representation, 1890–1930*. UNC Press Books, 2015, 1.

30. M. Omi and H. Winant, *Racial Formation in the United States*. Routledge, 2014.

31. R. Pérez, Brownface Minstrelsy: "José Jiménez," the Civil Rights Movement, and the Legacy of Racist Comedy, *Ethnicities*, vol. 16, no. 1 (2016): 40–67.

32. In addition to Boskin, *Sambo*, see M. L. Apte, Ethnic Humor Versus "Sense of Humor": An American Sociocultural Dilemma, *American Behavioral Scientist*. vol. 30, no. 3 (1987): 27.

33. See, for example, L. Bobo, J. R. Kluegel, and R. A. Smith, Laissez-Faire Racism: The Crystallization of a Kinder, Gentler, Antiblack Ideology," in *Racial Attitudes in the 1990s: Continuity and Change* (pp. 23–25). Praeger, 1997; E. Bonilla-Silva, *Racism Without Racists: Color-Blind Racism and the Persistence of Racial Inequality in America*. Rowman & Littlefield, 2013.

34. Feagin, *White Racial Frame*; J. Littlewood and M. Pickering, Gender, Ethnicity and Political Correctness in Comedy, in *Because I Tell a Joke or Two: Comedy, Politics, and Social Difference* (pp. 289–307). Routledge 1998.

35. L. Picca, and J. Feagin, *Two-Faced Racism: Whites in the Backstage and Frontstage*. Routledge, 2020; Pérez, Racist Humor.

36. D. T. Goldberg, *Are We All Postracial Yet?* Polity Press, 2015: https://www.humanities.uci.edu/SOH/calendar/story_details.php?recid=209

37. C. Davies, *Jokes and Targets*. Indiana University Press, 2011, 4.

38. Ibid., 5.

39. Ibid., 254.

40. Ibid., 66–68.

41. Ibid., 256.

42. Ibid.

43. C. Davies, *The Mirth of Nations*. Transaction Publishers, 2002, 157.

44. Ibid., 156. Emphasis in original.

45. Ibid., 157.

46. J. S. Pula, Image, Status, Mobility and Integration in American Society: The Polish Experience, *Journal of American Ethnic History*, vol. 16, no. 1 (1996): 74–95.

47. Davies, *Jokes and Targets*, 3.

48. Ibid., 257.

49. Ibid., 266–267.

50. For a further critique of Davies on this point see Mostafa Abedinifard's article, Jokes and Targets, by Christie Davies, *New Directions in Folklore*, vol. 11, no. 1 (2013): 57–61. Abedinifard also makes this point in his analysis of gender and humor. See M. Abedinifard, Ridicule, Gender Hegemony, and the Disciplinary Function of Mainstream Gender Humour, *Social Semiotics*, vol. 26, no. 3 (2016): 234–249. On Durkheim, see E. Durkheim, What Is a Social Fact? in *The Rules of Sociological Method* (pp. 50–59). Palgrave, 1982, 51.

51. C. W. Mills, White Ignorance, in *Race and Epistemologies of Ignorance* (pp. 13–38). SUNY Press, 2007.

52. C. W. Mills, *The Racial Contract.* Cornell University Press, 1997, 80.

53. Pérez, Racism Without Hatred?

54. Davies, *Mirth of Nations,* 189.

55. Ibid., 191.

56. B. Knott, *Truly Tasteless Jokes.* Ballantine Books, 1982/1983.

57. E. McDowell, Ethnic Jokebooks Flourish Despite Criticism, *New York Times* (July 30, 1983): https://www.nytimes.com/1983/07/30/books/ethnic-jokebooks-flourish-despite-criticism.html

58. Ibid.

59. A. Applewhite, Being Blanche: Coming Clean About Truly Tasteless Jokes, *Harper's Magazine* (June 2011): https://harpers.org/archive/2011/06/being-blanche/

60. Pérez, Racism Without Hatred?

61. McDowell, Ethnic Jokebooks Flourish.

62. Davies, *Birth of Nations.*

63. Ibid., 190.

64. P. Baker, Another Type of Joke Now No Laughing Matter, *Washington Post* (March 21, 1993): https://www.washingtonpost.com/archive/local/1993/03/21/another-type-of-joke-now-no-laughing-matter/49eb5db8-d499-406a-b5b6-d031d53ea789/

65. See J. Hartigan, Who Are These White People?:"Rednecks," "Hillbillies," and "White Trash" as Marked Racial Subjects, in *White Out* (pp. 100–116). Routledge, 2013.

66. A. Newitz and M. Wray, eds., *White Trash: Race and Class in America.* Routledge, 2013.

67. S. Hall, Racist Ideologies and the Media, in *Media Studies: A Reader,* P. Marris and S. Thornham, eds. (pp. 271–282). New York University Press, 2000, 279.

68. Feagin, *White Racial Frame.*

69. D. G. Embrick and K. Henricks, Discursive Colorlines at Work: How Epithets and Stereotypes are Racially Unequal, *Symbolic Interaction,* vol. 36, no. 2 (2013): 197–215; T. E. Ford, et al., Not All Groups Are Equal: Differential Vulnerability of Social Groups to the Prejudice-Releasing Effects of Disparagement Humor, *Group Processes & Intergroup Relations,* vol. 17, no. 2 (2014): 178–199.

70. J. Feagin, *Systemic Racism: A Theory of Oppression.* Routledge, 2013.

71. R. Pérez, Learning to Make Racism Funny in the "Color-Blind" Era: Stand-up Comedy Students, Performance Strategies, and the (Re)production of Racist Jokes in Public, *Discourse & Society,* vol. 24, no. 4 (2013): 478–503.

72. S. Weaver, *The Rhetoric of Racist Humour: US, UK and Global Race Joking.* Ashgate Publishing, 2011; S. L. Muhr, Entitlement Racism and Its Intersections: An Interview with Philomena Essed, Social Justice Scholar, *Ephemera*, vol. 18, no. 1 (2018): 183–201; Pérez, Racism Without Hatred?

73. Hall, Racist Ideologies and the Media.

74. V. Ray, A Theory of Racialized Organizations, *American Sociological Review*, vol. 84, no. 1 (2019): 26–53.

75. Lott, *Love & Theft*; D. R. Roediger, *The Wages of Whiteness: Race and the Making of the American Working Class.* Verso, 1999.

76. Pérez, Learning to Make Racism Funny in the "Color-Blind" Era.

77. Omi and Winant, *Racial Formation in the United States.*

78. Weaver, *Rhetoric of Racist Humour.*

79. Bonilla-Silva, *Racism Without Racists*; Bobo, Kluegel, and Smith, Laissez-Faire Racism; I. Haney-López, *Dog Whistle Politics: How Coded Racial Appeals Have Reinvented Racism and Wrecked the Middle Class.* Oxford University Press, 2015.

80. Apte, Ethnic Humor Versus "Sense of Humor"; Boskin, *Sambo*; A. A. Berger, *An Anatomy of Humor.* Routledge, 2017.

81. Bonilla-Silva, *Racism Without Racists*, 4.

82. S. Freud, *Jokes and Their Relation to the Unconscious.* Norton, 1960, 120.

83. Ibid., 118–119.

84. Picca, and Feagin, *Two-Faced Racism*, 69.

85. C. A. Sue and T. Golash-Boza, "It Was Only a Joke": How Racial Humour Fuels Colour-Blind Ideologies in Mexico and Peru, *Ethnic and Racial Studies*, vol. 36, no. 10 (2014): 1582–1598.

86. Ibid., 1595.

87. D. Apel, Just Joking? Chimps, Obama and Racial Stereotype, *Journal of Visual Culture*, vol. 8, no. 2 (2009): 134–142; G. S. Parks and D. C. Heard, Assassinate the N***** Ape: Obama, Implicit Imagery, and the Dire Consequences of Racist Jokes, *Rutgers Race and Law Review*, vol. 11 (2009): 259; Feagin, *White Racial Frame.*

88. M. K. Jung, *Beneath the Surface of White Supremacy: Denaturalizing U.S. Racisms Past and Present.* Stanford University Press, 2015, 48.

89. See Pérez, Learning to Make Racism Funny; Pérez, Racism Without Hatred?; Pérez, Racist Humor; Pérez, Brownface Minstrelsy.

90. Pérez, Racism Without Hatred?

Chapter 3

1. C. Gibson, "Do You Have White Teenage Sons? Listen Up." How White Supremacists Are Recruiting Boys Online, *Washington Post* (September 17, 2019):

https://www.washingtonpost.com/lifestyle/on-parenting/do-you-have-white
-teenage-sons-listen-up-how-white-supremacists-are-recruiting-boys-online/
2019/09/17/f081e806-d3d5-11e9-9343-40db57cf6abd_story.html

2. A. Feinberg, This Is the Daily Stormer's Playbook, *Huffington Post* (December 13, 2017): https://www.huffpost.com/entry/daily-stormer-nazi-style-guide_n
_5a2ece19e4b0ce3b344492f2

3. Ibid.

4. W. W. van Dijk and J. W. Ouwerkerk, eds., *Schadenfreude: Understanding Pleasure at the Misfortune of Others*. Cambridge University Press, 2014.

5. Q. Norton, Anonymous 101: Introduction to the Lulz, *Wired* (November 8, 2011): https://www.wired.com/2011/11/anonymous-101/

6. Ibid.

7. A. Morse and I. Sherr, For Some Hackers, Goal Is Prank, *Wall Street Journal* (June 6, 2011): https://www.wsj.com/articles/SB10001424052702304906004576367870123614038

8. J. Brito, "We Do It for the Lulz": What Makes LulzSec Tick? *Time* (June 17, 2011): http://techland.time.com/2011/06/17/we-do-it-for-the-lulz-what-makes
-lulzsec-tick/4/

9. L. O'Brien, The Making of an American Nazi, *The Atlantic* (December 2017): https://www.theatlantic.com/magazine/archive/2017/12/the-making-of
-an-american-nazi/544119/

10. M. Pearce, What Happens When a Millennial Goes Full Fascist? He Starts a New-Nazi Site, *Los Angeles Times* (June 24, 2015): https://www.latimes.com/
nation/la-na-daily-stormer-interview-20150624-story.html#page=1

11. D. E. Showalter, *Little Man, What Now?: Der Stürmer in the Weimar Republic*. Archon Books, 1982.

12. Pearce, What Happens When a Millennial Goes Full Fascist?

13. Ibid.

14. C. Miller-Idriss, *Hate in the Homeland*. Princeton University Press, 2020; G. Hawley, *Making Sense of the Alt-Right*. Columbia University Press, 2018.

15. C. Beltrán, *Cruelty as Citizenship: How Migrant Suffering Sustains White Democracy*. University of Minnesota Press, 2020; C. Beltrán, To Understand Trump's Support, We Must Think in Terms of Multiracial Whiteness, *Washington Post* (January 15, 2021): https://www.washingtonpost.com/opinions/2021/01/
15/understand-trumps-support-we-must-think-terms-multiracial-whiteness/

16. A. Nagle, The Lost Boys: The Young Men of the Alt-Right Could Define American Politics for a Generation, *The Atlantic* (December 2017): https://www
.theatlantic.com/magazine/archive/2017/12/brotherhood-of-losers/544158/

17. See A. Marantz, Inside the Daily Stormer's Style Guide, *New Yorker* (January 8, 2018): https://www.newyorker.com/magazine/2018/01/15/inside-the

-daily-stormers-style-guide The chapter opening quote from The Daily Stormer is in Marantz's article. See also Feinberg, This Is the Daily Stormer's Playbook.

18. Feinberg, A. (2017). This Is the Daily Stormer's Playbook.

19. K. Hankes, Propelled by the Trump Campaign and a New Focus on the "Alt-Right," the Daily Stormer Is Now the Top Hate Site in America, *Southern Poverty Law Center* (February 9, 2017): https://www.splcenter.org/fighting-hate/intelligence-report/2017/eye-stormer

20. See R. Pérez, Racist Humor: Then and Now, *Sociology Compass*, vol. 10, no. 10 (2016): 928–938; R. Pérez and G. Ward, From Insult to Estrangement and Injury: The Violence of Racist Police Jokes, *American Behavioral Scientist*, vol. 63, no. 13 (2019): 1810–1829; S. Weaver, *The Rhetoric of Racist Humour: US, UK and Global Race Joking*. Ashgate Publishing, 2011.

21. A. Nagle, *Kill All Normies: Online Culture Wars from 4chan and Tumblr to Trump and the Alt-Right*. John Hunt Publishing, 2017; V. S. Greene, "Deplorable" Satire: Alt-Right Memes, White Genocide Tweets, and Redpilling Normies, *Studies in American Humor*, vol. 5, no. 1 (2019): 31–69.

22. Greene, "Deplorable" Satire.

23. M. E. Hayden, Southern Poverty Law Center Says Pepe the Frog Meme Was "Hijacked" by Racists, *ABC News* (September 28, 2016): https://abcnews.go.com/Politics/southern-poverty-law-center-pepe-frog-meme-hijacked/story?id=42419782

24. G. Hawley, *Making Sense of the Alt-Right*. Columbia University Press, 2018, 20.

25. Ibid., 24–25.

26. Ibid.

27. In the following, I highlight these efforts among some of the most visible white supremacist propagandists and forums in the United States over the last three decades: the racist cartoons used by WAR (White Aryan Resistance) during the 1980s and 90s, racist joke forums and pages on Stormfront (the oldest and largest white supremacist website on the internet) and other far-right websites during the early to late 2000s, and the more recent use of racist memes and images circulating on websites like The Daily Stormer, 4chan, and Reddit in recent years.

28. Southern Poverty Law Center, Tom Metzger. https://www.splcenter.org/fighting-hate/extremist-files/individual/tom-metzger

29. Pérez, Perez, Racist Humor.

30. R. Pérez, Learning to Make Racism Funny in the "Color-Blind" Era: Stand-up Comedy Students, Performance Strategies, and the (Re)production of Racist Jokes in Public, *Discourse & Society*, vol. 24, no. 4 (2013): 478–503; R. Pérez,

Racism Without Hatred? Racist Humor and the Myth of "Colorblindness," *Sociological Perspectives*, vol. 60, no. 5 (2017): 956–974.

31. Associated Press, Metzger Agrees to Stop Portraying Bart as a Nazi, *Los Angeles Times* (June 5, 1991): https://www.latimes.com/archives/la-xpm-1991-06-05-me-128-story.html The chapter opening quote from Metzger is from this *Los Angeles Times* article.

32. See G. Michael, This Is War! Tom Metzger, White Aryan Resistance, and the Lone Wolf Legacy, *Focus on Terrorism*, vol. 14 (2016): 29–62.

33. Ibid., 42.

34. See J. R. Feagin and V. Hernan, *White Racism: The Basics*. Routledge, 2002, 102.

35. Figures 3.2 through 3.12 were previously published in issues of *White Aryan Resistance* from the late 1980s to the early 2000s, and some of them are available on Tom Metzger's website resist.com. In 2017, I retrieved an anonymously published compilation of hundreds of these images that were uploaded on a now defunct far-right website. These images have also continued to resurface online in various anonymous web forums and far-right and mainstream websites, including Stormfront, 4chan, and Reddit. Several of these images are also on display at the Jim Crow Museum of Racist Memorabilia at Ferris State University, in Big Rapids, Michigan.

36. J. Bernstein, The Surprisingly Mainstream History of the Internet's Favorite Anti-Semitic Image, *Buzz Feed News* (February 5, 2015): https://www.buzzfeednews.com/article/josephbernstein/the-surprisingly-mainstream-history-of-the-internets-favorit

37. M. Kleg, *Hate Prejudice and Racism*. SUNY Press, 1993, 205.

38. Miller-Idriss, *Hate in the Homeland*; M. Gardell, *Lone Wolf Race Warriors and White Genocide*. Cambridge University Press, 2021.

39. Pérez, Racism Without Hatred?

40. E. Oring, *Engaging Humor*. University of Illinois Press, 2010, 145.

41. Ibid., 56.

42. Ibid., 53.

43. S. F. Kovaleski, American Skinheads: Fighting Minorities and Each Other, *Washington Post* (January 16, 1996): https://www.washingtonpost.com/archive/politics/1996/01/16/american-skinheads-fighting-minorities-and-each-other/7807cc0e-9136-4e99-9c9c-67d358244634/

44. Ibid.

45. Michael, This Is War!, 44.

46. B. Denson, 1998 Story: Legacy of a Hate Crime: Mulugeta Seraw's Death a Decade Ago Avenged, Oregon Live (January 10, 2014): https://www.oregonlive.com/portland/2014/11/1998_story_legacy_of_a_hate_cr.html

47. Ibid.

48. B. O'Connor, Here Is What Appears to Be Dylann Roof's Racist Manifesto, *Gawker* (June 20, 2015): https://gawker.com/here-is-what-appears-to-be-dylann-roofs-racist-manifest-1712767241

49. Michael, This Is War!, 47. See also K. Davis, "A Dark Chapter of Hate Closes": Notorious Racist Leader Tom Metzger Dead at 82, *Los Angeles Times* (November 10, 2020): https://www.latimes.com/obituaries/story/2020-11-10/racist-leader-tom-metzger-dies

Chapter 4

1. R. Pérez and G. Ward, From Insult to Estrangement and Injury: The Violence of Racist Police Jokes, *American Behavioral Scientist*, vol. 63, no. 13 (2019): 1810–1829.

2. S. Dewan, When Police Officers Vent on Facebook, *New York Times* (June 3, 2019): https://www.nytimes.com/2019/06/03/us/politics/police-officers-facebook.html; The Plain View Project: https://www.plainviewproject.org

3. E. Hoerner and R. Tulksy, Cops Around the Country Are Posting Racist and Violent Comments on Facebook, *Injustice Watch* (2019): https://www.injusticewatch.org/interactives/cops-troubling-facebook-posts-revealed/

4. Ibid.

5. Ibid.

6. K. Epstein, Racist Posts from Police Oficcers' Social Media Accounts Trigger a Wave of Investigations, *Washington Post* (June 4, 2019): https://www.washingtonpost.com/nation/2019/06/04/racist-posts-police-officers-social-media-accounts-trigger-wave-investigations/

7. J. Stanley, We Need to Move Beyond the Frame of the "Bad Apple Cop," *ACLU* (March 19, 2015): https://www.aclu.org/blog/national-security/we-need-move-beyond-frame-bad-apple-cop; R. Ray, Bad Apples Come from Rotten Trees in Policing, *Brookings Institute* (May 30, 2020): https://www.brookings.edu/blog/how-we-rise/2020/05/30/bad-apples-come-from-rotten-trees-in-policing/

8. A. C. Thompson, Inside the Secret Border Patrol Facebook Group Where Agents Joke About Migrant Deaths and Post Sexist Memes, *ProPublica* (July 1, 2019): https://www.propublica.org/article/secret-border-patrol-facebook-group-agents-joke-about-migrant-deaths-post-sexist-memes

9. Ibid.

10. B. Mejia, Many Latinos Answer Call for the Border Patrol in the Age of Trump, *Los Angeles Times* (April 23, 2018): https://www.latimes.com/local/lanow/la-me-ln-citizens-academy-20180323-htmlstory.html

11. J. Fritze, Jeff Sessions Voices Concern About Use of Consent Decrees for Police, *Baltimore Sun* (January 10, 2017): https://www.baltimoresun.com/politics/bal-jeff-sessions-voices-concern-about-use-of-consent-decrees-for-police-20170110-story.html

12. E. J. Romero and K. W. Cruthirds, The Use of Humor in the Workplace, *Academy of Management Perspectives*, vol. 20, no. 2 (2006): 58–69; J. Mesmer-Magnus, D. J. Glew, and C. Viswesvaran, A Meta-Analysis of Positive Humor in the Workplace, *Journal of Managerial Psychology*, vol. 27, no. 2 (2012): 155–190; C. Cooper, Elucidating the Bonds of Workplace Humor: A Relational Process Model, *Human Relations*, vol. 61, no. 8 (2008): 1087–1115.

13. K. Holmes, Lawrence Police Department Uses Social Media, Humor to Engage Community, *KSHB Kansas City* (August 18, 2017): https://www.kshb.com/news/local-news/lawrence-police-department-uses-social-media-humor-to-engage-community

14. Staff, Lawrence Police's Hilarious Twitter Account Proves Humor Helps Spread Important Info, *Fox 4* (December 29, 2017): https://fox4kc.com/news/lawrence-polices-hilarious-twitter-account-proves-humor-helps-spread-important-info/

15. M. Seigel, *Violence Work: State Power and the Limits of Police*. Duke University Press, 2018.

16. E. Ortiz, George Holliday, Who Taped Rodney King Beating, Urges Others to Share Videos, *NBC News* (June 9, 2019): https://www.nbcnews.com/nightly-news/george-holliday-who-taped-rodney-king-beating-urges-others-share-n372551

17. Ibid.

18. Human Rights Watch, Los Angeles: The Christopher Commission Report (1998): https://www.hrw.org/legacy/reports98/police/uspo73.htm

19. Independent Commission on the Los Angeles Police Department (ICLAPD), Report of the Independent Commission on the Los Angeles Police Department (1991): http://michellawyers.com/wp-content/uploads/2010/06/Report-of-the-Independent-Commission-on-the-LAPD-re-Rodney-King_Reduced.pdf (p. i)

20. Ibid., xii.

21. L.A. Times Archives, The Christopher Commission on Tuesday Issued a 228-Page Report on the Activities of the Los Angeles Police Dept. Here Are Excerpts, *Los Angeles Times* (July 10, 1991): https://www.latimes.com/archives/la-xpm-1991-07-10-mn-1962-story.html

22. ICLAPD, Report, 14–15.

23. J. Chow, Sticks and Stones Will Break My Bones, but Will Racist Humor: A Look Around the World at Whether Police Officers Have a Free Speech Right to Engage in Racist Humor, *Loyola: International and Comparative Law Review*, vol. 14 (1991): 851; S. Holdaway, Blue Jokes: Humour in Police Work, in *Humour in Society* (pp. 106–122). Palgrave Macmillan, 1988; P. A. J. Waddington, Police (Canteen) Sub-Culture: An Appreciation, *British Journal of Criminology*, vol. 39, no. 2 (1999): 287–309.

24. ICLAPD, Report, 30.

25. R. Pérez, Racism Without Hatred? Racist Humor and the Myth of "Color-blindness," *Sociological Perspectives*, vol. 60, no. 5 (2017): 956–974.

26. Chow, Sticks and Stones Will Break My Bones, 858.

27. Waddington, Police (Canteen) Sub-Culture, 294. Emphasis in original.

28. Ibid., 295.

29. M. R. Pogrebin and E. D. Poole, Humor in the Briefing Room: A Study of the Strategic Uses of Humor Among Police, *Journal of Contemporary Ethnography*, vol. 17, no. 2 (1988): 183–210.

30. Ibid., 196–197.

31. Waddington, Police (Canteen) Sub-Culture, 300.

32. Ibid.

33. Pérez and Ward, From Insult to Estrangement and Injury; Chow, Sticks and Stones Will Break My Bones.

34. J. Galtung, Cultural Violence, *Journal of Peace Research*, vol. 27, no. 3 (1990): 291–305, at 291–292.

35. Pérez and Ward, From Insult to Estrangement and Injury; Chow, Sticks and Stones Will Break My Bones.

36. Waddington, Police (Canteen) Sub-Culture, 301.

37. G. N. Rosenberg, The 1964 Civil Rights Act: The Crucial Role of Social Movements in the Enactment and Implementation of Anti-Discrimination Law, *Saint Louis University Law Journal*, vol. 49 (2004): 1147.

38. K. Stainback and D. Tomaskovic-Devey, *Documenting Desegregation: Racial and Gender Segregation in Private Sector Employment Since the Civil Rights Act.* Russell Sage Foundation, 2012; Pérez and Ward, From Insult to Estrangement and Injury.

39. J. H. Skolnick, *Justice Without Trial: Law Enforcement in Democratic Society.* John Wiley & Sons, 1966.

40. Ibid., 73.

41. A. Silverstein, New Policy Will Focus on Conduct, *Star-News* (October 28, 1984): https://news.google.com/newspapers?nid=1454&dat=19841028&id=Y1ZOAAAAIBAJ&sjid=pRMEAAAAIBAJ&pg=6917,8313526&hl=en

42. Ibid.

43. ICLAPD, Report, 73.

44. M. J. Sniffen, State Police Academy Charged with Violating Anti-Bias Order, *Schenectady Gazette* (February 23, 1984): https://news.google.com/newspapers ?nid=1917&dat=19840223&id=twwhAAAAIBAJ&sjid=U3MFAAAAIBAJ&pg= 1128,1784476&hl=en

45. Ibid.

46. J. Newfield, An Anniversary for Attica, *New York Times* (September 13, 1972): https://www.nytimes.com/1972/09/13/archives/an-anniversary-for-attica .html

47. W. Turner, Two Desperate Hours: How George Jackson Died, *New York Times* (September 3, 1971): https://www.nytimes.com/1971/09/03/archives/ two-desperate-hours-how-george-jackson-died-two-desperate-hours-how.html

48. Newfield, An Anniversary for Attica.

49. L. Getlen, The True Story of the Attica Prison Riot, *New York Post* (August 20, 2016): https://nypost.com/2016/08/20/the-true-story-of-the-attica -prison-riot/

50. *United States v. State of NY*, 475 F. Supp. 1103 (N.D.N.Y 1979): https:// law.justia.com/cases/federal/district-courts/FSupp/475/1103/1688027/

51. Ibid.

52 State Police Academy Charged with Violating Bias Order, *Schenectady Gazette* (February 23, 1984): 2.

53. *United States v. State of N.Y.*, 593 F. Supp. 1216 (N.D.N.Y. 1984). https:// casetext.com/case/united-states-v-state-of-ny-2

54. ICLAPD, Report, 48.

55. Ibid, xii.

56. Ibid., 52.

57. Ibid., xii.

58. Chow, Sticks and Stones Will Break My Bones, 854.

59. ICLAPD, Report, 54–55.

60. Chow, Sticks and Stones Will Break My Bones, 854.

61. ICLAPD, Report, xii.

62. Ibid., 75.

63. Ibid., 34.

64. Ibid., xii.

65. Ibid., 79.

66. Ibid., 80.

67. Ibid., 78.

68. Ibid., 79.

69. Ibid., 82.

70. J. Wilgoren, LAPD Rejection over Racial Joke Raises Questions, *Los Angeles Times* (February 4, 1996): https://www.latimes.com/archives/la-xpm-1996 -02-04-mn-32283-story.html

71. Ibid.

72. The LAPD's Rampart Division would gain widespread notoriety during the late 1990s and early 2000s for being one of the most corrupt and violent police departments in the United States.

73. Wilgoren, LAPD Rejection over Racial Joke Raises Questions.

74. M. Marriott, Black Women Are Split over All Male March on Washington, *New York Times* (October 14, 1995): https://www.nytimes.com/1995/10/ 14/us/black-women-are-split-over-all-male-march-on-washington.html; M. Neal, *New Black Man*. Routledge, 2005, 16, 17.

75. J. K. Wilson, *The Myth of Political Correctness*. Duke University Press, 1995.

76. P. Baker, Another Type of Joke Now No Laughing Matter, *Washington Post* (March 21, 1993): https://www.washingtonpost.com/archive/local/1993/ 03/21/another-type-of-joke-now-no-laughing-matter/49eb5db8-d499-406a -b5b6-do31d53ea789/

77. D. Subotnik, The Joke in Critical Race Theory: De Gustibus Disputandum Est, *Touro Law Review*, vol. 15 (1998): 120.

78. Wilgoren, LAPD Rejection over Racial Joke Raises Questions.

79. Ibid.

80. Ibid.

81. B. Boyarsky, Laughing in the Face of Bureaucracy, *Los Angeles Times* (February 6, 1996): https://www.latimes.com/archives/la-xpm-1996-02-06-me -32926-story.html

82. S. Harris, When Do Jokes Become Racist? *Los Angeles Times* (February 8, 1991): https://www.latimes.com/archives/la-xpm-1996-02-08-me-33577-story .html

83. Boyarsky, Laughing in the Face of Bureaucracy.

84. Ibid.

85. Harris, When Do Jokes Become Racist?

86. K. Bentle, DOJ Investigations: 20 Departments Under Enforcement Agreements, *Chicago Tribune* (January 13, 2017): https://www.chicagotribune .com/news/ct-doj-investigations-police-departments-20170112-htmlstory.html

87. M. Alexander, *The New Jim Crow: Mass Incarceration in the Age of Colorblindness*. New Press, 2012.

88. S. Moughty, 17 Justice Dept. Investigations into Police Departments Nationwide, *Frontline* (September 10, 2011): https://www.pbs.org/wgbh/frontline/article/17-justice-dept-investigations-into-police-departments-nationwide/

89. Y. Alcindor, Mo. Gov. Declares State of Emergency, Curfew in Ferguson, *USA Today* (August 16, 2014): https://www.usatoday.com/story/news/nation/2014/08/16/ferguson-missouri-michael-brown-rally-protests/14160469/

90. M. Davey and J. Bosman, Protests Flare After Ferguson Police Officer Is Not Indicted, *New York Times* (November 24, 2014): https://www.nytimes.com/2014/11/25/us/ferguson-darren-wilson-shooting-michael-brown-grand-jury.html

91. U.S. Department of Justice (DOJ), Investigation of the Ferguson Police Department, *Civil Rights Division* (March 4, 2015): https://www.justice.gov/sites/default/files/opa/press-releases/attachments/2015/03/04/ferguson_police_department_report.pdf (pp. 4–5). The chapter opening quote is from this report.

92. DOJ, Investigation, 4.

93. E. Holder, Attorney General Holder Delivers Update on Investigations in Ferguson, Missouri, *United States Department of Justice* (August 26, 2015): https://www.justice.gov/opa/speech/attorney-general-holder-delivers-update-investigations-ferguson-missouri

94. DOJ, Investigation, 72.

95. Ibid., 71.

96. Pérez and Ward, From Insult to Estrangement and Injury.

97. T.-N. Coates, The Gangsters of Ferguson, *The Atlantic* (March 5, 2015): https://www.theatlantic.com/politics/archive/2015/03/The-Gangsters-Of-Ferguson/386893/ The chapter opening quote is from this article.

98. DOJ, Investigation, 72.

99. W. Lowery and K. Kindy, "These Are the Racially Charged Emails That Got 3 Ferguson Police and Court Officials Fired, *Washington Post* (April 3, 2015): https://www.washingtonpost.com/news/post-nation/wp/2015/04/03/these-are-the-racist-e-mails-that-got-3-ferguson-police-and-court-officials-fired/?utm_term=.119c41250485

100. T. Nashrulla and J. Anderson, Here Are the Racist Emails Between Ferguson Police and Court Officials, *Buzzfeed News* (April 3, 2015): https://www.buzzfeednews.com/article/tasneemnashrulla/here-are-the-racist-emails-between-ferguson-police-and-court

101. Lowery and Kindy, These Are the Racially Charged Emails.

102. Ibid.

103. San Francisco Cop at Center of Texting Scandal Speaks Out, *ABC 7 News* (March 17, 2015): https://abc7news.com/san-francisco-police-officers -investigated-racist/562166/

104. Ibid.

105. J. Serna and L. Romney, Racist, Homophobic Texts by San Francisco Police Trigger Case Reviews, *Los Angeles Times* (March 17, 2015): https://www.latimes .com/local/lanow/la-me-ln-racist-police-text-messages-review-20150317-story.html

106. S. Glover and D. Simon, "Wild Animals": Racist Texts Sent by San Francisco Police Officer, Documents Show, *CNN* (April 26, 2016): https://www.cnn .com/2016/04/26/us/racist-texts-san-francisco-police-officer/index.html

107. E. Sernoffsky, Muslim San Francisco Cop Alleges "Blatant Racism" on Job, *SF Gate* (April 10, 2018): https://www.sfgate.com/news/article/Muslim -San-Francisco-cop-blatant-sexism-racism-12822700.php

108. M. Flynn, Minneapolis Police Decorate Christmas Tree with Racial Stereotypes in Majority-Black Neighborhood, *Washington Post* (December 3, 2018): https://www.washingtonpost.com/nation/2018/12/03/minneapolis-police -erected-racist-christmas-tree-majority-black-neighborhood/

109. The Plain View Project: https://www.plainviewproject.org/

110. A. Stockler, 25 Dallas Police Officers Under Investigation for Allegedly Posting Racist, Threatening Content on Facebook, *Newsweek* (August 19, 2019): https://www.newsweek.com/25-dallas-police-officers-under-investigation -allegedly-posting-racist-threatening-content-1447879

111. The Plain View Project: https://cdn.plainviewproject.org/e317869b8 d819aff045aef6f765c69e4ccbd32b2.png

112. J. Cobb, Donald Trump Is Serious When He "Jokes" About Police Brutality, *New Yorker* (August 1, 2017): https://www.newyorker.com/news/news -desk/donald-trump-is-serious-when-he-jokes-about-police-brutality

113. Ibid.

114. J. Rodgers, Police Union Backs Trump for Re-Election in 2020, *Courthouse News Service* (September 9, 2019): https://www.courthousenews.com/ police-union-backs-trump-for-re-election-in-2020/

Chapter 5

1. See M. Tesler, *Post-Racial or Most-Racial? Race and Politics in the Obama Era.* University of Chicago Press, 2016; J. Jost and C. Ogletree, *The Obamas and a (Post) Racial America?* Oxford University Press, 2011.

2. W. E. B. Du Bois, "The Talented Tenth," in *The Negro Problem: A Series of Articles by Representative Negroes of To-day.* New York, 1903: https://glc.yale .edu/talented-tenth-excerpts

3. The chapter opening quote by Hughes was in response to backlash he received to his "non-exceptional" African American characters. See D. Roessel and A. Rampersad, eds., *Langston Hughes: Poetry for Young People*, Sterling Publishing Company, 2006, 6.

4. T. Donovan, Obama and the White Vote, *Political Research Quarterly*, vol. 63, no. 4 (2010): 863–874; A. Mazama, The Barack Obama Phenomenon, *Journal of Black Studies*, vol. 38, no. 1 (2007): 3–6; E. Bonilla-Silva and V. Ray, When Whites Love a Black Leader: Race Matters in Obamerica, *Journal of African American Studies*, vol. 13, no. 2 (2009): 176–183.

5. E. Bonilla-Silva and D. Dietrich, The Sweet Enchantment of Color-Blind Racism in Obamerica, *Annals of the American Academy of Political and Social Science*, vol. 634, no. 1 (2011): 190–206.

6. E. Bonilla-Silva, *Racism Without Racists: Color-Blind Racism and the Persistence of Racial Inequality in the United States*. Rowman & Littlefield Publishers, 2006.

7. See L. Bobo, J. R. Kluegel, and R. A. Smith, Laissez-Faire Racism: The Crystallization of a Kinder, Gentler, Antiblack Ideology, *Racial Attitudes in the 1990s: Continuity and Change*, vol. 15 (1997): 23–25; E. Bonilla-Silva, The Linguistics of Color Blind Racism: How to Talk Nasty About Blacks Without Sounding "Racist," *Critical Sociology*, vol. 28, no. 1–2 (2002): 41–64.

8. R. R. Banks, J. L. Eberhardt, and L. Ross, Discrimination and Implicit Bias in a Racially Unequal Society, *California Law Review*, vol. 94, no. 4 (2006): 1169–1190.

9. J. Kang, Trojan Horses of Race, *Harvard Law Review*, vol. 118, no. 5 (2005): 1489–1593.

10. L. H. Picca and J. R. Feagin, *Two-Faced Racism: Whites in the Backstage and Frontstage*. Routledge, 2020; N. Eliasoph, "Everyday Racism" in a Culture of Political Avoidance: Civil Society, Speech, and Taboo, *Social Problems*, vol. 46, no. 4 (1999): 479–502; Bonilla-Silva, *Racism Without Racists*.

11. S. Stephens-Davidowitz, *Everybody Lies: Big Data, New Data, and What the Internet Can Tell Us About Who We Really Are*. HarperCollins, 2017, 132.

12. Ibid.; S. Stephens-Davidowitz, The Cost of Racial Animus on a Black Candidate: Evidence Using Google Search Data, *Journal of Public Economics*, vol. 118 (2014): 26–40.

13. K. Severson, Number of U.S. Hate Groups Is Rising, Report Says, *New York Times* (March 7, 2012): https://www.nytimes.com/2012/03/08/us/number-of-us-hate-groups-on-the-rise-report-says.html

14. Stephens-Davidowitz, *Everybody Lies*,139.

15. W. D. Hund, C. W. Mills, and S. Sebastiani, eds., *Simianization: Apes, Gender, Class, and Race*. LIT Verlag Münster 2015: https://www.google.com/

books/edition/Simianization/HnZBCwAAQBAJ?hl=en&gbpv=1&printsec=
frontcover

16. Ibid.

17. W. E. B. Du Bois and K. A. Appiah, *Dusk of Dawn*. Oxford University
Press, 2007, 49: https://cominsitu.files.wordpress.com/2019/02/w-e-b-du-bois
-dusk-of-dawn-an-essay-toward-an-autobiography-of-a-race-concept-1.pdf

18. C. W. Mills, Bestial Inferiority. Locating Simianization Within Racism, in
Simianization.

19. Hund, Mills, and Sebastiani, *Simianization.*

20. Ibid.

21. Ibid., 30.

22. P. S. S. Howard, Drawing Dissent: Postracialist Pedagogy, Racist Literacy,
and Racial Plagiarism in Anti-Obama Political Cartoons, *Review of Education,
Pedagogy, and Cultural Studies*, vol. 36, no. 5 (2014): 386–402, at 391.

23. E. Chen, Bush Returns to Yale, Gives Graduates the Last Laugh, *Los Angeles Times* (May 22, 2001): https://www.latimes.com/archives/la-xpm-2001-may
-22-mn-1027-story.html

24. S. Bell, How Often Does a Leader of the Free World Come Along Who
Resembles a Monkey in Every Particular? *The Guardian* (December 12, 2005):
https://www.theguardian.com/politics/2005/dec/13/usa

25. V. S. Navasky, *The Art of Controversy: Political Cartoons and Their Enduring Power*. Knopf, 2013.

26. Bell, How Often Does a Leader . . . Come Along?

27. Ibid.

28. C. Orr, Monkey Business, *New Republic* (March 3, 2008): https://
newrepublic.com/article/40476/monkey-business

29. M. Calderone, Rush Limbaugh Apologizes to Obama, *Politico* (March 8,
2008): https://www.politico.com/blogs/michaelcalderone/0308/Rush_Lim
baugh_apologizes_to_Obama.html

30. L. Copeland, Shooting from the Hip, with a Smile to Boot, *Washington Post*
(October 1, 2008): https://www.washingtonpost.com/wp-srv/artsandliving/
style/features/2008/rhetoric/gallery.html

31. M. Stewart, Palin Hits Obama for "Terrorist" Connection, *CNN* (October 4, 2008): https://www.cnn.com/2008/POLITICS/10/04/palin.obama/

32. R. Smith, CBS Radio Fires Don Imus in Fallout over Remarks, *NPR*
(April 12, 2007): https://www.npr.org/templates/story/story.php?storyId=955
6159

33. Calderone, Rush Limbaugh Apologizes to Obama.

34. Ibid.

35. V. Jungkunz and J. White, Ignorance, Innocence, and Democratic Responsibility: Seeing Race, Hearing Racism, *Journal of Politics*, vol. 75, no. 2 (2013): 436–450.

36. Calderone, Rush Limbaugh Apologizes to Obama.

37. Ibid.

38. D. Ehrenstein, Obama the "Magic Negro," *Los Angeles Times* (March 19, 2007): https://www.latimes.com/la-oe-ehrenstein19mar19-story.html

39. C. Parsons, Limbaugh Draws Fire on Obama Parody, *Seattle Times* (May 6, 2007): https://www.seattletimes.com/nation-world/limbaugh-draws-fire-on-obama-parody/

40. Z. Chafets, Late-Period Limbaugh, *New York Times* (July 6, 2008): https://www.nytimes.com/2008/07/06/magazine/06Limbaugh-t.html

41. Ibid.

42. Ibid.

43. Ibid.

44. S. Cohen, Howard Stern's Blackface Video Is Painful to Watch, But Offers a Not-So-Shocking Lesson, *Forbes* (July 13, 2020): https://www.forbes.com/sites/sethcohen/2020/06/13/howard-sterns-blackface-video-is-painful-to-watch/?sh=22b3b8d76314

45. Chafets, Late-Period Limbaugh.

46. Restaurant Owner Drawing Heat for Obama T-Shirt, *WSFA 12 News* (May 14, 2008): https://www.wsfa.com/story/8323614/restaurant-owner-drawing-heat-for-obama-t-shirt/

47. Associated Press, Bar Owner's T-Shirts Link "Curious George" to Obama, *Daily News* (May 15, 2008): https://www.dailynews.com/2008/05/15/bar-owners-t-shirts-link-curious-george-to-obama/

48. Ibid.

49. Restaurant Owner Drawing Heat for Obama T-Shirt.

50. S. Conroy, Man at Palin Rally Displays Monkey Doll Donning Obama Sticker, *CBS News* (October 11, 2008): https://www.cbsnews.com/news/man-at-palin-rally-displays-monkey-doll-donning-obama-sticker/

51. B. Smith, Palin: Obama Birth Certificate "a Fair Question," *Politico* (December 3, 2009): https://www.politico.com/blogs/ben-smith/2009/12/palin-obama-birth-certificate-a-fair-question-023233

52. J. Sancton, Sean Delonas: Stupid, Racist, or Both? *Vanity Fair* (February 18, 2009): https://www.vanityfair.com/news/2009/02/sean-delonas-stupid-racist-or-both

53. L. Meckler, Obama Signs Stimulus into Law, *Wall Street Journal* (February 18, 2009): https://www.wsj.com/articles/SB123487951033799545

54. P. Krugman, The Obama Gap, *New York Times* (January 8, 2009): https://www.nytimes.com/2009/01/09/opinion/09krugman.html?_r=2

55. A. Johnson, Bush Signs $700 Billion Financial Bailout Bill, *NBC News* (October 2, 2008): https://www.nbcnews.com/id/wbna26987291

56. L. Halloran, Top Republicans: Yeah, We're Calling Obama Socialist, *NPR* (March 5, 2010): https://www.npr.org/templates/story/story.php?storyId=124359632

57. A. Newman, Pet Chimp Is Killed After Mauling Woman, *New York Times* (February 16, 2009): https://www.nytimes.com/2009/02/17/nyregion/17chimp.html

58. J. Bivens, Worst Economic Crisis Since the Great Depression? By a Long Shot, *Economic Policy Institute* (January 27, 2010).

59. O. Burkeman, New York Post in Racism Row over Chimpanzee Cartoon, *The Guardian* (February 18, 2009): https://www.theguardian.com/world/2009/feb/18/new-york-post-cartoon-race

60. Editorial Cartoon Stirring up Controversy, *CNY Central* (February 19, 2009): https://cnycentral.com/news/political/editorial-cartoon-stirring-up-controversy

61. A. Fantz, Racism Row over Chimp Cartoon Sparks Debate, *CNN* (February 19, 2009): https://www.cnn.com/2009/US/02/19/chimp.cartoon.react/index.html

62. R. Martin, NY Post Cartoon Is Racist and Careless, *CNN* (February 18, 2009): https://www.cnn.com/2009/POLITICS/02/18/martin.cartoon/

63. Fantz, Racism Row over Chimp Cartoon.

64. Martin, NY Post Cartoon Is Racist and Careless.

65. Fantz, Racism Row over Chimp Cartoon.

66. G. S. Parks and D. C. Heard, Assassinate the N***** Ape: Obama, Implicit Imagery, and the Dire Consequences of Racist Jokes, *Rutgers Race and the Law Review*, vol. 11, no. 2 (2010): 259–323.

67. P. Bump, Visualizing Threats Against President Obama, in 1 Chart, *Washington Post* (September 30, 2014): https://www.washingtonpost.com/news/the-fix/wp/2014/09/30/visualizing-threats-against-president-obama-in-1-chart/

68. Severson, Number of U.S. Hate Groups Is Rising.

69. K. Downs, FBI Warned of White Supremacists in Law Enforcement 10 Years Ago. Has Anything Changed? *PBS News Hour* (October 21, 2016): https://www.pbs.org/newshour/nation/fbi-white-supremacists-in-law-enforcement

70. R. Pérez-Peña, Murdoch Apologizes in Post for Cartoon of Chimpanzee, *New York Times* (February 24, 2009): https://www.nytimes.com/2009/02/25/nyregion/25cartoon.html

71. R. Sinderbrand, RNC Chairman Candidate Defends "Barack the Magic Negro" Song, *CNN* (December 26, 2008): http://edition.cnn.com/2008/POLITICS/12/26/rnc.obama.satire/

72. Associated Press, Los Alamitos Mayor Criticized for "Watermelon" E-Mail, *Los Angeles Times* (February 25, 2009): https://www.latimes.com/archives/la-xpm-2009-feb-25-me-watermelons25-story.html

73. J. L. Fletcher, Disgust over Mayor's White House Watermelon E-Mail, *Orange County Register* (February 25, 2009): https://www.ocregister.com/2009/02/25/disgust-over-mayors-white-house-watermelon-e-mail/

74. Associated Press, Los Alamitos Mayor Criticized.

75. Fletcher, Disgust over Mayor's White House Watermelon E-Mail.

76. J. Ridley, Sometimes a Racist Chimp Cartoon Just Isn't Enough, *NPR* (February 26, 2009): https://www.npr.org/sections/visibleman/2009/02/cause_sometimes_a_racist_chimp_1.html

77. Fletcher, Disgust over Mayor's White House Watermelon E-Mail.

78. R. Cathcart, Mayor Resigns over "Watermelon" E-Mail Message, *New York Times* (February 27, 2009): https://www.nytimes.com/2009/02/28/us/28resign.html

79. G. Gardner, GOP Mailing Depicts Obama on Food Stamps, Not Dollar Bill, *NPR* (October 16, 2008): https://www.npr.org/sections/newsandviews/2008/10/gop_mailing_is_mouth_watering.html

80. Ibid.

81. Associated Press, OC GOP Official Says Obama Photo Was Satire, Not Racist, *ABC 13 News* (April 20, 2011): https://abc13.com/archive/8085341/

82. J. Adams, O.C. Tea Party Member Sends Picture of Obama as Ape, *NBC 4 News* (April 19, 2011): https://www.nbclosangeles.com/news/local/oc-tea-party-member-sends-picture-of-obama-as-ape/1921463/

83. B. Martin, O.C. Republican Linked to Offensive Obama "Ape" Email, *Orange County Register* (April 17, 2011): https://www.ocregister.com/2011/04/17/oc-republican-linked-to-offensive-obama-ape-email

84. G. Flaccus, GOP Official Apologizes for Obama Chimp Email, *NBC News* (April 19, 2011): https://www.nbcnews.com/id/wbna42656911

85. Local GOP Official Assailed for Racist Email Against Obama, *Voice of OC* (April 17, 2011): https://voiceofoc.org/2011/04/local-gop-official-assailed-for-racist-email-against-obama/

86. OC GOP Official Says Obama Photo Was Satire, Not Racist, *ABC13* (April 20, 2011): https://abc13.com/archive/8085341/

87. Ibid.

88. L. Madison, GOP Official Apologizes for Sending Obama Chimp Image, Refuses to Step Down, *CBS News* (April 19, 2011): https://www.cbsnews.com/news/gop-official-apologizes-for-sending-obama-chimp-image-refuses-to-step-down/

89. P. S. S. Howard, Drawing Dissent: Post-Racialist Pedagogy, Racist Literacy, and Racial Plagiarism in Anti-Obama Political Cartoons, *Review of Education, Pedagogy, and Cultural Studies*, vol. 36, no. 5 (2014): 386–402.

90. K. Russell, Barack Gets It Right on Limbaugh's "Barack the Magic Negro" Parody, *Huffington Post* (May 10, 2007): https://www.huffpost.com/entry/barack-gets-it-right-on-l_1_b_48186

91. A. Wang, Did the 2011 White House Correspondents' Dinner Spur Trump to Run for President? *Chicago Tribune* (February 26, 2017).

Epilogue

1. C. Beltrán, To Understand Trump's Support, We Must Think in Terms of Multiracial Whiteness, *Washington Post* (January 15, 2021): https://www.washingtonpost.com/opinions/2021/01/15/understand-trumps-support-we-must-think-terms-multiracial-whiteness/

2. J. Wolcott, How Donald Trump Became America's Insult Comic in Chief, *Vanity Fair* (December 2015): https://www.vanityfair.com/culture/2015/11/wolcott-trump-insult-comic

3. J. Taranto, Trump the Insult Comic Dog, *Wall Street Journal* (August 15, 2015): https://www.wsj.com/articles/trump-the-insult-comic-dog-1438968585

4. J. Fan, The Atlanta Shooting and the Dehumanizing of Asian Women, *New Yorker* (March 19, 2021): https://www.newyorker.com/news/daily-comment/the-atlanta-shooting-and-the-dehumanizing-of-asian-women

5. A. France-Presse, Sex Addict or Racist? What We Know About Atlanta Shooting Suspect Robert Aaron Long, *South China Morning Post* (March 18, 2021): https://www.scmp.com/news/world/united-states-canada/article/3125937/sex-addict-or-racist-what-we-know-about-atlanta

6. A. Collman, People Are Pushing Back After Georgia Police Were Reluctant to Say Race Was a Factor in the Shooting Spree That Killed Mostly Asian Women, *Insider* (March 18, 2021): https://www.insider.com/people-question-narrative-ga-shooting-spree-wasnt-racially-motivated-2021-3

7. E. Shapiro, Georgia Sheriff's Department Under Fire After Official Says Spa Shootings Suspect Had "Really Bad Day," *ABC News* (March 18, 2021): https://abcnews.go.com/US/georgia-sheriffs-department-fire-official-spa-shootings-suspect/story?id=76533598

8. R. Sandler, Officer Who Said Atlanta Spa Shooter Was Having A "Bad Day" Promoted Racist Covid-19 T-Shirt on Facebook, *Forbes* (March 18, 2021): https://

www.forbes.com/sites/rachelsandler/2021/03/17/officer-who-said-atlanta-spa
-shooter-was-having-a-bad-day-promoted-racist-covid-19-shirt-on-facebook/?sh=
3c1cebea31ed

9. M. Papenfuss, Trump Uses Racist Terms "Kung Flu" And "Chinese Virus"
to Describe COVID-19, *Huffington Post* (June 20, 2020): https://www.huffpost
.com/entry/trump-kellyanne-conway-coronavirus_n_5eeebc5dc5b6aac5f3a4
6b45

10. N. Ruiz, J. M. Horowitz, and C. Tamir, Many Black and Asian Americans
Say They Have Experienced Discrimination Amid the COVID-19 Outbreak, *Pew
Research Center* (July 1, 2020): https://www.pewresearch.org/social-trends/
2020/07/01/many-black-and-asian-americans-say-they-have-experienced
-discrimination-amid-the-covid-19-outbreak/

11. P. Smolinski, Reports of Anti-Asian Hate Crimes Rose Nearly 150% in Major
U.S. Cities Last Year, *CBS News* (March 13, 2021): https://www.cbsnews.com/
news/asian-american-hate-crimes-up-150-percent-us/

12. V. T. Nguyen, From Colonialism to Covid: Viet Thanh Nguyen on
the Rise of Anti-Asian Violence, *The Guardian* (April 3, 2021): https://www
.theguardian.com/books/2021/apr/03/from-colonialism-to-covid-viet
-thanh-nguyen-on-the-rise-of-anti-asian-violence?fbclid=IwAR0C7uJojLpVW
8N1P76IEVEzpmJBcU3y4BH7B-A9LVvC_X-phBrpwPz3RZs

13. P. Gosar, Cartoon Depicts Real Life Policy Battle Against Illegal Immigration and Amnesty (November 14, 2021): https://gosar.house.gov/news/email/
show.aspx?ID=URE2JA5AWSMH67WQJVNM4ZQ4QQ

14. V. Romo, El Paso Walmart Shooting Suspect Pleads Not Guilty, *NPR* (October 10, 2019): https://www.npr.org/2019/10/10/769013051/el-paso-walmart
-shooting-suspect-pleads-not-guilty

15. J. Guerrero, Column: Paul Gosar's Anime Video of Killing AOC Is Not a
Joke. It Displays the New GOP's Violent Extremist Turn, *Los Angeles Times* (November 17, 2021): https://www.latimes.com/opinion/story/2021-11-17/gosar
-video-displays-gops-violent

16. Gosar, Cartoon Depicts Real Life Policy Battle.

17. D. Mangan, Trump "Strongly Condemns" Doctored Video Showing Him
Killing News Media Outlets and Political Foes, Press Secretary Says, *CNBC* (October 14, 2019): https://www.cnbc.com/2019/10/14/trump-condemns-video
-showing-him-killing-media-outlets.html

18. Guerrero, Gosar's Anime Video.

19. V. Stracqualursi, Marjorie Taylor Greene Posts Image of Herself with Gun
Alongside "Squad" Congresswomen, Encourages Going on the "Offense Against
These Socialists," *CNN* (September 4, 2020): https://www.cnn.com/2020/09/
04/politics/marjorie-taylor-greene-gun-post-squad/index.html

20. E. Relman, Facebook Took Down a Far-Right Congressional Candidate's Photo Showing Her Holding a Gun Next to Rep. Alexandria Ocasio-Cortez and the "Squad," *Insider* (September 4, 2020): https://www.businessinsider.com/facebook-deleted-gop-candidates-post-threatening-violence-against-aoc-2020-9

21. Transcript: The ReidOut, *MSNBC* (November 17, 2021): https://www.msnbc.com/transcripts/transcript-reidout-11-17-21-n1284081

22. Ibid.

23. J. C. Mueller, Producing Colorblindness: Everyday Mechanisms of White Ignorance, *Social Problems*, vol. 64, no. 2 (2017): 219–238.

24. Scroll Staff, Can a Dose of Obscenity and Humour Help Counter Racism? Philosopher Slavoj Žižek Thinks So, *Scroll.in* (January 12, 2017): https://scroll.in/video/826326/watch-can-a-dose-of-obscenity-and-humour-help-counter-racism-philosopher-slavoj-zizek-thinks-so

25. R. Pérez, Racist Humor: Then and Now, *Sociology Compass*, vol. 10, no. 10 (2016): 928–938; R. Pérez, Rhetoric of Racial Ridicule in an Era of Racial Protest: Don Rickles, the "Equal Opportunity Offender" Strategy, and the Civil Rights Movement, in *Standing Up, Speaking Out* (pp. 103–123). Routledge, 2016.

26. R. Liu and S. Shange, Toward Thick Solidarity: Theorizing Empathy in Social Justice Movements, *Radical History Review*, vol. 131 (2018): 189–198.

27. D. Obeidallah, Jay Leno and Other White Comic Icons Finally Address Racism in Comedy, *MSNBC* (March 29, 2021): https://www.msnbc.com/opinion/jay-leno-jimmy-fallon-other-white-comic-icons-finally-address-n1262237

28. S. Ford, Comedian Carlin's Point Is to Make Point, *Daily News* (November 24, 1974): http://news.google.com/newspapers?nid=1696&dat=19741122&id=O9seAAAAIBAJ&sjid=toYEAAAAIBAJ&pg=6926,3488437

29. CNN, How George Carlin Became George Carlin, *CNN* (1990): https://www.cnn.com/videos/entertainment/2017/01/09/george-carlin-1990-larry-king-live-interview.cnn

30. S. Hall, Racist Ideologies and the Media, in *Media Studies: A Reader*, eds. P. Marris and S. Thornham (pp. 271–282). New York University Press, 2000. The chapter opening quote is from p. 279.

INDEX

Note: Page numbers in italic type indicate illustrations.

Adachi, Jeff, 118
affirmative action, 61, 62, 63, 74, 101
African Americans: alleged inferiority
    of, 14–16, 22, 29–31, 128–31; dehu-
    manization of, 13, 16, 38–39, 87, 88,
    95–96, 104, 106, 114, 116–17, 130,
    133, 155; Du Bois on, 7; empathy
    for experiences of, 3–4; and excep-
    tionalism, 123–24; likened to apes/
    chimpanzees/monkeys, 104, 128,
    130–31, 136, 147, 155; New York
    discrimination case against, 98–101;
    racist representations of, 59,
    67–69, 109, 115–16, 120, 127, 142,
    150–53; self-caricature by, 16, 59; as
    targets of white contempt, 4–8
aggression, humor as means of, 28, 76
Ahmed, Sara, 9–11, 21, 24, 46, 168
alienation, humor as means of, 11, 13,
    19, 24, 26–29, 45, 103
Allan, Col, 147
All in the Family (television show), 59
alt-right: nationalist goals of, 52, 54,
    56; racist humor as tool of, 20,
    51–58, 82–83; support for Trump

from, 56, 161; white supremacist
    message of, 51–58. *See also* far right
American Recovery and Reinvestment
    Act, 145–46
Amos 'n' Andy (television show), 32
amused racial contempt: African Amer-
    icans as targets of, 6–7; Asians as
    targets of, 163–64; concept of,
    8–13, 47–48; critical evaluation
    of, 168–72; emotions associated
    with, 9; law enforcement use of,
    86, 89, 95, 102, 105, 106, 115–16,
    121; Obama as target of, 126–28,
    136–58; proliferation of, 48;
    Trump's use of, 161–63; unequal
    terrain of, 157; white attitude of,
    7–8; in white racist humor, 30, 43;
    white supremacy's use of, 53–56, 58,
    60–65, 68–69, 73–84, 160. *See also*
    pleasure and enjoyment, in racist
    humor; racist humor
Anderson, Elijah, 4
Angel, Tom, 12–13
Anglin, Andrew, 50, 52–56, 83
Animal House (film), 59

Anonymous (online activist group), 52
Anti-Defamation League, 20, 142–43
anti-Semitism: alt-right and, 51–55; of
    Farrakhan, 109; memes based on,
    51, 56; in Nazi Germany, 53; of
    white supremacists, *68*, 69, *70*. See
    also Jews
apes/chimpanzees/monkeys: Afri-
    can Americans likened to, 104,
    128, 130–31, 136, 147, 155; George
    W. Bush likened to, 133–36, *135*;
    Lincoln likened to, 131, *132*, 133;
    Obama likened to, 20–21, 115, 128,
    136–49, *143*, 154, *155*, 158
Aristotle, 8, 23
Aryan Youth Movement (AYM), 61
Asians, 72, 106, 119, 160, 162–64
Association of American Editorial
    Cartoonists, 148
Attack on Titan (anime series), 164
Attica Prison uprising, 99–100

Baker, Jay, 163
Baker-White, Emily, 87
bank bailout, 145–46
"Barack the Magic Negro" (song),
    140
Baugh, Scott, 154–55
Bell, Steve, cartoon depiction of Bush
    as an ape, 134–35, *135*
Bergson, Henri, 23
Bericat, Eduardo, 9
Billig, Michael, 27–28
birther conspiracy, 144, 154, 161–62
blackface minstrelsy: Black participa-
    tion in, 16; critiques of, 13–14, 32;
    defined, 5; historical legacy of, 140,
    142, 167; Obama likened to, 158;
    origins of, 14; popularity of, 13, 15,
    31, 55; post–civil rights era racist
    humor compared to, 69; racializa-
    tion effected by, 43; ridicule of

African Americans in, 14–15, 31;
    social functions of, 5, 16–17, 22–23
Black Lives Matter, 2, 56, 114, 120,
    121, 124
Black Power movement, 97
Blaxploitation films, 59
Bogren, Michael S., 2
Bones (stage character), 14, 15
Bonilla-Silva, Eduardo, 45
Border Patrol, 87–88
Boyarsky, Bill, 112
Boylan, Karie, 2
Boy's Club (online comic), 56
Bradley, Tom, 91
Brown, Cleon, 1–4, 37, 41, 90
Brown, Michael, 114–15
Bryant, John, 150–51
Bush, George W., 133–36, *135*, 145, 149

Campbell, Frank, 2
cancel culture, 40, 160
capitalism: positive psychology and, 28;
    racialization's role in, 6, 167; and
    rationalization of society, 35
Carlin, George, 170
Carnegie Corporation, 29
Chafets, Zev, 142
Chaffey Community Republican
    Women, 153
Chick, Laura, 111
chimpanzees. *See* apes/chimpanzees/
    monkeys
Chow, Josephine, 93
Christopher, Warren, 91
Christopher Commission Report, 91,
    104–7, 116
Ciara, Barbara, 147
Civil Rights Act, 96, 103
civil rights movement: condemna-
    tion of racist humor as outgrowth
    of, 31–32, 36, 39, 45, 47, 96, 126;
    critique of scientific basis of race

as outgrowth of, 131; sociocultural changes resulting from, 96–97; white racial frame challenged by, 79–80. *See also* post–civil rights era

Clark, Jamar, 120

class: *See* lower-class whites; middle-class whites; upper-class whites; ruling-class whites

class conflict, 6, 7, 167

Clay, Andrew Dice, 170

Clinton, Bill, 113

CNBC (television network), 62

Coates, Ta-Nehisi, 85, 116

Cobb, Jelani, 121, 147

collective effervescence, 17

Collins, Patricia Hill, 15

colonialism. *See* imperialism

colorblind era: blackface in, 167; Limbaugh in, 141–42; Obama presidency and, 124, 166; persistence of racism in, 20, 23, 45–46, 60, 69, 77, 80, 83–84, 92, 96, 121, 125, 144, 150, 159, 162; proclamations of, 33; racist humor in, 45–47, 50, 58, 62, 69, 75, 80, 144, 146. *See also* post–civil rights era; post-racialism

Connelie, William G., 100

conservative commentators: free speech appeals of, 138; Obama as target of, 136–37, 139; and political correctness, 40, 161; post-racial concept embraced by, 33; on racist humor, 40–41, 110, 161. *See also* Limbaugh, Rush

Cooper, Cecily, 11

critical race theory, 33, 42, 110, 131

Crusius, Patrick, 164

cultural violence, 95, 116

culture war, 56, 140, 161, 171

Cunningham, Phillipe, 120

Curious George, 137–39, 142–44

Daily Stormer, The (website), 52–55, 83

Dana, Bill, 32

Dark Mirror (television series), 3

Darwin, Charles, 25, 128, 130

Davenport, Marilyn, 154–56

Davies, Christie, 18, 33–41, 76–77, 110, 130, 169

Dees, Morris, 82

dehumanization: of African Americans and other non-whites, 13, 16, 38–39, 87, 88, 95–96, 104, 106, 114, 116–17, 130, 133, 155; of Asians, 163–64; humor as means of, 10, 11, 18–21, 39, 50, 104, 116–17, 119; of immigrants, 73; by law enforcement, 87, 88, 95–96, 104, 106, 114, 116–17; of Obama, 136; violence enabled by, 13, 20, 50, 82, 95, 116–17, 119; in Western societies, 38

Delonas, Sean, anti-Obama cartoon of, 145–50, *147*

Department of Justice, 20, 85, 86, 99, 101, 113–18; Civil Rights Division, 113

De Soucey, Michaela, 25–26

Dezecache, Guillaume, 25

double-consciousness, 7

Douglass, Frederick, 13

Du Bois, W. E. B., 1, 5–7, 29, 46, 48, 123, 130, 167; *The Souls of Black Folk*, 7; "The Souls of White Folk," 5–7, 48

Duke, David, 61

Dunbar, Robin, 25

Durkheim, Emile, 17, 34, 37

East Side White Pride, 81

economic elites, 7, 167

Ehrenstein, David, 140

election: *See* Obama; Trump

Emancipation Proclamation, 131, *132*
Emergency Economic Stabilization
    Act, 145–46
Emmet, Dan, 14
emotions, 8–10, 23, 45. *See also*
    pleasure and enjoyment, in racist
    humor
enjoyment. *See* pleasure and enjoy-
    ment, in racist humor
Enlightenment, 28
equal opportunity offender notion, 59,
    77, 93, 169
ethnic humor: in post-racial era, 33–34,
    37; racist humor compared to,
    34, 37–39, 102; scholarship on,
    18, 33–37, 169; social functions of,
    34–37; themes of, 34–35
evolution, 25, 128, 130
evolutionary theory, 25
exploitation, 6, 69

Facebook, 87–88
Farrakhan, Louis, 108
far right: alt-right racist humor, 51–58;
    defenses of racist humor, 40;
    growth of, in Obama presidency,
    127, 149; Metzger's *White Aryan
    Resistance* and, 58–84; racist
    humor as tool of, 19–20, 50–84,
    145–46, 150; social media's use by,
    50–52, 55; support for Trump from,
    161; and white victimhood, 58, 61,
    63–84. *See also* white supremacy
fascism, 29, 53, 54, 165
Feagin, Joe, 12, 37, 42
Fedele, Diane, 153–54
Feinberg, Ashley, 52
Fennelly, Drew, 89
Ferguson Police Department, 20,
    114–18
Fine, Gary Alan, 25–26
First Amendment, 83, 110

Floyd, George, 120, 121
Foley, James T., 100–102
food stamps, 153
4chan, 52, 55, 56
Fox News, 161
freedom of speech, 63–64, 79, 83, 110,
    138–43, 149, 160, 168
French, Antonio, 118
Freud, Sigmund, 24, 46, 126
Fuhrman, Mark, 109
Furie, Matt, 56
Furminger, Ian, 118–19

Galtung, Johan, 95
Goldberg, David Theo, 33
Goldberg, Jackie, 111
Golden, James, 141
Google searches, 126–27
Gore, Al, 133
Gosar, Paul, 164–66
Great Recession, 145–46
Greene, Marjorie Taylor, 165–66
Griffin, John Howard, *Black Like Me*,
    3–4
Grose, Dean, 150–52, 154, 156
Guerrero, Jean, 165

Haley, Alex, *Roots*, 2
Hall, Stuart, 42–43, 159, 171
happiness/happy objects, 10–11,
    24–25, 27
Harold, Sandra, 146
Harper's Weekly, 131
Harris, Scott, 112
Hastings Police Department, 1–3
hate crimes, *67*, 82, 149
hate groups, 127
hate symbols, 20
Hawley, George, 56–57
Henke, Rick, 117
Hispanic population. *See* Latino popu-
    lation; Mexican Americans

Hitchens, Christopher, 62–64
Hobbes, Thomas, 8, 23
Holdaway, Simon, 93
Holder, Eric, 114–15
Holliday, George, 90
Holocaust, 56–57
homophobia, 12, 51, 86, 93, 118–19, 145
Hoopes, George, 112
Houghton Mifflin Harcourt, 143
Howard, Philip S. S., 131
Hughes, Langston, 123, 199n3
humor/jokes: aggression theory of, 28, 76; alienating effects of, 11, 13, 19, 24, 26–29, 45, 103; conflict theory of, 36; disregard of negative effects of, 10–11; evolutionary theories of, 25; happiness produced by, 10, 24–25, 27; incongruity theory of, 23–24; as means of establishing social order/control, 4, 10–15, 27, 37–38; positive interpretations of, 10–11, 17–19, 24–25, 27–28; relief theory of, 24, 46; rhetorical function of, 27, 44–45; social alignment/bonds established through, 10–11, 24–27, 89, 92–94, 168; social context for, 168–72; superiority theory of, 8, 23; theories and analysis of, 8, 10–12, 18–19, 21–29, 33–37, 41–43, 45–47, 76–77, 126, 168–69; Western ideals betrayed by negative forms of, 28–29. See also ethnic humor; racist humor; white racist humor
Hyde, Volney E., 112

immigrants, 72–73, 73, 120, 160, 164–65
imperialism: forms of humor linked to, 28; racialization's role in, 6, 38, 128, 130, 167, 171, 179n1
implicit bias, 88, 125–26

Imus, Don, 137–38
International Union of Police Associations, 121
Involvement of Mexican Americans in Gainful Endeavors (IMAGE), 32
Ioanide, Paula, 9
Irish, denigration of, 36, 38, 130

Jackson, George, 99
Jews, 38, 53, 65, 68–69. See also anti-Semitism
Jim Crow (stage character), 14
Jiménez, José (stage character), 32
John Birch Society, 60
jokes. See humor/jokes
Jung, Moon-Kie, 47

Kant, Immanuel, 23
Kennedy, John F., 32
King, Larry, 170
King, Martin Luther, Jr., 62, 63
King, Rodney, 70, 90–92, 95, 103–5, 107, 113
King Kong (film), 130
KKK. See Ku Klux Klan
Knowles, James, 117
Ku Klux Klan (KKK), 56, 57, 60, 83

Lai, Jason, 119
Latino population, 98–101. See also Mexican Americans
law enforcement: alleged moral superiority of, 94, 96; "bad apples" myth about, 87, 88, 102, 117–18; behavioral policies adopted by, 96–98, 107; criticisms of, 86; dehumanizing language of, 87, 88, 95–96, 104, 106, 114, 116–17, 119; discipline and supervision in, 96–98, 104–13, 117; DOJ investigations of, 113–15; fellow officers as target of racist humor, 1–3, 106;

law enforcement (*continued*)
functions of humor used by, 89,
92–96, 101; positive uses of humor
by, 89; public attitudes toward,
87, 105, 112; racism endemic in,
87–91, 102–3, 105, 113–20; racist
humor of, 1–3, 12–13, 20, 86–122;
recruitment and training scandals
involving, 98–104, 107–12; social
bonding of, through humor, 13,
89, 92–94, 116; support for Trump
from, 121, 161; use of violence by,
90–92, 95, 103–7, 112; us-them
mentality in, 94–96, 113–14; as
victims, 71–72, *72*, 111; violence ad-
vocated/celebrated by, 87, 95, 104,
116, 120–21; white supremacists in,
84, 149
Lawrence Police Department, 89
Leno, Jay, 170
libertarianism, 169–70
Limbaugh, Rush, 40, 110, 136–42, 157,
161
Lincoln, Abraham, 131, *132*, 133
Liu, Roseann, 169
Long, Robert Aaron, 162–63
Los Angeles City Council, 111
Los Angeles Police Department
(LAPD), 70, 90–92, 95, 97,
104–12, 196n72
Los Angeles Times (newspaper), 53, 60,
108, 112, 140, 165
Los Angeles uprising (1992), 70–71, *71*,
72, 107
Lott, Eric, 15
lower-class whites: alleged racial su-
periority of, 6–7, 16–17, 79; social
status of, 6–7, 16–17, 79–80; as target audience of white supremacists,
66, 69; as targets of humor, 42
lulz, 52
LulzSec, 52

Mansfield, Jeff, 2
Martin, Trayvon, 53
Mazzella, Dave, 81
McCain, John, 137, 142, 144
McDonnell, Katey, 152
McDowall, Marjorie, 151
Mehringer, Bud, 108, 111
Mehringer, Randy, 108–12
memes, 20, 23, 51, 53, 55, 56, *57*, 82, 87,
120, 127, 166
Metzger, John, 61–64, 77
Metzger, Tom, 19, 50, 58, 60–64, 77,
81–84, 149, 162, 165
Mexican American Anti-Defamation
Committee (MAADC), 32
Mexican Americans, 12, 32, 72–73, *73*,
88. *See also* Latino population
microaggressions, 4
middle-class whites, 14, 162
Mieske, Ken, 80–82
Million Man March, 108–9
Mills, Charles, 37–38, 130
Minneapolis Police Department, 120
monkeys. *See* apes/chimpanzees/
monkeys
Morreall, John, 25
Mudd, William, 117
Murdoch, Rupert, 145, 148
Muscular Dystrophy Association, 143
Muslims, 87, 119, 120, 127, 144, 160
Myrdal, Gunnar, 22, 29–30, 37
My Space, 56

NAACP. *See* National Association
for the Advancement of Colored
People
Nash, Charla, 146
National Association for the Ad-
vancement of Colored People
(NAACP), 32
nationalism. *See* white nationalism
Nation of Islam, 108

Native Americans, 1–2, 6
Nazis, 38, 53, 56, 60
Negro Problem, 29
neo-Nazis, 52, 56, 80–81
NewsCorp, 145
New York Post (newspaper), 145–50
New York State Police Academy, 98–100
New York Times (newspaper), 4, 39–40
Nguyen, Viet Thanh, 164
N*****mania.com, 109
"n***** moments," 4
Norman, Mike, 142–43

Obama, Barack: birther conspiracy about, 144, 154, 161–62; criticisms of, 124; death threats against, 149; effects of racist humor on political fortunes of, 21, 126–27; likened to apes/chimpanzees/monkeys, 20–21, 115, 128, 136–49, *143*, 154, *155*, 158; Limbaugh's attacks on, 136–42; opposition to legislation promoted by, 145–48; public response to campaign and election of, 123–25, 127, 136, 140; racist humor aimed at, 20–21, 47, 115, 126–28, 136–58
Ocasio-Cortez, Alexandria, 88, 164–66
Occupy Wall Street, 52, 124
Odumosu, Temi, 29
Omar, Ilhan, 165–66
Omi, Michael, 5, 44
Orange County Register (newspaper), 151–52
Orange County Republican Party, 155
Oring, Elliot, 76–77, 80, 82
others. *See* us-them mentality

Palin, Sarah, 137, 144, 161
Patterson, Pat, 107–8

Peele, Jordan, 3
"Pepe the Frog" (meme), 20, 56, *57*
Plain View Project (PVP), 87, 120
Plato, 8
pleasure and enjoyment, in racist humor, 5, 8, 10–12, 14–17, 22–24, 31, 41, 46, 61, 75, 83, 103, 121, 126, 150, 156, 158, 160, 166–67, 170. *See also* social alignment and bonding
Pogrebin, Mark, 94
police. *See* law enforcement
Police Protective League, 110
Polish American Congress, 36
Polish jokes, 35–36, 38, 39
political correctness: attacks on, 39, 40, 58, 71, 75, 110, 119, 138–42, 144, 160–62, 167–69; cultural sensibilities of, 32, 46, 62, 69, 71, 75, 138; racist humor and, 31–32, 39, 46, 59, 69, 77, 96, 144, 158, 160, 167–68; white oppression fostered by, 75
political discourse, shaped by racist humor, 128, 136, 139, 142, 144, 156–57
political populism, 7, 15, 21
Poole, Eric, 94
positive psychology, 28
positivism, 28
post–civil rights era, racist humor in, 19–20, 23, 32, 39, 40, 48, 51, 58–64, 69, 85–86, 144, 157–58. *See also* civil rights movement; colorblind era; post-racialism
post-racialism: blackface in era of, 167; ethnic humor and, 33–34, 37; Limbaugh in, 141; Obama presidency and, 123–24, 158; persistence of racism in era of, 33, 83, 92, 121, 125, 144, 150, 158, 159–60; proclamations of, 33; racist humor in era of, 39–40, 45–47, 75, 144. *See also* colorblindness era; post–civil rights era

Powell, Laurence, 91–92
Pratt, Jeff, 2
Price, Keyanus, 151
ProPublica, 87–88, 120
pundits. *See* conservative
    commentators

race: alleged biological basis of, 6,
    128–31; construction of, 5–6, 179n1
racial formation, 5, 44, 48, 84, 96,
    160. *See also* racialization
racial ignorance. *See* white epistemo-
    logical ignorance
racialization: blackface minstrelsy's
    role in, 14–15; emotions linked to,
    9, 23, 45; as means of establish-
    ing social order/control, 6, 9;
    racist humor as means of, 4–5,
    43–45; role of, in imperialism and
    capitalism, 6, 38, 128, 130, 167, 171;
    sociocultural means of, 44; and
    white racial frame, 12, 30. *See also*
    racial formation
racism: colorblind, 45–46; implicit
    bias as explanation of, 88, 125–26;
    post-racialism and, 33, 83; racialized
    emotions and, 23; reinforcement
    of, by racist humor, regardless of
    intentions, 42–45, 59, 136, 148–49,
    154, 156, 158; reverse racism, 62, *67*,
    70, 74; "scientific" basis of, 128–31,
    129; social solidarity underlying, 18,
    26–27, 48, 166; in twenty-first cen-
    tury, 17–18. *See also* colorblind era;
    post-racialism; systemic racism
racist humor: criticisms of, 23, 31–32,
    40, 45; deflection of criticisms of
    ("just a joke"), 3, 13, 18–19, 21, 36–
    37, 40–41, 47, 76–77, 82, 84, 89,
    92–96, 101–3, 106, 111, 133, 146–50,
    153–58, 165–66, 171; dehumanizing
    effects of, 10, 11, 18–21, 39, 104,

116–17, 119; ethnic humor com-
    pared to, 34, 37–39, 102; historical
    legacy of, 30–31, 54, 55, 58, 60, 147,
    149, 166–67; as means of establish-
    ing social order/control, 4, 10–15,
    26, 29, 43–44, 48, 79, 94–95, 103,
    159; in nineteenth century, 13–17;
    non-whites' use of, 12, 41–43, 59,
    88, 119, 159; in political discourse,
    128, 136, 139, 142, 144, 156–57; ra-
    cialization effected by, 4–5, 43–45;
    research on, 48–49; rhetorical
    function of, 44–45; social align-
    ment/bonds established through,
    17, 19, 26, 45, 46, 54, 75–76, 86,
    103, 144, 156, 166, 168–69; social
    functions of, 4–5, 16–17, 22, 26,
    29, 30, 54, 94, 144; social solidar-
    ity underlying, 170; theory of, 41;
    in twentieth century, 39–40; in
    twenty-first century, 17–19; white-
    ness constructed by, 16–17, 160;
    whites as targets of, 41–42; white
    supremacy fostered by, 8, 16–17,
    19–20, 31, 51, 54, 57–64, 159–60,
    166–67, 171. *See also* amused racial
    contempt; blackface minstrelsy;
    ethnic humor; humor/jokes;
    pleasure and enjoyment, in racist
    humor; white racist humor
Raines, Sheila, 153
Rall, Ted, 148
Ray, Victor, 43
Reddit, 55, 109
Republican Central Committee of
    Orange County, 154
Republican National Committee, 150
Republican Party, 133, 135–37, 139, 142,
    144–46, 150–55, 164–65
reverse racism, 62, *67*, 70, 74
Reynolds, William Bradford, 98
Rice, Thomas D., 14

ridicule, 27
right-wing politics. *See* alt-right; conservative commentators; far right
Roediger, David, 16
Roof, Dylann, 53, 54, 83
Ruff, Cliff, 110
ruling class whites, 6

Saltsman, Chip, 150
Sambo (stage character), 14
San Francisco Gate (newspaper), 119
San Francisco Police Department
   (SFPD), 118–19
satire, political, 134
Saxton, Alexander, 15
schadenfreude, 8, 52, 160
Schroeder, Joanna, 51
Seraw, Mulugeta, 80–82, 84
Sernoffsky, Evan, 119
Sessions, Jeff, 88
sexism, 12, 15, 40, 51, 86, 88, 90, 93,
   165
Shange, Savannah, 169
Shanklin, Paul, 140
Sharpton, Al, 140, 146–48
Silverman, Sarah, 170
simianization, 130
Simpson, OJ, 109
Simpsons, The (television show), 59, 60
Sixteen Candles (film), 59
skinheads, 57, 58, 80–83
Skolnick, Jerome, 97
slavery, defenses of, 15–16
social alignment and bonding: humor
   as means of, 10–11, 24–27, 89, 92–
   94, 168; of police, 13, 89, 92–94,
   116; racist humor as means of, 17,
   19, 26, 45, 46, 54, 75–76, 86, 103,
   144, 156, 166, 168–69; of white
   supremacists, 26–27, 54–56, 58, 75.
   See also pleasure and enjoyment, in
   racist humor

social media: far right's use of, 50–52,
   55; law enforcement's use of,
   87–88, 94. *See also* memes
social order/control: emotions as tool
   for establishing, 9–10; humor as
   means of establishing, 4, 10–15,
   26, 27, 29, 37–38, 43–44, 48, 79,
   94–95, 103, 159; racialization as
   tool for establishing, 6, 9
Sotiropoulos, Karen, 15
Southern Poverty Law Center, 20, 82,
   127
Spencer, Herbert, 24
Stanley, Jason, 165
Stephens-Davidowitz, Seth, 21, 126
stereotypes: about Poles, 36; of African
   Americans, 59, 67–69, 109, 115–16,
   120, 127, 142, 150–53; Black perpetuation of, 16; of immigrants,
   72; implicit bias stemming from,
   125; law enforcement use of, 94,
   108, 115, 120; in the media, 109; in
   popular culture, 59; in racist humor, 22, 27, 31, 62, 68, 142; white
   racial frame reinforced by, 42. *See
   also* apes/chimpanzees/monkeys
Stern, Howard, 142
stimulus bill, 145–46
Stormfront (website), 55, 127
Streicher, Julius, 53
Stretz, Tom, 151
Strother, David H., cartoon of Lincoln
   as a monkey, 131, *132*
Stürmer, Der (newspaper), 53
Subotnik, Dan, 110
systemic racism: in law enforcement,
   87–91, 102–3, 105, 113–20; racialized emotions at root of, 23; racist
   humor linked to, 12, 23, 36, 43, 47,
   64, 136, 159–60; in United States,
   29–30, 50, 64; white racial frame as
   foundation of, 30

Talk Live (television show), 62
Tambo (stage character), 14, 15
Tea Party, 154, 161
Thomas, Mark Ridley, 111
Thompson, A. C., 88
Tlaib, Rashida, 165
Total Fascism (website), 53
Travis (chimpanzee), 146
Truly Tasteless Jokes series, 39–40, 59
Trump, Donald: campaign of, 161–62; capitalization of, on existing white grievance, 157; election of, 127; far right and alt-right support for, 56, 161; law enforcement support for, 121, 161; as target of Obama's jokes, 157; use and encouragement of racist humor by, 47, 51, 161–63, 165, 170; violence advocated/celebrated by, 121
Tuchman, Barbara W., 40
Tumblr, 56
Twitty, Mary Ann, 117

United States: national sense of humor in, 14, 17; systemic racism in, 29–30, 50, 64
United States v. State of New York, 99–100
upper-class whites, 162
U.S. Marine Corps, 60
us-them mentality: emotions as tool of, 9–10; in law enforcement, 94–96, 113–14; racist humor as tool of, 8, 11–13, 24, 27

violence: cultural, 95, 116; dehumanization as legitimation for use of violence, 13, 20, 50, 82, 95, 116–17, 119; humor linked to, 77–84, 91–92, 95–96, 103–5, 121–22, 149, 162–66; Obama as intended target of, 145–50, *147*; police advocacy/

celebration of, 87, 95, 104, 116, 120–21; police use of, 90–92, 95, 103–7, 112; as "self-defense," 64, 80; white supremacists' advocacy of, 62–64, 77–84, *81*; white supremacists' perpetration of, 80–83
Violent Crime Control and Law Enforcement Act, 113

Waddington, P. A. J., 93–96
WAR. *See* White Aryan Resistance
Washington Post (newspaper), 149
watermelons, 150–52, *152*
Weaver, Simon, 44
White American Political Association, 60
White Aryan Resistance (newspaper), 19, 58, 61–84, *63, 66–68, 70–74, 78, 81*, 149
White Aryan Resistance (WAR), 58, 60–84
white epistemological ignorance, 37, 139, 151, 154, 156
white flight, *66*
White House Correspondents Dinner, 157
white nationalism, 20, 21, 52–56, 127, 157
whiteness: construction of, through racist humor, 16–17, 160; divisions within, 6; Du Bois on, v, 1, 6–7, 46, 48; Obama's presidency as foil for, 156–57; and white supremacy, v, 1, 6–7
white racial frame: challenging of, 79–80; defined, 12, 30; humor as expression of, 12, 30–31, 32; ignorance underlying, 37; naturalization/normalization of, 6, 15, 17, 31, 42–43, 79, 130, 133, 166; systemic racism based on, 30; in United States, 30–31

white racist humor: alignment and bonding through, 16–17; Black inferiority as theme of, 14–15; criticisms of, 31–32, 45; persistence of, 32; power and contempt underlying, 43; in twentieth century, 30–32; white racial frame maintained through, 12, 30–31, 32. *See also* amused racial contempt; blackface minstrelsy; racist humor

White Student Unions, 61–62

white supremacy: alleged biological basis of, 6–7, 128–31; calls to action, 65–84; historical legacy of, 157, 158; law enforcement and, 84, 149; Obama's election as challenge to, 125, 128, 156; promotion of, 52, 53; racist humor as tool of, 8, 16–17, 19–20, 31, 51, 54, 57–64, 159–60, 166–67, 171; social construction of, 6–7; social solidarity underlying, 26–27, 75; in twentieth century, 29; victim mentality of, 58, 61, 63–84, 162; violence associated with, 62–64, 77–84, *81*; whiteness and, v, 1, 6–7; working-class whites as target audience of, 66, 69; young people as target audience of, 51, 54–58, 61–62. *See also* alt-right; far right

WikiLeaks, 52

Williams, J. S., 97

Wilmington Police Department, 97

Wilson, Darren, 114–15

Winant, Howard, 5, 44

Wind, Timothy, 91–92

working-class whites. *See* lower-class whites

youth, 55, 56, 58, 61, 151

YouTube, 55

Žižek, Slavoj, 168–69

Zimmerman, George, 53–54

Zip Coon (stage character), 14

Lightning Source UK Ltd.
Milton Keynes UK
UKHW010747110822
407134UK00002B/83